Pacific Asia

Pacific Asia has witnessed arguably the most dynamic economic growth and social transformation in the world since 1945. Inspired by the example of Japan, a number of high-performing economies have emerged in the region.

Pacific Asia explores this extraordinary pace of development and explains the various factors that lie behind it. It introduces the complex politics of development and sets Pacific Asia in its geographical and sociocultural context.

As well as Japan, the role model of development, *Pacific Asia* examines the experiences of Malaysia, Indonesia, Thailand, Singapore, South Korea and Taiwan.

Yumei Zhang was Senior Lecturer in Politics at the University of Luton before joining the Guernsey Financial Services Commission in November 2001.

The Making of the Contemporary World
Edited by Eric Evans and Ruth Henig
University of Lancaster

The Making of the Contemporary World series provides challenging interpretations of contemporary isues and debates within strongly defined historical frameworks. The range of the series is global, with each volume drawing together material from a range of disciplines – including economics, politics and sociology. The books in this series present compact, indispensable introductions for students studying the modern world.

Titles include:

Pacific Asia
The politics of development

Yumei Zhang

Routledge
Taylor & Francis Group

LONDON AND NEW YORK

First published 2003
by Routledge
11 New Fetter Lane, London EC4P 4EE

Simultaneously published in the USA and Canada
by Routledge
29 West 35th Street, New York, NY 10001

Routledge is an imprint of the Taylor & Francis Group

Typeset in Times by
Prepress Projects Ltd, Perth, Scotland
Printed and bound in Great Britain by
TJ International Ltd, Padstow, Cornwall

British Library Cataloguing in Publication Data
A catalogue record for this book is available from the British Library

Library of Congress Cataloging in Publication Data
Zhang, Yumei, 1964–
    Pacific Asia : the politics of development / Yumei Zhang.
        p. cm. – (The making of the contemporary world)
    Includes biographical references and index.
    1. East Asia–Politics and government. 2. East Asia–Economic
    policy. 3. Asia, Southeastern–Politics and government–1945– 4. Asia,
    Southeastern–Economic policy. I. Title. II. Series.

JQ1499.A792 P5395 2002
320.95 – dc21   2002011675

ISBN 0-415-18489-4 (pbk)
ISBN 0-415-18488-6 (hbk)

Contents

Conclusion 149

List of abbreviations

AFTA	ASEAN Free Trade Area
AMF	Asian Monetary Fund
AP	Alliance Party (Malaysia)
APEC	Asia Pacific Economic Cooperation Forum
ASEAN	Association of Southeast Asian Nations
BN	Barisan National (Malaysia)
CDS	capitalist developmental state
CECD	Council for Economic Cooperation and Development (Taiwan)
CPF	Central Provident Fund (Singapore)
DPP	Democratic Progressive Party (Taiwan)
DPR	People's Representative Council (Indonesia)
EAEC	East Asian Economic Caucus
EAEG	East Asian Economic Grouping
EC	European Community
EDB	Economic Development Board (Singapore)
EOI	export-oriented industrialisation
EPB	Economic Planning Board (South Korea)
EPZs	export processing zones
EU	European Union
EWYB	*Europa World Year Book*
FDI	foreign direct investment
FEER	*Far Eastern Economic Review*
GATT	General Agreement on Tariffs and Trade
GDP	gross domestic product
GLCs	government-linked companies (Singapore)
GNP	gross national product
HDB	Housing Development Board (Singapore)
HPAEs	high-performing Asian economies
IMF	International Monetary Fund
IPE	international political economy

ISI	import-substitution industrialisation
JSP	Japan Socialist Party
KMT	Kuomintang, the National Party (Taiwan)
KRWE	*Keesing's Record of World Events*
LDP	Liberal Democratic Party (Japan)
MCA	Malaysian Chinese Association
MIC	Malaysian Indian Congress
MITI	Ministry of Trade and Industry (Japan)
MNCs	multinational corporations
MPR	People's Consultative Assembly (Indonesia)
NAFTA	North American Free Trade Agreement
NDCs	newly democratised countries
NECs	newly exporting countries
NEP	New Economic Policy (Malaysia)
NGOs	non-governmental organisations
NHI	National Health Insurance
NICs	newly industrialised countries
NPP	National Pension Programme
OECD	Organization for Economic Cooperation and Development
PAP	People's Action Party (Singapore)
PRC	People's Republic of China
SMEs	small and medium-sized enterprises
SNTV	single non-transferable vote
UMNO	United Malays National Organisation (Malaysia)
WP	Workers' Party (Singapore)
WTO	World Trade Organization

Introduction

Since the end of World War II, Pacific Asia, the part of Asia on the west coast of the Pacific Ocean, has been home to the world's most dynamic region of economic growth and social transformation. Inspired by Japan, the region's first industrial nation, and helped by its financial and technological support, a number of high-performing economies have emerged in the area over the decades. These include the now newly industrialised countries (NICs) of South Korea, Taiwan and Singapore and the three Southeast Asian countries on the verge of 'NIC-dom', namely, Malaysia, Indonesia and Thailand. These high-performing Asian economies (HPAEs), as the World Bank (1993) describes them, are the only post-war economies that have combined high growth rates with declining income inequality to a greater or lesser degree. Shared growth, according to the World Bank, has greatly improved human welfare. Between 1960 and 1990, the period of rapid growth, life expectancy in the HPAEs increased from 56 years to 71 years, and the proportion of people living in absolute poverty decreased from 58 per cent to 17 per cent.

The rise of Pacific Asia in the world economy has had a profound intellectual and political impact on international politics. From the early 1980s, when, for the first time in history, the United States began to trade more with Pacific Asia than with Western Europe, increasing numbers of scholars and politicians began to speculate about the coming of the 'Pacific century' (Linder 1986; Borthwick 1992). This refers to the perceived shift of the political–economic centre of gravity from the Western-dominated Atlantic region to the Asian-dominated Pacific region. Perhaps more importantly, it also refers to the perceived decline of the Western intellectual hegemony in social sciences. In short, the 'new Asian renaissance' was seen to be challenging Western political and philosophical dominance in international politics. Notions such as 'Asian capitalism', 'Asian democracy' and 'Asian welfare system' were widely used to portray alternative and better models of human development.

Until 1997, the year in which the Asian financial crisis broke out, the notion of the 'Pacific century' was widely invoked in the West by politicians and professors alike to urge economic and social reforms in their own societies (Rodan 1996). The West, i.e. Western Europe, North America and the Antipodes, it was argued, was suffering from various economic and social malaises resulting from 'excessive liberalism' and thus needed to learn from Pacific Asia. So great were the cultural differences between the East (i.e. Asia), whose hallmark was seen to be its attachment to collectivism, and the West, with its alleged obsession with individualism, as Huntington (1993a) argued, that their conflict was expected to be the major theme of post-Cold War international politics. Within Pacific Asia itself, politicians and some intellectuals regularly resorted to the 'Asian values' rhetoric to instil national pride, to exhort further collective endeavour and to warn against corrosive 'Westernisation'.

The 1997–8 Asian financial crisis marked a turning point in both the region's development and the study of it. Not only has it shattered the much-hyped Pacific century hubris, but it has also led to a more sober analysis of the region's development successes and failures. As the region embarks on its post-crisis recovery and grapples with new issues of development that stem from changed domestic and international environments, more scholars are re-examining the region's development experiences in the light of the Asian crisis.

This book is written in the aftermath of the 1997–8 Asian financial crisis. As a study of Pacific Asia's extraordinary experience of development, characterised by its rapid rise in the international political economy followed by an equally unpredicted fall in 1997–8, in this book I seek to understand the various factors that lay behind this. In so doing, I hope to achieve two broad aims: to introduce students of politics to the development experiences of Pacific Asia and to achieve a deeper understanding of the complex issue of development, a policy goal that still eludes the majority of the world's humanity.

As is clear, the organising theme of the book is the concept of development, and the countries that will be studied are the six HPAEs, together with Japan, once the role model of these economies. To facilitate understanding, there is thus a need in this introduction to explain briefly the meaning of development and to draw a geographical and sociocultural map of the region in which these economies are located. This will then be followed by an introduction to the themes, methodologies and structure of the book.

THE MEANING OF DEVELOPMENT

Since the end of World War II, development has been the most important term used to describe economic, social and political changes in what have come to be known as Third World countries, most of which had been former colonies of the Western powers. However, as a normative term, often implicitly associated with progress, a legacy of eighteenth-century Western Enlightenment thought, development is a *contested concept*. Its meaning is a product of personal preference and reflects value judgement. An important source of this contestation lies in its multidimensional nature. As Huntington (1987) argues, as a condition, development entails at least five goals: economic growth, social equality, political democracy, order and stability, and national autonomy. As part of a process, however, he continues, these goals invariably come into conflict with each other and there is no universal agreement on the best way of their integration.

Another reason for the lack of universal agreement on the meaning of development is the fact that it creates costs as well as benefits to different groups of people in society. This is what Goulet (1992: 470) means when he defines development as 'a two-edged sword which brings benefits, but also produces losses and generates value conflict'. In the benefit category, Goulet lists improvements in material well-being, technological gains – which relieve people from hard physical labour – institutional specialisation, increased freedom of choice, a higher degree of tolerance and some form of democracy. As losses, he lists the destruction of culture and community and the rise of acquisitive personal orientations. To these may also be added environmental damage.

In this book, I share Huntington and Goulet's conceptions of development by defining it as a multidimensional change that encompasses all aspects of social life. These include: economic development, which generates growth and its equitable distribution; social development, which generates well-being in terms of health, education, housing and employment; political development, which creates a system of government based on protection of human rights, political freedom and democracy; and cultural development, which leads to the emergence of a vibrant civil society as a means by which citizens freely express their self-identity and collective belonging.

Obviously, this list of the dimensions of development is helpful only to the extent that it provides us with analytical categories with which to organise our study. Of itself, it reveals neither value conflict nor the costs associated with development. These can only be revealed by analysing the actual development experiences of nations.

PACIFIC ASIA AS A REGION: SIMILARITY AND DIVERSITY

The seven countries under study are all located in Pacific Asia, alternatively known as East Asia. As with other regions in the world, shared space has brought about some shared historical and contemporary experiences among the region's otherwise diverse societies. In this section, I make a broad-brush sketch of these similarities and diversities in order to situate our study in concrete geographical, historical–cultural settings.

Pacific Asia is a region with diverse cultures and traditions. It is home to three of the world's major religions: Hinduism, Buddhism and Islam. In addition, societies across the region also differ enormously in size, natural resources, social structure, levels of economic development, and political system. Broadly speaking, however, the region can be divided into two subregions according to traditions and social structure. These are Northeast Asia, characterised by the dominant cultural tradition of Confucianism and a homogeneous social structure, and Southeast Asia, characterised by multiculturalism and a heterogeneous social structure. The one thing that unites the two subregions is their common historical experience of colonialism, although the details of that experience have varied between nations.

The coming into contact with the West in the seventeenth century marked the beginning of the incorporation of Pacific Asia into the emerging world capitalist economy and hence the dawning of its modern era. Besides capitalism, nationalism was the other product of Western influence, which inspired a demand for national self-determination and a desire for 'modernisation'. Japan and Thailand were the only two countries to escape colonisation, although both societies had to carry out substantial social and political reforms to survive the age of colonialism. Japan's modernisation, by adopting Western technology and social and political institutions during the late nineteenth century, had been so rapid that by the end of the century it had not only repealed all the 'unequal treaties' that it had been forced to sign with the Western powers but also conquered Taiwan and Korea as its colonies. During the Pacific War, Malaysia, Singapore and Indonesia all came under Japanese occupation, and Thailand formed a strategic alliance with Japan to avoid a similar fate. All the states gained their independence first from Japan, then from their old Western colonialists, within the first decade or so of the end of World War II. As will be seen in later chapters, colonial legacies, of both the Japanese and the Western variety, are still having an impact on development in the region.

Broadly similar historical experience apart, Northeast Asia and Southeast Asia are very different in terms of resource endowment, social structure and cultural practice. While Japan, South Korea and Taiwan are all resource-poor countries, Malaysia, Indonesia and Thailand are all rich in natural endowments such as oil, natural gas, tin, rubber and timber, as well as a range of agricultural products. Singapore, the only NIC in Southeast Asia, has virtually no natural resources of any kind.

Differences in natural endowments have been an important factor in influencing development strategies and outcomes, as will become clear later. The traditional importance of agriculture in Southeast Asia (with the exception of Singapore), for instance, explains the relatively low level of urbanisation (i.e. the proportion of people living in cities) of these societies in comparison with Northeast Asia. Although less than a third of Thailand's population lives in the cities, 100 per cent of Singaporeans do.

The social structures of Northeast Asia and Southeast Asia are also very different. While Indonesia consists of thousands of islands and hundreds of languages and dialects, Japan, South Korea and Taiwan are among the world's most homogeneous societies in terms of ethnicity, language, religion and culture. Although less so than Indonesia, which has the reputation of being the 'Yugoslavia of Asia', Malaysia, Thailand and Singapore are all multicultural societies consisting of several ethnic, linguistic and religious groups. As we will see, ethnic politics often adds another layer of complexity to the already difficult task of development. Except in Singapore, where ethnic Chinese forms the overwhelming majority, all other Southeast Asian societies are beset, to different degrees, by 'the Chinese problem', which affects their development policies. The heart of the problem is the monopoly by the Chinese minorities of the industrial and commercial sectors in these societies, provoking popular resentment.

Northeast Asia, together with Singapore, is commonly described as a Confucian region, referring to the dominant tradition of Confucianism in these societies. *Confucianism* is a type of social and political thought, associated with the ancient Chinese scholar Confucius (551–479 BC). Owing to the pre-eminence of Chinese civilisation in Pacific Asia prior to the latter's encounter with the West, Confucian thought spread to Korea, Japan, Singapore and Vietnam, and it became the most influential secular ethical tradition in these societies. Its core values are social hierarchy, respect for authority, family centredness, filial piety (i.e. the obligation of offspring to look after their elderly parents), benevolent government by virtuous leaders, and individual self-improvement through education. In the Confucian ethos, contempt for commercial activities, and thus merchants, is matched by reverence for accomplished scholars, who serve the ruler.

In Southeast Asia (with the exception of Singapore), Buddhism and Islam are the dominant belief systems. In Thailand, 95 per cent of the population is Buddhist, whereas in Indonesia 88 per cent of the population is Muslim.

In Malaysia, Islam is the officially designated religion for the 60 per cent or so of the Malay population, and the rest of its people believe in a range of other religions, including Buddhism, Hinduism and Sikhism, to name but a few. Although these religions are all very different from Confucian belief as well as from each other, they also have some similarities. For example, while both Buddhism and Hinduism share the Confucian disdain for commerce, Hinduism also shares the Confucian respect for social hierarchy in the form of the caste system. Islam, like Christianity, is amenable to wide variations. But apart from its belief in theocracy, or rule by God, the core Islamic belief is otherwise very similar to that of Confucianism in that both advocate the suppression of the individual's desires and interests in favour of those of society.

I have devoted a considerable amount of attention to the belief systems of Pacific Asia. The reason for this is its relevance to one of the influential perspectives advanced to explain the development experiences of the region. This is the cultural perspective that attributes the region's development success to its cultural similarities. This perspective also underlies the 'Asian values' discourse noted earlier in the introduction. At this stage, I will simply note that whereas it is possible to identify some cultural similarities across the region, such as collectivist orientations that put the community before the individual, it is equally true that the region's cultural heritages are diverse and changing. The implications of this observation will be explored in later chapters.

ABOUT THIS BOOK: THEMES, METHODOLOGIES AND STRUCTURE

Having explained the meaning of development and made a brief survey of Pacific Asia's history, society and culture, we now move to the final section, in which a brief introduction to the book is in order.

We noted earlier the contested nature of development, both as a condition and as a process. This basic fact inspires the main concerns of this book: How is development defined and pursued in Pacific Asia? Why? And with what consequences? In effect, what we are interested in is the politics of development in Pacific Asia, as the title of the book indicates. To study the politics of development, therefore, involves investigating the way in which the meaning of development is thrashed out and the policy consequences that ensue. Since development brings about changes in the authoritative allocation of values and distribution of resources in society, to examine the politics of development is thus essentially to examine the way in which power is exercised in the struggle for development.

To this end, comparative analysis is a major methodological approach adopted in this book. Cross-national comparison not only gives us a richer insight into the differences and similarities of the development experiences of the countries under study but is also the best means by which these patterns can be related to competing theories of development. In other words, comparison enables us to test theories of development and hence enrich our general understanding of the nature of development.

The book consists of ten chapters. Chapter 1 briefly reviews the two dominant theories of development in order to set the scene for our subsequent study. Chapter 2 is an overview of the various theoretical issues raised by the rapid development of HPAEs. The main purpose of this chapter is twofold: to identify the intellectual links between these issues and the main concerns of the two theories of development and to foreshadow the main areas of contention to be addressed in subsequent chapters. Chapters 3 and 4 compare the economic development of all seven nations from the perspective of political economy, which examines the interaction between economics and politics at both national and international levels. Differences and similarities in development patterns are identified and explained in terms of the dynamic interaction between domestic and international political forces shaped by history and geopolitics. Chapters 5 to 7 examine the political development of the seven nations. Chapter 5 focuses on the nature of Japanese democracy with a view to scrutinising the culturalist argument that Japan has pioneered a unique model of 'illiberal democracy' for other Pacific Asian countries. Chapter 6 compares the different trajectories of the democratisation of Taiwan, South Korea and Thailand with a view to explaining their successful moves to democracy. Chapter 7 compares political development in Singapore, Malaysia and Indonesia to identify reasons for these three societies' failure to democratise. A common theme running through the three chapters is an emphasis on the key role of politics, i.e. the struggles over power, instead of culture, in shaping a nation's political development. Chapter 8 compares social development within Pacific Asia to assess the impact of 'Asian values' on social policy. Policy similarities and differences are explained in terms of the political logic of the developmental state rather than local cultures.

The last two chapters focus on the changing national, international and regional context of development for Pacific Asia. Chapter 9 examines the causes and impact of the 1997–8 financial crisis in Asia with a view to drawing some lessons for future development in Pacific Asia. Chapter 10 examines the development of regionalism in Pacific Asia from the perspective of international political economy by focusing on the various factors affecting the emergence of regional identity and cooperation in the region. Finally, this book concludes by drawing together the main arguments developed throughout the text.

1 Development theories

Following the end of World War II, a large number of societies, mainly in Africa, Asia and Latin America, gained national independence from the Western colonialists. The emergence of these newly independent, or post-colonial, states, which later collectively came to be known as the Third World because of their common 'backwardness', led to the formulation in the West of the first theory of development: modernisation theory (MT). Until the end of the 1960s, MT was the dominant perspective on development. After that, it came under serious criticism in the wake of widespread development disasters in the Third World. At the same time as MT was being reformulated, a more radical critique emerged, known as dependency theory (DT), calling for a complete rejection of MT. Events and intense intellectual exchanges, however, led to the revision of DT itself, resulting in world system theory (WST). The emergence of the HPAEs in Pacific Asia was the major empirical basis on which WST was built.

In this chapter, I will review the two dominant theories of development by focusing on three of their main concerns: the conception of development, the political economy of development and the culture of development. I will conclude by noting the areas of convergence between the two perspectives.

MODERNISATION THEORY

As a theory of social change, MT went through two stages of development: an early stage, characterised by a linear conception of development and a liberal approach to development strategy, and a revisionist stage, which emphasised the political precondition of development. What was revised in its later version was not the goal of development but the way of achieving it.

The linear conception of development

In early MT, development was construed as an evolutionary process in which all societies progressed through an identifiable series of stages to become 'modern'. Writing in the mid-nineteenth century, Karl Marx famously predicted that 'the country that is more developed industrially only shows to the less developed the image of its own future' (Harrison 1988: 2). A century later, modernisation theorists had little doubt that the experience of the modernised West was about to be repeated in the newly independent states. For example, in the mid-1960s Eisenstadt (1966: 1) could write that modernisation was 'the process of change towards those types of social, economic and political systems that have developed in Western Europe and North America from the seventeenth century to the nineteenth century and have spread to other European countries'.

Based on the Western experience, early modernisation theorists envisaged all other societies beginning modernisation from industrialisation, which lays the foundation for economic development. Economic development in turn lays the foundation for social development, such as urbanisation, the rise in literacy through mass education and the spread of the mass media. Social development in turn enables the populace to participate in politics, which ultimately leads to the creation of a competitive political system of democratic rule. In this linear conception of development, therefore, the final stage of modernisation is a Western-style industrialised democracy. Lipset (1959) summarises nicely this key modernisation thesis by asserting that the more affluent a society is, the more likely it is to become a democracy.

As economic development was seen as the driving force of modernisation, the early modernisation theorists were particularly concerned with the preconditions for it. On this point, two complementary perspectives prevailed: the neo-classical political economic perspective and the cultural perspective.

Economic development: neo-classical political economic perspective

Originating with the eighteenth-century Scottish philosopher and political economist Adam Smith, the neo-classical political economic perspective on economic development sees the capitalist market economy as the most powerful engine of economic development. In this kind of economic system, the individual, guided by his or her own self-interest, functions as the prime agent of change by engaging in profit-maximising economic exchanges in the marketplace. The state, on the other hand, plays a supportive role by providing a secure and stable environment in which these exchanges can take place. The major roles of the state include acting as a legal enforcer of commercial contracts freely entered into by individuals, protecting private property rights, providing systems of law and order, external defence and internal security, and providing a basic education to equip individuals with the right skills to participate in the economy. In short, modernisation theorists believe that the Western nation-state enables the individual to function as the agent of social change through the marketplace.

From this perspective, the economist Rostow (1960) proposed a general theory of economic growth based upon five stages. In the first, traditional, stage, it is very difficult to expand production beyond a limited ceiling because society is based on pre-Newtonian technology and science and pre-Newtonian attitudes towards the physical world, i.e. the belief that the external world is not subject to knowable laws and is thus not capable of productive manipulation. Such societies are agrarian and hierarchical, with family and clan connections being the dominant social structure, allowing little scope for social mobility. As a result, the dominant attitude is one of 'long-run fatalism', the belief that the range of possibilities open to one's grandchildren will be just about the same as they were for one's grandparents.

In Western Europe, the translation of the insights of modern science into both agricultural and industrial production during the late seventeenth and early eighteenth centuries initiated the transition from traditional to pre-take-off stage. This is the stage in which the preconditions for economic take-off are developed. In the Third World countries, however, Rostow believed that such preconditions could not come from within society itself but had to come from some external intrusion by more advanced societies. Such intrusion, he argued, shocks the traditional society and begins or hastens its undoing; but it also sets in motion ideas and sentiments that initiate the process by which a modern alternative to the traditional society is constructed out of the old culture. The new attitude sees economic progress as not only possible but also desirable, whether for higher profits, national dignity or general well-being.

During the transition from traditional society to economic take-off, major changes take place in both the economy itself and the balance of social values, both of which lay the preconditions for take-off. But to Rostow, changes in the political system are often a decisive precondition of economic take-off. Essentially, this involves the building of an effective centralised national state based on 'new nationalism', a kind of nationalism that opposes both traditional landed regional interests and the colonial power.

Once traditional values and resistance to steady economic growth are finally overcome, a society makes its decisive break from its past by entering the third stage, that of economic take-off, in which growth becomes its normal condition. What makes growth steady and sustainable during this stage is the coming into political power of a group prepared to regard the modernisation of the economy as 'serious, high-order political business'. In other words, the values favouring economic progress become the dominant values in society during this stage.

Economic take-off is followed by the drive to maturity, during which the economy extends modern technology over the whole front of its economic activity. During this stage, production becomes more complex and technologically more refined; the make-up of the economy changes constantly as old industries decline and new ones emerge. Consequently, society as a whole is also constantly balancing the new against the older values and institutions, or revising the latter in a way that supports rather than retards the growth process.

The final stage of economic development is the age of high mass-consumption, in which leading sectors of the economy move into the manufacture of consumer durables and the provision of services. This stage can only be reached when a large proportion of the population has an average income sufficient to move its consumption needs beyond basic food, shelter and clothing. At the time of Rostow was writing (the late 1950s), only the United States, Western Europe and Japan were seen to have reached this stage.

Rostow's writing was clearly in the tradition of neo-classical political economy. For the Third World countries, although the initial stimulus to modernise comes from outside, through examples set by the West, the basic problem of taking off is entirely internal to the economies concerned. Essentially, it is to produce enough individuals with entrepreneurial abilities (Randall and Theobald 1998: 25). The role of the state is to help these individuals to function effectively in a stable and secure environment, secured by the rule of law.

Although economic growth was his main concern, Rostow saw its achievement as an outcome of a combination of factors: attitudinal, institutional, and political, as well as technological. Changes in social and political institutions are seen to contribute simultaneously to economic growth and be the inevitable outcomes of such growth.

Economic development: cultural perspective

Like most other early modernisation theorists, Rostow was also a Eurocentric writer, in believing that non-European cultures were incapable of generating pro-capitalist values on their own. Therefore, apart from their linear conception of development, early modernisation theorists were also culturalists, in that they saw culture as having the independent capacity to determine socioeconomic development.

The cultural perspective on economic development drew its inspiration from the German sociologist Max Weber, whose seminal work *The Protestant Ethic and the Spirit of Capitalism* (first published in 1904–5) argued that the Protestant ethic provided a set of values and orientations that enabled capitalism to originate in Western Europe. Weber also studied Asian religions, such as Confucianism, Hinduism and Buddhism, and found them all fostering negative attitudes to capitalist development. Based on Weber, early modernisation theorists, such as Lerner (1958) and McClelland (1961), put great emphasis on cultivating 'modern man' in Third World countries through 'cultural diffusion', what Rostow called cultural invasion. It was believed that once sufficient numbers of 'modern mankind', educated in Western values, emerged as risk-taking entrepreneurs, economic take-off in Third World countries might take a shorter time to materialise with the help of Western technology.

Modernisation revisionism

Towards the end of the 1960s, the Third World witnessed a series of development disasters, which swept away the optimistic and linear conceptions of development characteristic of early modernisation theorists. Contrary to their belief, the adoption of Western political, social and economic institutions in the post-colonial states did not lead inexorably to development in these societies. Instead, there was continuing poverty, increasing inequality and communal violence. As conflict and instability gave way to development, increasing numbers of modernisation theorists began to question earlier assumptions based on evolutionary optimism. Modernisation revisionism, a result of the rethinking of MT, moved away from such a linear conception and focused instead on the *primacy of politics,* rather than culture, in bringing about change. At the same time, some also questioned the Eurocentric negativism about non-European cultures and sought to show the instrumental role of the latter in development. But on this matter, there remains ambiguity over whether non-Western cultures are inherently anti-capitalist, despite the argument that they may adapt to and even assist capitalist development (Rudolf and Rudolf 1967).

The case for a strong state

What set modernisation revisionists apart from earlier writers was their realisation of the very different political context in which development was to occur in the Third World. In Western Europe, societies had not only taken centuries to evolve but had also established an effective political system, in the form of the nation-state, before they embarked on industrial capitalism (Almond and Powell 1966). The hallmark of the nation-state is the institutional capacity of the national bureaucracy to integrate and regulate society. Therefore, as Rostow had earlier argued, the nation-state was a decisive political condition for Europe's economic take-off.

However, the lack of this key political condition in the Third World was overlooked by early modernisation theorists. As Myrdal (1968) and Huntington (1968) pointed out, a major problem with post-colonial states is their weakness or 'softness'. Despite their trappings of Western states, such as bureaucracy and parliament, they have neither the institutional capacity nor the political legitimacy to make and implement policies. Too often, tribal loyalty over-rides national identity, and the bureaucracy is riddled with kinship-based patronage and corruption. As a result, 'governments simply do not govern' in these countries (Huntington 1968: 2).

The realisation of these problems, associated with a weak state, led modernisation revisionists to abandon the linear conception of development in favour of a strong state as a guarantor of a smooth transition in the long run. Without a strong state providing order and stability, Huntington (1968: 2) argued, economic development is either practically impossible or generates such pressures on the political system that it could lead to political instability and decay instead of stability and democracy. Therefore, what matters for economic development in the Third World is 'not their form of government but their degree of government' (Huntington: 1968: 1). There is, in effect, a need to construct and strengthen government institutions capable of effective policy making, a process Huntington described as *political institutionalisation*.

The call for a strong state by modernisation revisionists did not signal the modernisation theorists' abandonment of democracy as the ultimate goal of political development. Rather, a strong state, authoritarian if need be, was seen as the best guarantee of the smooth transition from economic development to democracy. Undirected economic development was seen to be more likely to generate political breakdown and violence than stable democracy. In short, political direction is vital for both economic development and ultimately democracy.

The greatest contribution of modernisation revisionism to development thinking was its move away from linear economic determinism, which saw economic development in the Third World not only to be relatively trouble-free once the cultural barrier to economic growth was broken down but also to lead inexorably to a stable democracy. Modernisation revisionism argued for strong and effective government institutions, both to provide the political preconditions for economic development and to manage the social and political conflict inevitably generated by economic growth. The implication of this analysis is that political failure can lead to economic failure.

DEPENDENCY THEORY

At the same time as MT was undergoing its revisionist transformation by focusing on the primacy of politics, a strong and effective state in particular, a radical critique emerged calling for its complete rejection. Dependency theory (DT), as the critique is known, challenged both of the core theses of MT: that a strong state is essential for development and that changes in cultural values, by imitating the West, are necessary for economic take-off. For dependency theorists, one single factor has long sealed the fate of all the Third World countries and condemned them to eternal underdevelopment, and this is the existence of a single capitalist world economy.

According to dependency theorists, since the late fifteenth and early sixteenth centuries, there has been a progressive spread of capitalism from Western Europe to other parts of the world through conquest and colonisation. As a result, the entire world today is integrated into a Western-dominated capitalist economy, geared towards transferring economic surplus from the Third World periphery to the Western core nations. Systematic exploitation of the periphery by the core is thus the hallmark of the global economic structure, which delivers development to the West at the expense of the rest. So development and underdevelopment are but two sides of the same historical process: the West developed by 'underdeveloping' the rest (Frank 1969; Amin 1976).

Trapped in the exploitative global economic structure, dependency theorists argue, state autonomy is not possible and indigenous culture does not matter in Third World development. The state, instead of pursuing independent development policies that would benefit its people, is no more than an instrument in the hands of local comprador capitalists, who are agents of foreign capital. Similarly, local culture is neither here nor there as it is subjugated to the over-riding ideology of capitalism. The result of this economic and ideological dependency on the West, it is argued, is permanent impoverishment of the people of the Third World, who are unlikely to see either development or democracy. To achieve these goals, radical solutions are called for, including 'de-linking' from world capitalism, trading with 'progressive', i.e. socialist, countries, striving for self-sufficiency through import-substitution industrialisation (ISI) and socialist revolution.

'Dependent development'

During the late 1960s and early 1970s, DT provided powerful ideological rationalisation for a number of Third World states in their choice of socialist development strategies. But the subsequent failure of these states to achieve development, in contrast with the noticeable economic development of the East Asian NICs, brought the theory under severe criticism. Divergent development experiences, critics argued, demanded a far less deterministic theoretical framework that is sensitive to the political factors of the peripheral country, its social classes, state institutions, ideologies, etc. Unfortunately, other than claiming that underdevelopment at the periphery originated at the centre, DT has nothing to say on these factors. Therefore, more critical dependency theorists, while recognising the usefulness of the concept of a world capitalist economy, were uneasy with DT's 'simple reductionism [that] can remove from history all its ambiguities, conjectures and surprises' (Cardoso 1977: 21).

Meanwhile, through the detailed study of several Third World countries, a number of dependency theorists were able to demonstrate both the theoretical possibility and the empirical reality of 'dependent development' (Cardoso 1973; Evans 1979; Cardoso and Faletto 1979). They argued that, despite dependency, the peripheral state is by no means a mere agent of metropolitan interests. A range of international, historical and internal factors, not least the different internal class configurations, can allow the state relative autonomy in its pursuit of national development. These studies eventually forced DT to shed its 'mechanical and deductive determinism' (Bernstein and Nicholas 1983: 621) in favour of a more detailed analysis of national political dynamics, a process that resulted in world system theory.

WORLD SYSTEM THEORY

WST shares DT's conception of the world economy as one single system. But instead of seeing the system as divided along a core–periphery dichotomy, it envisages an intermediate semi-periphery, which is inhabited by upwardly mobile developing countries and downwardly mobile developed countries. This three-tiered world economic system, argues Wallerstein (1979), the founder of the theory, is a far more realistic conception of the international political economy because a dichotomous system characterised by a permanent domination–subjugation relationship is an inherently unstable one. The existence of the semi-periphery not only allows for the possibility of change in the relative position of individual national economies, but in so doing it also plays a vital role in the maintenance of the system. Therefore, WST is also a dynamic, as opposed to a static, framework for the analysis of development.

In Wallerstein's WST, the political dynamics in the peripheral economy is a key to its upward mobility in the international system. Crucial factors include the nature of its state organisation, its coercive power and its ideology. The Asian NICs were seen to be exemplary of the power of the state in development. However, unlike modernisation theorists, Wallerstein, together with dependency theorists, does not see capitalist democracy as the end-state of development. Instead, socialism is envisaged to ultimately transcend capitalism.

Like modernisation revisionism, the contribution of WST to development thinking is in its abandonment of crude economic reductionism by taking into account the role of national politics in development. As a result, the international system is increasingly seen 'not as a rigidly determinate structure but rather as a set of shifting constraints within which states can learn and expand their range of manoeuvre' (Haggard 1990: 22). This realistic and dynamic approach to development has been increasingly appreciated since the 1980s, during which time the economic interdependence between nations has intensified and the economic success of the Asian NICs has become widely noted. By the 1980s, DT was rarely mentioned as the world's socialist regimes, beginning with China in the late 1970s and followed by the Soviet bloc a decade later, abandoned autarky and eagerly embraced the world capitalist economy. Since then, development thinking has tended to focus on 'national strategies in an international context', as reflected in the apt title of the book by Bienefeld and Godfrey (1982).

CONCLUSION

Being the two dominant theories of development, MT and WST share some similarities despite their considerable differences. Both are derived from European experience and are formulated by intellectuals socialised into European political thought. As a result, both see, more or less explicitly, non-Western traditions and cultures as incapable of generating capitalist development. While cultural orientation to development is of crucial importance to modernisation theorists, the ideology of development is far more important to world system theorists in determining development outcomes. Because of this, what is seen as a development handicap in the form of a lack of a pro-capitalist culture by modernisation theorists is seen by world system theorists as a positive factor for socialist development. So despite their similar conceptions of the development process, whereby all societies move from premodern to modern forms, MT and WST have very different visions of the end-state of development. Unlike modernisation theorists, who see capitalist democracy as the end-state of development, world system theorists envisage socialism as transcending capitalism.

But, since the 1980s, there has been a convergence between the two theories on the role of the state in development. In recognising the vital importance of the state in development, both theories have had to shed their original economic determinism to address the primacy of politics in national development. Within MT, the strengthening of the state's capacity for effective policy making is seen to be essential for bringing about socioeconomic development, which is deemed necessary for democracy. Economic development is therefore seen to be both determining and determined by politics. Within WST, the state is seen as both constrained by the world economy and possessing the relative autonomy to take advantage of it in pursuit of national development. As we will see in Chapter 2, this shared recognition of the necessity of a 'strong state' for national development gave rise to the developmental state perspective, which has, since the 1980s, been one of the dominant perspectives on development in Pacific Asia.

2 Development in Pacific Asia

Since the 1980s, the concept and theories of the developmental state have dominated intellectual thinking on development, thanks largely to Pacific Asia's remarkable development record. As a result, many old issues and themes, first raised and discussed in the two dominant theories of development, have been either reinterpreted or reinforced with new empirical investigations. On the one hand, the concept of the developmental state itself can be seen to reflect the convergence between modernisation theory and dependency/world system theory over the indispensable role of the state in economic development. On the other hand, the various theoretical perspectives on the nature and conditions of the developmental state have revived old debates on the relative importance of factors such as culture and external environment.

In this chapter, I trace the origin of the concept of the developmental state and examine the three dominant theoretical perspectives on it with a view to bringing out as far as possible their complementary aspects as well as their contentions. In so doing, our own approach to the development experiences of Pacific Asia will be elucidated.

The chapter consists of three sections. In the first, a brief introduction is given to the spread of economic development in Pacific Asia by way of explaining the term 'the flying geese formation', which demonstrates the leadership role played by Japan in terms of its material and ideological influence on the region's new tiger economies. The second part traces the concept of the developmental state in the context of Japan's and the East Asian NICs' development experiences. Major characteristics of the developmental state are discussed. The third part then examines the nature and conditions of the developmental state from the three dominant theoretical perspectives of liberal institutionalism, culturalism and globalism. Finally, I will conclude by making the case for taking an integrated approach to Pacific Asian development, which centres on institutionalism and draws on aspects of culturalism and globalism.

THE FLYING GEESE FORMATION OF DEVELOPMENT

Students of economic development in Pacific Asia often come across the term 'the flying geese formation', describing the orderly pattern of industrialisation in the region. Broadly speaking, industrialisation in Pacific Asia spread from Northeast Asia to Southeast Asia, with Japan playing a central role – being the head goose – in the process. Being the first country in the region to become industrialised (Japan joined the Organization for Economic Cooperation and Development (OECD) in 1964), Japan became both the region's chief supplier of capital and technology and its development model, leading the spread of industrialisation from South Korea, Taiwan and Singapore to Malaysia, Indonesia and Thailand. To a great extent, the emergence of such a pattern of regional development fulfils the theoretical prediction first made by the Japanese economist Kaname Akamatsu (1896–1974), who coined the term 'the flying geese formation' (Korhonen 1994).

In Akamatsu's original formulation, the theory of the flying geese formation described the technology-led process of economic 'catch-up' in developing countries. According to the theory, an economically advanced nation serves as both a role model of development and a source of capital and technological know-how for the less advanced. By receiving material help and following the example of the lead nation, the followers gradually close their technological gap from the lead nation and move up the economic ladder. As they take up the leading role, they repeat the same process with their own less advanced followers. Over the years, however, this metaphor for economic development has acquired social and political dimensions. As the Japan-centred economic integration in the region deepened (see Chapter 10), political leaders across the region increasingly looked to Japan as a model not just of economic development but also of social and political development. Both the Japanese welfare system, with its emphasis on the limited role of the state, and its political system, with its stable one-party domination, came to be widely admired.

The Malaysian prime minister, Dr Mahathir, was among the most outspoken of political leaders in expressing the need for other Pacific Asian countries to 'look East' (i.e. to Japan), as opposed to West, for policy inspiration. In other words, the flying geese formation is increasingly used to refer to the underlying cultural similarities that are seen to be orienting all the countries towards a particular pattern of development distinct from the West. Western political scientists such as Pye (1985; 1988) and Huntington (1993a, b) also agree with this culturalist view in claiming that shared Asian values are in the process of forging a distinctive Asian model of development based on Japan.

I will come back to this cultural perspective in a later part of the chapter. At this stage, I will simply note that the flying geese formation has become associated with Pacific Asia's perceived common pattern of development, pioneered by Japan. In what follows, I will first trace the origin of the term developmental state and then move on to examine the nature and conditions of the developmental state from the three contending theoretical perspectives of liberal institutionalism, culturalism and globalism.

DEVELOPMENTAL STATES IN PACIFIC ASIA

The term 'developmental state' was first coined by Chalmers Johnson (1982) to describe modern Japanese economic development. However, despite its recent origin, the concept owes its intellectual debt to mid-nineteenth-century continental European writing on national political economy (Leftwich 1995; 1996). In advocating an alternative path of economic development for Germany, based on its late development, the German political economist Friedrich List was probably the first to articulate the ideas of the developmental state. Central to List's argument was the mercantilist idea that late-industrialising countries, such as Germany, needed strong state protection of their infant industries to enable them to compete successfully at a later stage with developed economies, such as Britain. Essentially, the Listian mercantilist case for protectionism was an argument for the delayed adoption of free-trade liberal economics, advocated by Adam Smith and associated with the British experience of economic development (Levi-Faur 1997).

List's idea was later picked up by the economic historian Alexander Gerschenkron, who described the industrial history of continental Europe as 'an orderly system of graduated deviation' from the first industrialisation of Britain (Gerschenkron 1962: 44). What was common about the European economies was the central role played by the state in their industrialisation, a role Gerschenkron argued to be necessitated by their common status as late developers.

In his study of Japan's economic history, Johnson further developed the notion of late development, which he saw as a product of a conscious political decision to industrialise. Late developers, Johnson (1995a: 45) argued, require mobilisation regimes to force their economic priorities on society. According to him, there were two fundamental types of such mobilisation regimes: the Leninist–Stalinist totalitarian model and the Bismarckian–Meiji authoritarian model. Both involved the setting of social goals, forced saving, mercantilism and bureaucratism. The second model, the capitalist developmental state (CDS), with imperial Germany and modern Japan being the prototypes, relies on market-conforming methods for economic intervention. Unlike the first model, which seeks to abolish market economy in its state-led industrialisation, the CDS uses the market as an instrument of industrialisation.

The Japanese developmental state

During the first two decades after World War II, in which the Japanese economy outgrew other Western economies, neo-classical economic theory dominated Western scholarship on Japanese economic development. Effectively, this perspective saw Japan's extraordinary growth as the product of a laissez-faire state, which does no more than get the business environment right for individual entrepreneurs to pursue their economic interest in the marketplace. Evidence used to support this view often included, for example, Japan's low level of taxation and public spending on government administration (which was significantly lower than the OECD average), and its resultant small bureaucracy, its low public spending on social policy, and its resultant minimalist welfare system, and the virtual absence of public ownership. The Japanese government, declared neo-classical economist, has always let the market allocate resources and in so doing has achieved the optimal level of economic efficiency (Patrick and Rosovsky 1976).

This interpretation of Japan's economic development, however, was seriously challenged in 1982, when Chalmers Johnson published his seminal work *MITI and the Japanese Miracle*. In his detailed study of the historical evolution of industrial policy in Japan, Johnson coined the term CDS ('capitalist developmental state') to describe Japan's post-war political economy. His main concern in using this term was to demonstrate that neo-classical economic theory is an inappropriate framework for understanding post-war Japanese economic success. Instead of being an orthodox free-market economy, as suggested by neo-classical theorists, Johnson argued, Japan is a CDS, which actively guides the market to serve political, not economic, ends. And later he wrote: 'The Japanese pursue economic activities primarily to achieve independence from and leverage over potential adversaries rather than to achieve consumer utility, private wealth, mutually beneficial trade, or any other objective posited by economic determinists.' (Johnson 1995b: 105).

Economic nationalism, authoritarianism and industrial policy

In Johnson's formulation, the Japanese developmental state is characterised by three key ingredients: economic nationalism, which is the driving force for development, authoritarian rule, which is the political context in which policy priorities are set, and the pursuit of strategic industrial policies by a technically competent bureaucracy. The roots of Japanese economic nationalism go back to the Meiji reforms of the 1870s, when the state led industrialisation in order to defend the country against Western imperialism. During the inter-war years, Japanese imperialism drove industrialisation; and in the post-war period, export promotion and competition for world market share has substituted for imperial expansion and war. Therefore, since the 1870s, the central role of the Japanese state has been to pursue economic development, construed as growth, productivity and competitiveness, as a means of ensuring national survival rather than maximising consumer benefits.

At the centre of Johnson's model of the Japanese developmental state is an authoritarian elite, which perpetuates itself through a conservative alliance. Since the war, the key actors in the alliance have been the pro-business Liberal Democratic Party (LDP), which dominates Japanese politics, and the bureaucrats that make and implement policies. This elite promotes national pride to motivate development and to deflect attention from constitutional development. Democracy is but a façade in post-war Japan, where the LDP, with the support of business, routinely achieves a parliamentary majority. Once in power, politicians 'reign' while bureaucrats 'rule' in collaboration with business. This tacit division of labour between politicians and bureaucrats, Johnson argues, is what gives the bureaucrats both the legitimacy of their rule and the necessary space in which to pursue national economic policies free from sectional societal pressure. In other words, the Japanese political arrangement makes bureaucratic rule both legitimate and insulated from social demand.

But authoritarianism is only a partial feature of the Japanese developmental state. The other equally important feature is bureaucratic competence, exemplified by Japan's highly successful industrial policy. According to Johnson, the industrial policy is the defining feature of the Japanese developmental state, which is highly interventionist in its attempt to structure the domestic industry to enhance its international competitiveness. Government not only allocates credit to strategic industries and provides financial support for export but also sets clear performance standards against which companies are rewarded or punished. Despite their commitment to free enterprise and markets, as Johnson (1982) noted, Japanese industrial planners were convinced that market forces alone would never have made Japan the industrial giant it is today. Goals such as this were typically set by the elite state bureaucracy in Japan, 'but in order to implement the goals, they must enter the market and manipulate and structure it so that private citizens responding to the incentives and disincentives make the market work for the state' (Johnson 1995a: 46).

The Ministry of International Trade and Industry (MITI) is the 'pilot agency' charged with formulating and implementing industrial policy. Its main duties are to identify the industries to be developed, select the best means of support to be made available to the targeted industries, and supervise competition in the designated sectors to ensure their economic health and effectiveness (Johnson 1982: 315). Apart from the political insulation noted earlier, Johnson identified three specific institutional factors that are crucial to the success of the bureaucracy. These are: the merit-based recruitment system, which brings into the bureaucracy highly talented individuals, the concentration of bureaucratic power within this single agency, and the establishment of close government–business ties, both formally and informally, which facilitates communication, consultation, policy formulation and implementation.

Johnson's model of the Japanese developmental state is basically that of a mobilisation regime, centred on a conservative alliance seeking to perpetuate its rule through unrelenting economic conquest in the world market. This alliance, consisting of politicians, bureaucrats and businesses, sets up an elaborate policy network of interaction to harness the market for the national mercantilist and productionist goals of economic development based on promoting export and production and discouraging import and consumption.

The NICs as BAIRs

Johnson's explanation of Japan's economic development soon became the new orthodoxy on Japanese political economy. His conceptual framework, the CDS, was subsequently applied to the entire region as industrialisation spread. The central role of the state in economic development was seen to be a common feature of all the tiger economies although it was recognised that, in individual countries, this role differed in form and effectiveness (Amsden 1985; 1989; Cumings 1987; Alam 1989; Wade 1990; Castells 1992; Rodan *et al.* 1997).

The East Asian NICs were seen to bear a particular resemblance to the Japanese developmental state, due partly to the historical legacy of Japanese colonial rule (in the cases of South Korea and Taiwan) and partly to the common cultural heritage of Confucianism. Like the Japan of the late nineteenth century, economic development in these nations was driven by a 'historic mission' of national survival and legitimating the regime. The resultant capacity of the state to promote and sustain economic development derived as much from its coercive ability to dominate and over-ride societal interests as from its institutional capacity to lead and persuade these interests to comply with policies (Johnson 1987; Weiss and Hobson 1995).

To distinguish post-war Japan from the East Asian NICs, Cumings (1987) characterises the latter as BAIRs: bureaucratic–authoritarian industrialising regimes. The BAIRs share with Japan a similar form of political economy: a market that is the engine of economic growth and an authoritarian state as the driver of the engine (Simone and Feraru 1995: 163). However, whereas post-war Japan relied largely on the 'soft authoritarianism' of persuasion and negotiation to ensure private business compliance with government guidance, the BAIRs have often relied on the blatant authoritarian methods of coercion and command. The Leninist-style party-states of Taiwan and Singapore and the military rule of South Korea were seen as the functional equivalents of post-war Japan's dominant party rule.

THEORETICAL PERSPECTIVES ON THE DEVELOPMENTAL STATE

The great emphasis on the developmental capacity of the state in Pacific Asia led to different theoretical perspectives on the nature and conditions of the developmental state. Broadly speaking, three such perspectives exist: liberal institutionalism, culturalism, and globalism. While the first perspective tends to emphasise the universal nature of the developmental state, the other two tend to emphasise contingent factors such as culture, geographical location and timing. In what follows, I will critically examine each of these perspectives with a view to highlighting their relevance to the subsequent chapters.

Liberal institutionalism

As the developmental state theory emerged in response to what its proponents saw to be the erroneous interpretation of the East Asian economic miracle, it was initially greeted by neo-classical writers with the criticism of being a 'statist' theory. However, as evidence mounted that the states in these countries did intervene not just in a 'market-conforming' but also in a 'market-guiding' manner, the critics were forced to moderate their positions. Consequently, neo-classical economic writers began to modify their minimalist conception of the state in favour of a liberal view of 'competent state intervention' (World Bank 1991a). What this amounts to was a recognition of the institutional foundations of capitalism, the importance of which for economic development neo-classical writers had hitherto ignored.

The institutionalist understanding of the developmental state sees it as neither a description of, nor a prescription for, the state overtaking market. Rather, it moves the debate beyond the arid concern about the relative merits of markets and government action. Such a question, as Krueger (1992: 35) argues, is 'inherently unanswerable', because it fails to consider the institutional context of the market. What, in the institutionalist view, the developmental state theory demonstrates is both the reality and the desirability of the appropriate mixture of market orientation and state intervention in a manner that promotes efficient late industrialisation (Onis 1991; Weiss and Hobson 1995). In this mixture, the extent (i.e. how much) of state intervention matters less than the quality (i.e. what kind) of intervention (Evans 1995: 11). Strategic targeting and institution building are the key ingredients of successful intervention.

The emphasis on institution building is thus the main concern of the institutionalist perspective. The intellectual basis of this concern goes back to Polanyi (1944), who argued that competition and markets are not spontaneous social phenomena; rather, they are shaped and made possible by an underlying framework of institutions and social practices, such as patterns of property ownership, the legal system, modes of corporate organisation, managerial practices, ideologies and norms of socialisation. According to this view, a neo-classical laissez-faire capitalism can exist only in libertarian fantasies, because capitalism is congenitally incapable of reproducing the mainsprings of its own internal logic without the aid of extra-capitalist social infrastructures. Its common inborn fatal weaknesses include the free-riding problem, i.e. the tendency for market participants to reap benefits from markets without having to pay for them, its tendency to generate a systematic social inequality that threatens its long-term efficiency, and its inability to protect cultural values that are threatened by commercial interests. The efficient operation of the market, therefore, requires highly developed institutional frameworks for the regulation of economic activity and for running social welfare programmes (Doner 1992; Haggard and Kaufman 1992). Furthermore, only the state is in a position to construct these frameworks, which can address such issues as free-riding and collective interests.

The institutionalist view, which sees the market as a conscious political construct involving the state rather than a self-regulating technical mechanism, has had a huge impact on development thinking and policy. Nowhere is this more evident than in the policy shift of the World Bank, for long a major source of influence on development thinking and policy in the Third World, not least because of its financial contributions. Since the early 1990s, the Bank has become increasingly concerned with the issue of the institutional capacity for economic development. In one of its discussion papers, it states that 'without the institutions and supportive framework of the state to create and enforce the rules [to make markets work more effectively], to establish law and order, and to ensure property rights, production and investment will be deterred and development hindered' (World Bank 1991b: 3). The Bank's 1993 study *The East Asian Miracle: Economic Growth and Public Policy* also goes some way towards acknowledging the developmental role of the East Asian states, a role it thinks lacking in their Southeast Asian counterparts.

But hitherto the most revealing sign of the Bank's embracing the institutionalist agenda was reflected in its *World Development Report 1997: The State in a Changing World*. In this report the Bank not only dismisses as 'extreme' its erstwhile long-held view of the minimalist state but also declares such a state to be 'ineffective'. The minimalist view, it argues, is at odds with the evidence of the world's development success stories, be it the development of the industrial economies in the nineteenth century or the post-war growth 'miracles' of East Asia. It thus concludes that 'development requires an effective state, one that encourages and complements the activities of private businesses and individuals. . . . Without it, sustainable development, both economic and social, is impossible.' One of the greatest challenges for development in the twenty-first century, it thus concludes, is neither to shrink the state into insignificance nor to expand it to dominate the market but to make it effective.

The conceptual framework within which the World Bank pursues the institutionalist agenda is the notion of governance. Essentially, this refers to the idea that fundamental changes in political and administrative structures in Third World countries are a prerequisite for development. Although the Bank recoils from using terms such as democracy, constrained mainly by its articles of association, the components of 'good governance' that it has specified in its successive Development Reports (World Bank 1992; 1997) can be easily associated with democratic governance. For good governance is construed as encompassing elements such as accountability, whereby 'public officials must be held responsible for their actions'; the rule of law, which is enforced by 'independent judicial bodies'; and information and transparency, whereby information concerning public policy is available to the public for analysis and debate. While all these institutional capacities are couched in technical terms, as if they were pieces of readily transferable technology, the Bank also talks of the need to construct 'mechanisms to compensate those who stand to lose from reforms. In other words, institutional reform is far from being a technical process; rather, it is an intrinsically political process involving contending social interests.

The move from neo-classical liberalism to liberal institutionalism in development thinking since the early 1990s can be seen to closely parallel the emergence of modernisation revisionism in the late 1960s. Like modernisation revisionism, liberal institutionalism sees capitalist economic development as the driving force for modernisation, without falling prey to the simplistic economic determinism associated with neo-classical liberalism, which Johnson so forcefully criticised in his work. The institutionalist perspective on the developmental state not only sees the capitalist market as a political construct but also envisages the state adapting its role to the continuing changes in the political economy. Many theorists of the developmental state, for example, expect to see the state acting in a more authoritarian vein during the early stages of industrialisation, when the capacity to apply vast amounts of capital and labour is decisive (Krugman 1994). Echoing Huntington (1968), Leftwich (1996: 287) argues that the weakness of civil society may well be a condition for the emergence and consolidation of the developmental state. However, as Evans (1992) cogently argues, in an era of deregulation and liberalisation, the state, which was once the solution, may well turn out to be the problem if new institutional capacities are not built.

In stressing the social and political embeddedness of the developmental state, institutional political economists clearly see economic development in general, and the developmental state in particular, as a product of politics. In this view, the obstacles to building an effective state that facilitates economic development would invariably lie in political arrangements in which anti-development interests prevail. However, this view is shared by neither the culturalist nor the globalist, who tend to emphasise the unique nature of the developmental state. I will now turn to the cultural perspective of the developmental state.

New Orientalism

The cultural perspective on the developmental state stems from its interest in the common cultural heritage of Japan and the NICs. Why is it, asks the culturalist, that the developmental state has appeared only in the Confucian part of Pacific Asia and not in other regions such as Africa and Latin America? In seeking to answer this, culturalists have rediscovered the Weberian perspective on the relationship between culture and capitalism (see Chapter 1). However, unlike Weber and his followers, who until the 1970s had routinely dismissed Oriental religions and cultures as unconducive to development, 'New Orientalists', as Woo-Cumings (1993:

138) dubbed them, seek to argue just the opposite. The Asian development miracles, they say, have proved that 'Asian values' are key determinants of their success.

New Orientalists agree with the institutionalist on the sociocultural embeddedness of the East Asian developmental states. However, unlike the institutionalist, they tend to elevate culture as the single most important factor shaping the East Asian developmental states. Asian cultures, they argue, rather than being inhospitable to capitalism, are in fact fostering an 'Oriental model' of capitalism different from Western capitalism. Unlike the Western 'rational model' of capitalism, based on 'Western' values such as 'efficiency, individualism and dynamism', the 'Oriental model', or *Asian* capitalism, is based on 'human emotional bonds, group orientation and harmony' (Tai 1989; Mahathir and Ishihara 1995). According to this view, all the major institutional characteristics of Asian capitalism are best understood in terms of their common cultures. These institutional aspects include: authoritarian–paternalistic state leadership, competent official guidance, harmonious corporate management based on personal family-like relations, characterised by respect for authority, and societal commitment to education, meritocracy and the work discipline (Pye 1988; Rozman 1992; Sakakibara 1993; Yoshihara 1994).

The cultural perspective on the developmental state sheds some insight into the cultural values that mould East Asian capitalism. Many would perhaps agree with its core idea that cultures and traditions provide social actors with the 'mental models . . . that will shape choices' (North 1994: 366–7). However, the key weakness of this perspective is its apolitical conception of culture, which fails to address the issue of the political basis of culture, namely the social relations of domination and subjugation from which it emerged and which it seeks to legitimise. This failure is primarily manifested in the essentialist conceptualisation of culture, which sees its essence as virtually unchangeable throughout time as a result of what it sees as the benign process of socialisation. Therefore, an immediate problem facing the culturalist is the question of timing, namely, why did Asian cultures fail to play a catalytic role in capitalist development only a few decades ago? Surely if culture does not change easily, something else must have changed, which enables presumably the same culture to function in such opposing ways – from a brake on development to a catalyst for development.

A closer look into the apparently unchanging culture invariably reveals the underlying political process at work, a process that involves using the language of culture to legitimise changing political priorities. In other words, culture is often used as a powerful political weapon, an official ideology, so to speak, either to rationalise the status quo or to mobilise public support for change. This is particularly true in authoritarian regimes, in which there is little opportunity for the public to challenge the officially sanctioned version of the society's putatively shared culture. As a result, what is seen to be a culturally determined phenomenon is often a product of public policy, despite the utterances to the contrary of political leaders.

The political psychology of justifying policy in terms of age-old tradition was first systematically studied by Hobsbawm and others in a seminal collection of essays edited by Hobsbawm and Rangers (1983). Authors in this collection had discovered that many 'traditions', which appear or claim to be old, are often quite recent in origin and sometimes invented, and that many aspects of the 'national culture' in Europe belong to this category. In his study of Europe during the period 1870–1914, for example, Hobsbawm (1983a: 267–8) showed how the widespread progress of electoral democracy and the consequent emergence of mass politics dominated the invention of official traditions designed to restore, quoting Edmund Burke, 'the pleasing illusions which made power gentle and obedience liberal'. Furthermore, it was argued that 'all invented traditions, so far as possible, use history as a legitimator of action and cement of group cohesion' (Hobsbawm 1983b: 12). And finally, the process of inventing tradition itself invariably involves 'fabrication of facts, selective remembering and partial forgetting' of the nation's 'kaleidoscope of historical facts and contradictory cultural phenomena' (Befu 1993:4).

The distinction between culture and the political use of culture is thus the key to understanding the culturalist conundrum on the timing of development in Pacific Asia. As our studies will show, a combination of changing international and domestic situations have been crucial to the resort to the political use of culture in Pacific Asia in its quest for development. In the next section, I will highlight the international aspect of the developmental state by focusing on the globalist perspective.

Globalism

Like the culturalist, the globalist also emphasises the contingent nature of the developmental state in Pacific Asia; the only difference is that historical/ geopolitical specificity replaces cultural specificity. In the globalist view, international politics and global economy have been the key factors shaping the emergence and characteristics of the developmental state in Pacific Asia. Specifically, these have included the Cold War and the resultant geopolitical interactions between the United States and Pacific Asia, geostrategic security concerns at the regional level, and the long post-war economic boom, which lasted until the mid-1970s.

According to the globalist, international and regional geostrategic rivalry played a key role in generating the 'political will to develop' in the East Asian NICs, and the mechanisms by which this worked varied between states faced with different domestic issues. For South Korea and Taiwan, the Cold War created powerful 'brother enemies' in terms of both ideology and military strength, generating a heightened sense of national vulnerability. For Singapore, its forced independence in the wake of its expulsion from Malaysia provoked a 'crisis of survival', which motivated a concerted national struggle for development. For all three societies, therefore, economic development was a matter of national efficacy rather than simple economic efficiency. As Wade (1992: 314) observed, 'whereas the governments of most other developing countries know they can fail economically and not risk invasion, the governments and elites of these countries know that without fast economic growth and social stability this could well happen.' The imperative of survival also produced a greater degree of public tolerance to authoritarian rule.

The Cold War, together with the cyclical upturn in the world economy, also provided Pacific Asia with the opportunities for economic expansion, which would otherwise have been more difficult (Cumings 1987; Haggard 1989). Essentially, the region benefited disproportionately in comparison with other developing regions from favourable US aid, trade, and financial policies, motivated by its foreign policy objective of containing communism in Asia. Although South Korea and Taiwan both benefited directly from US military and economic aid because of their strategic geopolitical positions, Japan and all East Asian NICs saw their economies boosted by the Vietnam War, which lasted from the early 1960s to the mid-1970s. On top of these, the United States also opened its market to the region and tolerated the mercantilist policies pursued by the developmental states, an act made easier by the long post-war boom in the world economy, which lasted until the mid-1970s.

The unique international security and economic environment in which East Asian developmental states emerged led some to argue that the developmental state was a historically contingent phenomenon unlikely to emerge elsewhere in the post-Cold War world (Strange 1996: 6–7). This view also sees the East Asian developmental states as primarily a product of good fortune, i.e. their critical geopolitical importance to the US anti-communist foreign policy. However, as Weiss and Hobson (1995: 183–90) pointed out, the differences in the degree of state effectiveness in promoting economic development in the region, for example between Northeast Asia and Southeast Asia, suggest a tendency to overplay the external factors in shaping the developmental state. After all, a central feature of the developmental state, it is argued, involves its institutional capacity to adapt to and mediate external influences.

CONCLUSION

In this chapter I have taken an overview of the development experiences of Pacific Asia in the context of the conceptual and theoretical framework of the developmental state. Although there are different theoretical perspectives on the nature and conditions of the developmental state, it is possible to adopt an integrated approach to Pacific Asian development that is centred on the liberal institutionalist perspective and incorporates culturalist and globalist insights. Essentially, this would require recognition of the political–institutional foundation of development, which shapes and is shaped by culture and which mediates the effect of international exigencies outside the control of the state. From this synthesised perspective, economic development must no longer be analysed as a technical phenomenon but as a political outcome, which can only take place within a framework of effective state institutions capable of regulating economic activities and reconciling conflicting social interests. In short, what is called for is a political economic approach to development, which examines the dynamic interaction between politics and economics.

3   The political economy of 'Confucian' capitalisms

South Korea, Taiwan and Singapore were the first group of countries to join Japan as Asia's NICs after undergoing sustained hyper-growth during the 1960s to 1970s. Although they were later joined by the three Southeast Asian tiger economies of Malaysia, Indonesia and Thailand, known as NECs (newly exporting countries), the differences between the two groups of economies were widely noted. Whereas the NICs, together with Japan, were often characterised as 'Confucian capitalism', based on strong, effective state traditions, the NECs were described as 'ersatz capitalism', which was based on weak, inefficient state traditions (Yoshihara 1988).

There are undoubtedly important differences between the NICs and the NECs in terms of their institutional settings and state effectiveness, an aspect I will pick up in the next chapter. But in this chapter, I will focus on the four so-called 'Confucian capitalisms' with a view to identifying and explaining the similarities and differences in their trajectories of economic development. As the use of 'Confucian' suggests the centrality of culture in these political economies, our study will therefore focus on the extent to which, and the manner in which, Confucianism has influenced their development. By comparing the institutional settings of capitalism in these countries, and the government–business relations in particular, I seek to demonstrate a common pattern of development, characterised by adept elite use of Confucian *ideology* to construct very different institutions to suit unique national situations. In other words, authoritarian regimes in all these countries selected aspects of Confucianism to rationalise their particular form of capitalism.

The chapter consists of two parts. The first will give an overview of the institutional forms of the four capitalisms. In the second, I will compare these forms by situating them in their national–historical and international contexts. Finally, I will conclude by noting the political basis of development that is common to all four capitalisms.

CONFUCIAN CAPITALISMS: AN OVERVIEW

In the developmental state literature, the state in the four Confucian capitalisms is commonly seen to be strong, a notion that mainly involves two aspects: the combination of political authoritarianism with technocratic competence, and a more or less institutionalised fusion of economic and political power in the form of close government–business relations (Onis 1991; Weiss and Hobson 1995). New Orientalists usually attribute the strong state to the Confucian heritage, which is common to all the developmental state societies.

However, despite the common strong state tradition, the four capitalisms vary a great deal in terms of their political–institutional forms. Just as European industrialisation progressed as a graduated deviation from the initial industrialisation process in Britain, the developmental states of the three NICs were not simple replications of the Japanese model. Apart from the rhetoric of Confucianism, all three constructed very different institutions to suit their respective historical and international positions. National variations, in terms of both the institutional context of state intervention and the industrial structure of these economies, therefore, militate against any simplistic generalisation about the Confucian influence on capitalism in East Asia.

Of the three NICs, South Korea and Taiwan were seen to be closest to Japan in their development experiences, largely because of their colonial occupation by Japan. Yet even this perception needs an important qualification as both South Korea and Taiwan differed not only a great deal from Japan but also from each other. Japan and South Korea both relied on large-scale conglomerates for industrialisation; however, in Japan, small businesses and their close links with both the conglomerates and the long-ruling LDP (Liberal Democratic Party) were an essential part of Japanese 'alliance capitalism' (Hamilton and Biggart 1988; Gerlach 1992; K.-R. Kim 1993; 1994). In South Korea, by contrast, the large, diversified family-run conglomerates, *chaebol*, dominated the political economy in terms of both their market position and their close relationship with the military regime. Korean capitalism was thus essentially *chaebol* capitalism with economic power concentrated in the hands of the *chaebol* (Amsden 1989; K.-R. Kim 1998).

Taiwan and Singapore displayed further differences. Unlike Japan and South Korea, Taiwan's economic structure was dominated by small and medium-sized enterprises (SMEs) operating in the private sector, which existed alongside a large, state-owned sector run by a quasi-Leninist one-party state, the KMT state (Wade 1990; Cheng 1989). The SMEs were the backbone of Taiwan's crucial export sector, accounting for two-thirds of total exports during the 1980s (Lam and Clark 1998: 120). Most of the SMEs were family-based networks of subcontractors with linkages with multinational corporations (MNCs), and relied largely on their own family savings, a cooperative savings network and limited government bank credits for business finance.

The government–business relationship in Taiwan was thus more 'cool and distant' than collaborative and close (Chu 1989), as reflected in both the dual economic structure and the limited government financial support for the SMEs. The success of Taiwan's 'family capitalism' was nevertheless inextricably linked to an active rather than laissez-faire state, which provided excellent physical and social infrastructure and a protectionist environment (Greenhalgh 1988; Redding 1990). Taiwan was the first country to pioneer the idea of export-processing zones (EPZs), which offered integrated infrastructure and fiscal incentives to foreign companies wishing to operate in Taiwan. This practice subsequently became widespread in the region, copied by ostensibly communist China and Vietnam.

Finally, Singapore offered yet another institutional model of capitalism, which is best described as transnational capitalism. At the centre of this model was the alliance between the Leninist party-state and the MNCs. Because of its small size, Singapore opted for a development strategy centred on two aspects: actively attracting foreign direct investment (FDI) to the manufacturing sector, and bringing key enterprises under state control (Gayle 1989). As a result, Singapore has the largest dependency in Pacific Asia on FDI for its capital formation; more than 80 per cent of its investment in the manufacturing sector comes from FDI (Islam and Chowdhury 1997: 203). Foreign enterprises were thus the most important agents of industrialisation in Singapore.

Meanwhile, the state exerted enormous influence over the domestic economy through statutory boards and state-owned enterprises, many of which entered into joint ventures with MNCs. In 1988, government-linked companies (GLCs) were responsible for 60.5 per cent of total realised profits (Vennewald 1994: 25–8). Senior civil servants, ministers and former ministers all had seats on the boards of hundreds of public and private firms (Regnier 1991: 235). The leading business entrepreneurs in Singapore are effectively government bureaucrats, who are also the main source of membership of the People's Action Party (PAP), which has ruled Singapore since 1959 (Khong 1995). Capitalism in Singapore is thus effectively dominated by close alliance between the PAP state and the MNCs.

Having drawn a sketch of the four Confucian capitalisms, I will now turn to their detailed analysis. In what follows, I will seek to make sense of the differences by situating each in its respective national political context and examining them from both comparative and international perspectives.

THE MAKING OF CONFUCIAN CAPITALISMS: A COMPARATIVE ANALYSIS

Japan: alliance capitalism

The rapid transformation of the post-war Japanese economy is well documented, and there is not much dispute about the developmental capacity of the Japanese state. So what interests us is the historical and international context in which the Japanese developmental state was wrought.

There has long been a tradition, both in Japan and beyond, of attributing the Japanese developmental state to the unique Japanese, i.e. Confucian, culture, which is said to underpin the essential characteristics of Japan's alliance capitalism. According to this view, the Japanese political economy is the epitome of the Confucian image of the family, bound by fatherly benevolence and filial piety. Like all family members, the hierarchy of the rights-/duties-based social relations all pull in the same direction for the sake of the Japanese nation. While the state stands at the apex of the hierarchy, providing welfare to and commanding obedience and loyalty from the population, the firm is the backbone upon which the state depends for effecting its duties. Japanese firms are in turn portrayed as corporate fathers, who treat their employees with benevolence, for example by organising enterprise unions, to which both managers and employees belong, and by offering job security and rewarding loyalty through seniority pay increases (Morishima 1982; Dore 1987; Sakakibara 1993; Yoshihara 1994).

However, a closer examination of the origin of the Japanese developmental state reveals the profound influence of politics on these apparently cultural traits of Japanese capitalism. External threats, perceived and real, symbolised in the historic landing of Commodore Perry's 'black ships' at Tokyo Bay in 1853, proved to be decisive in the nation's drive to Westernise in the name of restoring traditional values (Gluck 1985). Under the Meiji Restoration in 1868, led by the samurai (warriors), who overthrew the 265-year-old Tokugawa feudal regime, Confucianism was successfully reworked as part of the Shinto doctrine of the Emperor cult. In the name of Shintoism, which justified unconditional obedience to the Emperor, Father of the Japanese nation, the far-reaching Meiji reforms were introduced with the aim of creating 'a rich country and a strong army'. The army and the school became the two key instruments of this 'nation-building' project, which, argues Williams (1994: 8), is 'the most singular achievement of Japanese public policy over the past twelve decades'.

The Meiji period (1868–1912) thus marked the beginning of Japan's developmental state. The traditions of state intervention and close government–business collaboration, together with other major elements of the economic structure, had their origins during the Meiji period and the inter-war years, when military ambition drove Japan towards industrial expansion. Since then, despite the upheavals of its defeat in World War II and the subsequent US-led radical restructuring of its society and economy, these basic patterns have continued well into the 1990s.

The Meiji reforms created a bureaucratic–authoritarian state, modelled on Bismarckian Germany. A powerful bureaucracy and military stood at the centre of the state apparatus. Two decades after becoming directly involved in heavy industry, financial difficulties forced the state to sell non-military operations to big combined family businesses, the *zaibatsu*. This marked the beginning of close government–business relations as the *zaibatsu* were used as instruments of state policy aimed at integrating profits with patriotism. With the help of the state, the *zaibatsu* grew into giant conglomerates, combining industrial, financial and trading activities, organised around a central holding company. They in turn became major financial supporters of the then two main conservative political parties in exchange for continued state support (Eccleston 1989: 13, 109). After the war, the *zaibatsu* were revamped into *keiretsu*, which, in alliance with the ruling LDP, played a key role in post-war Japanese economic reconstruction.

After the late 1920s, state–business collaboration intensified both in response to international economic crises and as a result of the rise of militarism. Many of the post-war industrial interventionist practices originated from this period, including the state assuming powers to forge cartels, to persuade *zaibatsu* members to reorganise production capacities, to approve investments designed to expand facilities, to license production and to sponsor a limited group of capital intensive firms to pioneer technical change. The bureaucracy, the Ministry of Commerce and Industry (MCI), dubbed 'the economic general staff', which was responsible for all these policies, was to be reincarnated in 1949 as the famous MITI, the engine room of the post-war Japanese economic miracle. At the same time, the labour movement and political parties advocating class confrontation were either brutally repressed or banned outright, while moderate articulations were tolerated and co-opted by both the management and the state (Garon 1987; Fukui 1992: 201–2).

But by far the most far-reaching achievement of the state was its success in inventing a 'culture of harmony' as a normative economic value for the emerging industrial society (Kinzley 1991). Using the familiar symbolism of the Confucian family, and through its agency the Kyochokai (Cooperative and Harmony Society, created in 1919), the state articulated and successfully promoted the vision of a future Japanese society based on industrial harmony and cooperation. The success was also buttressed by a substantial programme of social and economic reforms, which centred around labour legislation aimed at providing minimum benefits to workers.

During the inter-war years, thousands of 'patriotic industrial associations', comprising management and workers, were organised with both explicit support and covert coercion by the state (Garon 1987). These associations were the forerunners of the unique Japanese *enterprise union*, so often portrayed as an icon of Japanese culture. After the war, these associations 'simply shed their old skins and continued their existence' with the explicit sanctions of the US forces, which, influenced by the Cold War, became more interested in taming the unions than promoting industrial democracy.

Another distinctive feature of the post-war Japanese economy, which also originated during the inter-war years, was the institutionalised subcontracting link between small firms and the *keiretsu*. Just as the enterprise union was not a result of a 'natural' Japanese inclination to identify with the larger community, this owed equally little to Japanese culture, which was based on 'hierarchical but personalised long-term relationships of trust and patronage'. Instead, it resulted from large firms hiving off much of their production to smaller firms that used 'cheaper and more dispensable labour'. Its continuing existence after the war was the outcome of both deliberate government policies and reciprocal benefits generated for both sides (Eccleston 1989: Ch. 2 and 4; Francks 1999: 252).

It is thus clear that economic nationalism dressed up in the Confucian/Shinto language of family/state loyalty was the driving force of the Japanese developmental state, which relied on a two-pronged strategy of ideological construction and ameliorative social reforms to achieve its modernisation objectives. How then did the Japanese state manage to preserve its continuity after World War II?

The answer to this lies mainly with the Cold War-induced international geopolitics. At the end of the war, Japan came under occupation by the US-led Allied Powers. Having forced the Japanese government to adopt a US-written democratic constitution, the US occupying forces initiated a radical reform programme, centred on demilitarising, decentralising and democratising the Japanese regime. However, except for demilitarisation, the programme was soon blown off course by the onset of the Cold War. The new foreign policy priority of strengthening Japan as a bulwark against communism in Asia led the United States to pursue a 'reverse course', which either abandoned or diluted the original reform programme. As a result, the bureaucracy was strengthened, retaining 80 per cent of the pre-war bureaucrats who had worked at the centre of Japan's war machine. Those who stayed in MITI were then given a free hand to reconstruct *keiretsu* out of the wartime *zaibatsu*.

Neutralisation of the burgeoning labour militarism, supported by the Japanese Communist Party, was another important consequence of the reverse course that ensured the continuity of the Japanese political economy.

This was carried out with the explicit support of the US occupying forces by a host of tactics involving dismissal, co-option, and cultural mobilisation (Eccleston 1989: 69–85). In order to fragment the labour movement, the state effectively forced the workers to be organised in enterprise unions. Potential dissenters were labelled as either pro-communists, bent on destabilising Japan, or traitors to the Japanese nation, who were corrupted by Western individualist values (Clark 1979: 175). To reward workers who joined the enterprise union, the management offered a small proportion of them lifetime employment and wages based on seniority and promotion in the name of Confucian benevolence. Furthermore, while managerial prerogative was tightly guarded, practices such as group decision making, group responsibility and the minimisation of status differences between managers and workers were introduced (Yoshihara 1994: 151). The state helped to reinforce this cultural legitimation of group solidarity by setting up the Japan Productivity Centre in 1955, which instituted consultations between management and labour and introduced the zero defect movement and quality control circles.

This period of 'authoritarian liberalism' (Kabashima 1993), which lasted until the early 1960s and was characterised by intense ideological confrontation (see Chapter 5), gradually faded into the political background as the ruling elite concentrated on economic growth. With the pre-war power structure intact, the post-war Japanese political economy continued to be dominated by the iron triangle of the ruling party (the LDP, established in 1955), the bureaucracy and big business. 'Corporatism without labour' was thus the essence of the 'soft authoritarian' approach to post-war Japanese economic management (Pempel and Tsunekawa 1979; Johnson 1982).

South Korea and Taiwan: *chaebol* capitalism versus family capitalism

South Korea and Taiwan were Japanese colonies for 35 and 50 years, respectively, before they gained independence in 1945. Consequently, the development experiences of the two countries were deeply influenced by Japan. Like Japan, neither society was well endowed with natural resources, yet both achieved rapid economic development within two decades or so. By the late 1980s, both South Korea and Taiwan, together with Japan, had become significant foreign investors in Southeast Asia. Since the late 1980s, democracy in both societies has also been firmly entrenched. At the time of writing, South Korea is the world's eleventh trading economy and Taiwan the fourteenth, both enjoying a living standard similar to that of the industrialised West. However, different national situations meant that economic development in the two societies was achieved under very different institutional settings.

The regimes under which industrialisation took place in both societies were 'hard authoritarian', similar to pre-war Japan. In South Korea, a period under a nominally democratic regime (1945–61) brought economic chaos and political instability, which ended in 1961 in a military coup led by General Park Chung Hee. Economic development took off under Park's quasi-military rule, which ended in his assassination in 1979. The two 5-year plans (1962–6 and 1967–71), which launched Korea on export-oriented industrialisation (EOI), laid solid foundations for Korea's economic progress. In Taiwan, economic development was presided over by the National Party (or the KMT (Kuomintang) in its Chinese abbreviation), whose supporters fled mainland China in 1949 after the party's defeat by the Chinese Communist Party in the civil war. The regime was a quasi-Leninist one as the KMT controlled all levels of governmental and military units through its central organisations. Under martial law, which lasted until 1986, the ruthless KMT apparatus hunted down political dissidents and banned the formation of all independent parties and civic associations, while setting up its own as a means of both penetrating society and co-opting social organisations into its fold.

However, the foundation of the state's infrastructural capacity to take the economic lead in both societies was laid during Japanese colonial rule. The military style of the Japanese colonial administration, with its emphasis on hierarchy, discipline and efficiency, meant that both societies inherited a relatively efficient bureaucracy when they embarked on post-war development (Amsden 1985; Cumings 1987). In addition, the Japanese-sponsored land reform in the two societies also strengthened the state, as the transformation of the agricultural system into one of small-holding cultivation led to the elimination of the feudal landlord class, which was often a major barrier to industrialisation in developing countries.

As in Meiji Japan, the political will for economic development in both societies was motivated by the 'crisis of survival', occasioned by a combination of domestic political crises and 'external shocks'. At the end of World War II, Korea was divided into two parts along the thirty-eighth parallel, with the North occupied by the communist USSR and the South by the capitalist United States. The outbreak of the Cold War institutionalised the division. In 1950, South Korea was invaded by the North, which provoked the 3-year Korean War. During this period, massive US assistance and military aid was crucial to the country's survival (Haggard and Cheng 1987: 87). Until the late 1950s, aid from the United States was a major source of South Korea's capital investment.

When General Park came to power in 1961, he was faced with two immediate problems. The first was the need to overcome the problem of legitimacy and lack of social support. The second was the impending withdrawal of US economic aid at a time when South Korea still lagged behind the North in its per capita income, industrial production capacity and military strength. This acute sense of national and regime vulnerability drove the government to commit the whole nation 'to industrial mobilisation for a development war against North Korea' (Burmeister 1990: 202). 'Nation-building through exports' became the guiding principle of the Park regime, which pursued a strategy of 'forced expansion' of exports and investment to achieve 'growth at any cost' (Song 1990: 90, 91).

Taiwan's experience was similar, except that the KMT lost no time in toying with democracy following the flight to Taiwan. Until the early 1960s, industrialisation was motivated solely by the KMT's desire to retake mainland China by military means. Consequently, state-owned heavy industry was given development priority. China's involvement in the Korean War meant that Taiwan, like South Korea, also received massive economic and military assistance from the United States. However, the shock came in 1963 when the United States announced its intention to terminate aid in 1965. This forced President Chiang Kai-shek to quickly shift his priorities 'from a military campaign against the mainland to the economic independence of Taiwan' (Johnson 1987: 155). Consequently, the Council on the United States Aid was quickly converted into the Council for Economic Cooperation and Development (CECD), which was charged with the task of policy formulation and coordination, a role similar to Japan's MITI and South Korea's Economic Planning Board (EPB).

However, unique national situations led to different strategies for economic development. In South Korea, the state promoted Japanese-style conglomerates known as *chaebol* and helped them grow into the backbone of the Korean economy. Close government–business relations centred on the state allocation of banking credit to strategically targeted industries in exchange for *chaebol* compliance with government-set performance targets (Amsden 1989: 14). Throughout the Park era, industrial policy making was highly centralised; the EPB was made directly accountable to the president. Similarly, policy implementation was often heavy handed, sometimes involving the secret police; businessmen who evaded or refused state direction were threatened with confiscation of assets or prosecution (Weiss 1995: 175). A failed entrepreneur who had taken state subsidies might even be imprisoned (Gibney 1992: 57). Kwan S. Kim (1997: 95) suggests that the heavy reliance of Korean business on state-controlled bank credits, which supplied over two-thirds of the cash flow of manufacturing firms, was a deliberate government policy to put private business in a weak bargaining position vis-à-vis the state.

The KMT regime in Taiwan followed a different interventionist path largely because of the historical legacy of political schism between the 'mainlanders', the KMT followers who arrived in Taiwan in 1949, and the 'Taiwanese', the indigenous majority who had migrated to Taiwan (also from China) about three centuries earlier. The brutal suppression of the native Taiwanese by the KMT upon coming to Taiwan resulted in a Malaysian-style implicit division of labour between the two communities which was to last until the 1980s. This was the arrangement in which the mainlanders monopolised government offices and large state-owned enterprises while the Taiwanese were free to set up their own businesses. As a result, a dual economy developed, with the state-owned large firms dominating the 'commanding heights' of the economy and Taiwanese family-owned SMEs dominating the export sector (Gold 1986; Tien 1989). Limited government–business collaboration also prevented the growth of large firms in the private sector (Fields 1995). In comparison with Korea, Taiwan's dual economic structure and distant government–business financial relationship made the government 'relatively slow' in promoting structural change in the private sector (Chu 1989: 667).

Policy on FDI was another area in which South Korea and Taiwan diverged, although neither economy relied on FDI as an important tool of industrialisation. However, restrictions on foreign companies to set up direct operations in both economies were motivated by different political considerations. For South Korea, having historically been at the centre of rivalry among the regional powers, China, Japan and Russia, and having suffered the brutal rule of Japanese colonialism, national independence was paramount. Consequently, the Park regime positively *discouraged* FDI, Japanese in particular, as a source of both capital and advanced technology to avoid the nation's excessive dependence on foreign influence. Instead, the state resorted to other methods of raising capital, such as borrowing from international organisations and commercial sectors and accessing advanced technology, such as licensing. For those foreign firms that were allowed in, standards of technology transfer and export performance were stringently enforced.

The situation in Taiwan was less straightforward. Following the loss of its UN seat to the communist People's Republic of China (PRC) in 1971, the KMT regime pursued an official policy of encouraging the inflow of FDI as a means of avoiding the nation's international isolation. Despite this, the state exercised tight control on the process to ensure that MNCs operated in compliance with national priorities. In approving projects, priority was given to firms committed to technology transfer, to exports and to fostering economic linkage with local economy, i.e. by purchasing inputs from local producers. As a result, FDI in the first part of the 1980s accounted for a mere 2 per cent of Taiwan's gross domestic product (GDP) and 25.6 per cent of its total exports, only slightly higher than in South

Korea (Purcell 1987: 81). Since the late 1980s, however, both South Korea and Taiwan have liberalised their policies on FDI, which began to rise thereafter (Ramstetter 1998: 197–200).

As in Meiji Japan, states in both societies used Confucianism to legitimate repressive labour market intervention. In particular, Confucian rhetoric was used to inculcate patriotism as a means of exhorting the workers to work hard for the nation. However, behind the common rhetoric lay very different approaches to labour discipline as a means of providing cheap labour for industrialisation.

South Korea is often considered to be the most Confucian society in East Asia (K. S. Kim 1997: 100). Yet, ironically, South Korea also has the most militant labour movement in East Asia. Labour resistance and unrest has been present throughout Korea's entire period of rapid economic growth, making Korea politically the most unstable economy in East Asia. The reason for this lies mainly with the highly brutal methods used by successive military governments to subjugate the workforce. Under both Park and his successor, General Chun Doo Hwan (who came to power through another coup in 1981 and ruled Korea until 1987), unions were forbidden and worker activists were severely repressed, constantly harassed and intimidated (Lie 1991: 71). Workers were concentrated in large factories organised by quasi-military management, a situation itself favouring the emergence of militant trade unionism, and were forced to work the longest hours in the world, 60 hours per week being the norm. But both their working and housing conditions were kept at the lowest possible standards. Korean workers also suffered the most unequal distribution of income among the East Asian tiger economies. The improvement of their general standard of living was largely a result of economic growth rather than any paternalistic government social provision, unlike in Singapore and Taiwan (Castells 1992). The highly repressive and exploitative regime thus led to the formation of the most militant labour movement in East Asia despite Confucian ethics of harmony.

Unlike South Korea, where the state was brutal and exploitative, Taiwan relied on a combination of repression, co-option and state-mandated company paternalism to manage labour. Apart from repression, labour organisations under the KMT patronage were actively promoted as a means of pre-empting opportunities for the development of autonomous trade unions. The co-option of labour also ensured close monitoring of its activities. Meanwhile, in addition to providing subsidised health for private sector workers, the state also passed laws that required employers to provide a number of employment benefits covering death, disability, severance and retirement. State paternalism in Taiwan was a result of the desire of the KMT to achieve political legitimacy in its new insular home so as to avoid the political catastrophe it had suffered on the mainland. A combination of political co-option and proactive social legislation, together with rapid economic growth and a relatively equal distribution of income, therefore made labour relations in particular, and economic development in general, far more peaceful in Taiwan than in Korea.

Singapore: transnational capitalism

Singapore has a similar, if not better, economic development record to that of Taiwan and South Korea. Within two decades, it was transformed from a resource-poor fishing village to a modern industrial and financial metropolis. Singaporeans today enjoy a higher standard of living than many people in the West, including in Britain, its former colonial ruler. Yet, unlike South Korea and Taiwan, economic development in Singapore has not led to full democratisation of the polity. Its ruling party, the Leninist-style PAP, has been in power since 1959, a year after Singapore became an autonomous state within the British Commonwealth. Singapore's ability to continue with authoritarian developmentalism has enabled its political and intellectual leadership to lead the attack on 'Western' culture in favour of 'Asian' values and an 'Asian' model of development.

Singapore is probably the world's only non-communist country in which extensive and pervasive state policies to organise the people and influence their values and attitudes are an integral part of the state-led drive for economic development (Fong *et al.* 1989; Chua 1995). While this practice originated in the traumatic founding experience of Singapore, the experience itself has, over the years, been successfully implanted into the innermost psyche of every Singaporean thanks to the PAP state's relentless political campaigns about 'national survival' (Chan 1971; 1993). Cultural engineering has been a powerful weapon in the hands of the PAP state, which is concerned with fashioning an overarching national identity in a multi-ethnic society consisting of Chinese (75 per cent of the population), Malays (15 per cent), Indians (7 per cent) and various other ethnic groups (3 per cent).

When independence was thrust upon Singapore in 1965, the nation was united by one thing only: a profound sense of apprehension over its ability to survive. Cut off from the resource-rich Malaysian hinterland and its market, the PAP leadership found itself presiding over a society beset by crises: high unemployment, high population growth, poor public health and housing conditions, and hostile neighbours worried about the potential link between local Chinese and communist China. Furthermore, there was little political identification with the new nation on the part of the immigrant population, which was oriented more towards its homelands than towards Singapore. Faced with this grave situation, the PAP government moved quickly to construct an 'ideology of survival' based on the notion of a 'tightly organised society'. The thrust of this ideology was economic development based on discipline and sacrifice for the nation.

Parliamentary democracy, a legacy of British colonial rule, was thus severely curtailed for the sake of national unity. Any practices that could be deemed to promote 'sectional' interest, be it based on race or class, were outlawed. Not surprisingly, the lack of political and civil liberties had over the years enabled the PAP to win all parliamentary elections and put into practice its idea of economic development through collective endeavour. Like South Korea and Taiwan, economic development in Singapore was presided over by an authoritarian government.

Labour discipline was a crucial part of the tightly organised society. Under the PAP rule, trade unions were legally required to 'support management and government in a joint effort to realise our full potential', in the words of Lee Kuan Yew, Singapore's prime minister from 1959 to 1990 (Rodan 1989). Although union power on issues of wages and working conditions was severely restricted by law, the PAP regime resorted to Confucian rhetoric to foster a culture of mutual trust and cooperation between the workers, the employers and the state. Furthermore, tripartite institutions, such as the National Wages Council and the Committee on Productivity, were set up for this purpose. When the unions subsequently grew larger and more powerful, they were dismembered and replaced by smaller industry-based and Japanese-style company unions. The Japanese-style management ethos of 'teamwork' was also actively promoted, through such institutions as quality control circles and work improvement teams (Rodan 1989: 161–5).

During the early years of rapid industrialisation, the 1960s and 1970s, the PAP state promoted the value of 'rugged individualism' to encourage Singapore's immigrant population to work hard for personal and, by extension, national economic survival. Individualism also underpinned the government's effort to construct an efficient and meritocratic bureaucracy that rewarded individual talent and effort. Since the 1980s, however, the perceived growth of consumerism and political assertiveness in the society has led to 'a certain intentional amnesia on the part of the PAP government in its criticism of individualism' and promotion of Confucian/Asian values of collectivism (Chua 1995: 26–7). Cultural engineering in Singapore, as in Japan, South Korea and Taiwan, is politically selective and instrumental, only on a far more extensive scale.

The subordination of the workers put Singapore in a good position from which to launch its EOI using FDI as a major tool, a strategy different from South Korea and Taiwan and necessitated by Singapore's small population size and lack of domestic capital and entrepreneurs. However, the state played a pivotal role in attracting and channelling foreign industrial capital to its 'pioneer' industries. Initiatives included the provision of physical infrastructure, such as transport and communications, building of industrial estates (similar to EPZs), which provided centralised infrastructural facilities at low cost, and fiscal incentives. State provision of education and housing also offered an attractive social infrastructure to MNCs. The Economic Development Board (EDB), nicknamed the 'multinational corporate godfather', was charged with the overall responsibility of coordinating diverse policy initiatives aimed at attracting FDI (Gayle 1989: 66). By the 1970s, MNCs employed nearly half of the nation's workforce and accounted for 60 per cent of its total output and 84 per cent of its manufactured exports (Yoshihara 1976).

Alongside the MNCs was the Singapore state, which largely dictated the private sector's participation in Singapore's economy through its control of key industries and financial resources, such as the compulsory social security scheme, the Central Provident Fund (CPF) (see Chapter 8) and the Post Office Savings Bank. Many GLCs set up joint ventures with MNCs and, in so doing, facilitated not only the inflow of FDI but also the structural transformation of the manufacturing sector from labour-intensive, low-skilled production to high-value-added, highly skilled production.

The policy priority on foreign industrial capital and the strategic alliance between GLCs and MNCs, together with the extensive economic and political reach of the state, meant that local firms were marginalised as they depended on the state for business contracts, which only served to co-opt the local bourgeoisie into the PAP-dominated political economy (Rodan 1997: 160). The relatively corruption-free standing of the government, partly a legacy of British colonial rule and partly a result of the introduction and enforcement of strict profitability principles into public enterprises, played an important role in sustaining the hegemony of the PAP state in Singapore's political economy.

CONCLUSION

In this chapter, I have examined the making of the developmental state in Japan and the East Asian NICs from both historical and international perspectives. Our comparative analysis reveals a common pattern of nation building through economic development. In all four economies, the politics of survival was facilitated by the official promotion of Confucian culture, which worked as a hegemonic ideology legitimating the emerging industrial societies. A range of policies and practices were rationalised by resorting to selective Confucian values, from bureaucratic meritocracy to enterprise unions and the subordination of the workforce to the state and the management. At the same time, the four developmental states also displayed very different institutional architectures in terms of government–business relations, ranging from close interaction in Japan and South Korea to Taiwan's 'cool' detachment and Singapore's one-way state domination of the local bourgeoisie. The approaches to the labour market also differed. While Japan, Taiwan and Singapore all used a combination of state and company paternalism and brutal repression to neutralise workers, South Korea relied more on coercion and repression to discipline its labour force. In short, the unique national history and politics of each developmental state moulded particular institutional forms of Confucian capitalism.

4 The political economy of 'ersatz capitalism' in Southeast Asia

Following the successful elevation of South Korea, Taiwan and Singapore to NIC status in the 1980s, Malaysia, Indonesia and Thailand became the second tier of exporting tiger economies in Pacific Asia. Rapid economic development in the three NECs began in the 1960s and 1970s and gained momentum in the late 1980s before it was brought to a stop by the 1997–8 financial crisis. During this period of rapid growth, the annual increase in GDP of all three averaged about 7%, although income distribution was less equal than that in the NICs, especially between regions and ethnic groups. The reduction of absolute poverty was nevertheless a great achievement in all three countries.

However, despite their rapid economic development, the Southeast Asian NECs have been widely observed to display some common structural weaknesses in comparison with the East Asian NICs. Unlike the NICs, in which a *fusion* of economic and political power was institutionalised, argues McVey (1992: 22), the NECs institutionalised an '*apartheid* between political and economic power'. An important reason for this was the historical legacy of the 'Chinese problem', present in all three societies. As a result, state intervention in these economies was generally seen to lack rigorous discipline and effectiveness. In describing these economies as 'ersatz capitalism', Yoshihara (1988: 130–1) thought that 'Technological backwardness, the low quality of government intervention, and Chinese discrimination are the three most difficult problems afflicting the capitalism of Southeast Asia.'

In this chapter, I seek to understand these features of Southeast Asian capitalism by means of a two-way comparative process: between the NICs and the NECs on the one hand and between the individual NECs on the other. In so doing, I hope to show both the different historical–cultural context of development between the two blocs of economies and the dynamics of national politics within each of the NECs in mediating the influence of those legacies, especially those of the 'Chinese problem'.

SOUTHEAST ASIA IN COMPARATIVE AND HISTORICAL–CULTURAL PERSPECTIVES

Cultural diversity

Southeast Asia has a long history of open economy and cultural diversity due to its distinctive geography. Lying astride the world's major historic sea-trading route between the great empire of China to the north and India to the west, the peninsular and archipelagic territories had had nearly 1,000 years of history of maritime trading before they were incorporated into the capitalist world economy in the seventeenth century (Reid 1988). Unlike the NICs (with the partial exception of Singapore), all three Southeast Asian NECs are characterised by ethnic, cultural and religious diversity. While Islam is the dominant religion of Malaysia and Indonesia, Thailand is a predominantly Buddhist society. Each country also has significant ethnic and religious minorities, the most prominent of which are ethnic Chinese, who dominate the commercial sector in all the economies. The European colonial heritage of the region is equally diverse. While Thailand, like Japan, was never colonised by an external power, Malaysia was a British colony between 1826 and 1957 and Indonesia a Dutch colony between 1619 and 1949.

The origin of the 'Chinese problem'

The large-scale emigration of the Chinese to Southeast Asia in the late nineteenth century ushered in racial stereotyping in the region, which still persists today. The concentration of the Chinese in the commercial sector across the region led the Thai King Rama VI to infamously call the Southeast Asian Chinese 'the Jews of Asia' in the early twentieth century. In all three countries, industrialisation was profoundly influenced by the historical legacy of the 'Chinese problem'.

The origin of the problem went back to the European colonial expansion into the region. Attracted to expanding employment opportunities and often driven to escape domestic catastrophe resulting from misrule in the declining Chinese Empire, these Chinese immigrants were concentrated in the commercial world for lack of other alternatives. In Malaysia and Indonesia, the colonial powers exploited Chinese labour for the emerging mining and infrastructural building industries while denying them any hope of integration into indigenous society and government. A colonial division of labour was institutionalised. While Western enterprises dominated the 'commanding heights' of the economy, largely the capital-intensive primary exporting sector, the Chinese minority were either forced to work in the mines and ports or allowed to work as middlemen monopolising most lower-level commercial operations. The indigenous population functioned overwhelmingly as peasants, labourers and colonial servants, while the land-owning elite was absorbed into the colonial bureaucracy. This colonial enforced division of labour thus gave rise to racial stereotyping, for example 'entrepreneurial Chinese' and 'lazy Malays' (Alatas 1977).

Post-colonial social and political structure

Unlike in the East Asian NICs, decolonisation and the coming into power of modern constitutional government brought little disruption in its wake to the social structures of the three societies. There was no East Asian-style land reform, and the native aristocratic classes continued to dominate society and politics through Western-style institutions such as political parties, bureaucracy and the military. This historical and social continuity led to the emergence of what Jomo (1988) described as an 'administocratic' power structure in these societies, namely the oligarchic concentration of power in the hands of the aristocrats turned civil and military bureaucrats and, later, business leaders. This in turn gave birth to 'rentier capitalism' in Southeast Asia, which was characterised by a low level of technocratic competence.

In Thailand and Indonesia, post-monarchical and post-colonial governments, respectively, responded to long-harboured anti-Chinese communal sentiment by pursuing a nationalist economic policy that sought to promote indigenous entrepreneurship at the expense of Chinese or other foreign businesses (Golay *et al.* 1969). To defend their interests in the face of popular hostility and government discrimination, the Chinese communities developed clientelistic links with powerful indigenous officials in the civil and military bureaucracies while keeping a low social and political profile. Hence the birth of rentier capitalism in Southeast Asia, in which government officials charged 'rents' for their protection of the Chinese 'pariah entrepreneurs' (Riggs 1966).

In Malaysia, the first decade after independence (in 1957) entrenched the colonial division of labour in the form of an 'ethnic bargain' struck between the three ethnic parties for the Malays, Chinese and Indians respectively (Jomo 1988). This elite-led ethnic accommodation worked fairly well until 1969, when racial riots broke out, which resulted in a complete reorientation of the economic policy. The maintenance of the status quo by a largely laissez-faire state gave way to an activist state committed to re-establishing 'the primacy of Malay political power' (Ahmad 1993: 153). As a result, native Malays, known as the *bumiputra*, or 'sons of the soil', were accorded constitutionally protected preferential access to government jobs, business licences, education and land ownership.

This legally entrenched discriminatory practice was further extended in 1970 under the New Economic Policy (NEP), the major objective of which was to create a *bumiputra* business community by reducing Chinese economic power. Like post-colonial Indonesia and post-coup Thailand (after 1932), the NEP state created its own version of rentier capitalism known as the 'Ali Baba phenomenon', in which well-connected Malays sat on the boards of Chinese companies only to reap the 'rents' that derived from their ability to obtain preferential business opportunities for the company (Means 1991: 313). Historically, military and civilian officials formed the major part of the rent-seeking state in the Indonesian and Thai political economies, deriving their benefits from control of political power. The expansion of Malaysian bureaucracy under the NEP went hand in hand with the emergence of a rent-seeking state, the officials of which offered business contracts to companies related to the Malay political party, the United Malays National Organisation (UMNO) (Means 1991; Gomez 1994), to enrich themselves. This patron–client relationship between political officials and business elites thus benefited the Chinese and well-connected indigenous elites to the exclusion of the masses. Business success in Southeast Asia therefore has less to do with market competitiveness than with political connections.

The international context of development

As in Confucian East Asia, international politics and economy has been an important influence on Southeast Asian development. The concerted effort of the three economies to shift from ISI to labour-intensive EOI in the mid-1980s was a case in point. Like the NICs, in which geopolitics exacerbated a sense of national vulnerability and helped to focus their minds on EOI, the collapse of primary commodity prices in the world market in the mid-1980s had a similar effect on the NECs, which had relied heavily on primary export. The shift to EOI stimulated the latest wave of rapid economic growth in the NECs (Ariff and Hill 1985; Rodan *et al.* 1997). Malaysia's earlier switch to MNC-led EOI coincided with the increasing globalisation of production in the 1970s when, in response to the economic slowdown in the West in the wake of the oil crisis, many labour-intensive industries, such as textiles, garments and electronics, began to relocate in world peripheries to take advantage of cheap and unorganised labour.

Similarly, Thailand and Indonesia benefited greatly from Western economic aid in the early period of their economic development because of their geostrategic importance. Immediately after General Suharto came to power in Indonesia through a military coup in 1967, the United States, Japan and other Western countries, together with multilateral institutions such as the International Monetary Fund (IMF) and the World Bank, formed the Inter-Governmental Group on Indonesia (IGGI) to coordinate their aid policies. During the Cold War, the United States placed few conditions on aid to Suharto's repressive regime for fear that the 'sleeping giant of Southeast Asia' might otherwise fall to communism and set in motion the domino effect in Asia. Huge credits granted by Western countries, together with growing private investment by MNCs, enabled Suharto's military regime to regain control of the economy and promote the rapid development of the modern exporting sector of the economy. The first decade of Suharto's rule also relied on US-trained technocrats, the 'Berkeley Mafia', for economic management (Bresnan 1993: 83).

From the mid-1950s, Thailand was considered by the United States to be another key ally in its campaign to contain communism in Southeast Asia. US aid increased gradually from that time and then dramatically during the height of the Vietnam War (Girling 1981: 235–6). The offer of Thailand as the US military base for the Vietnam War attracted enormous benefits, as the US military built transport and communication infrastructures across the country. Between the mid-1950s and 1976, when the Americans closed their bases, a combination of US economic aid, military spending and increased Thai exports to South Vietnam stimulated a Thai economic boom, which laid the foundation for subsequent EOI expansion in the 1980s. Vietnam's invasion of Cambodia in the early 1980s restored US economic and military aid, which was crucial to revive the confidence of foreign investors in the Thai economy, suffering from a crisis induced by the 1979–80 oil-price shocks (Dixon 1995: 982).

The concerted drive to push for EOI and to attract FDI in all three economies in the mid-1980s coincided with the worldwide currency realignment initiated by the 1985 Plaza Accord. The sharp rise of the Japanese yen, followed by the currencies of the NICs, added to the cost pressures already faced by export manufacturers in these increasingly labour-short, high-wage economies. The result was a massive outflow of industrial investment from Japan and the NICs to Southeast Asia from the late 1980s. This process was accelerated by the United States' removal in 1989 of the Generalised System of Preferences from the NICs, which had allowed their goods to enter the US market at lower tariff rates. The massive injection of capital spurred record levels of economic and industrial growth in Southeast Asia after 1987 (Jomo *et al.* 1997).

The examination of the historical and international context of Southeast Asian economic development has shown that the three NECs were faced with very different historical legacies in comparison with the NICs. A common phenomenon in all three was a high level of social fragmentation, which gave rise to a patron–client relationship between the indigenous-dominated government and the economically powerful Chinese. Rentier capitalism also extended into the relationship between indigenous political and business elites thanks to the historical and social continuity that accompanied the transition from colonial rule to independence (from monarchical to post-monarchical rule in the case of Thailand). Instead of facing a national crisis of survival at the founding of the new state, as in the NICs, which served to discipline the state apparatus, the NECs continued with the old structure of power, dominated by land-owning aristocrats turned bureaucrats or politicians. Industrialisation, especially the prolonged ISI stage in which protective trade and investment policies were implemented, later provided the political power holders with both monopoly business opportunities and enormous scope for patronage. As a result, capitalism in Southeast Asia was essentially based on political patronage rather than technocratic competence. Of course, the same problem of patronage was also inflicted on the NICs, but the lack of large landowners and acute sense of crisis served to restrain its spread.

However, the above comparison between the two blocs of countries could be misleading unless it is realised that the three NECs, like the NICs, have taken different political initiatives to grapple with similar historical legacies in their own national settings, and that this has also led to very different development outcomes. This is the topic to which I will now turn.

'ERSATZ CAPITALISM': A COMPARISON

Malaysia: ethnic capitalism

With the highest per capita income and a relatively equal distribution of the fruits of its economic growth, Malaysia is widely tipped to become the leading NIC in Southeast Asia in the near future. This remarkable achievement can be attributed to the fact that the Malaysian state was the only one in Southeast Asia to adopt a comprehensive, and *controversial*, economic policy to address the issue of ethnic disparity in its society. This was the two-decade-long NEP (1970–90), which was introduced in the wake of the 1969 racial riots to address the ethnic inequality that had been sanctioned by the post-colonial government a decade earlier.

The introduction of the NEP marked the end of a decade-long laissez-faire capitalism in post-colonial Malaysia in which the state had been limited by the ethnic bargain to act more autonomously. During the NEP era, the state became the leading actor in Malaysian economic development, acting as a strategic planner, a regulator, an entrepreneur and, above all, a provider of economic opportunities to the Malays. As an unashamedly 'ethnic state' symbolising Malay nationalism (Majstorovic 1997), the NEP state pursued a range of initiatives aimed at combining economic growth with ethnic redistribution in order to reduce and limit the 'identification of race with economic function' (Islam and Chowdhury 1997: 236). In particular, it aimed to create a Malay business community by means of the preferential allocation of state funding to Malay businesses.

Judging by the concrete target it set of 30 per cent *bumiputra* corporate ownership by 1990, the NEP undoubtedly failed as it only delivered 20 per cent (Rasiah 1997: 128, Table 5.2). In addition, it was also criticised for widening the income gap *within* the Malay population as the increased business ownership went overwhelmingly to the already wealthy, i.e. the traditional princely land-owning families and politicians and bureaucrats. And finally, despite the massive programme of affirmative action involving large sums of public funding, the extent of poverty reduction among the *bumiputras* was the least in comparison with that among the Chinese and Indians, the other two major ethnic groups in Malaysia (ibid.: 127, Table 5.1). To critics, all these failures were attributable to the ineffective state, which was plagued by outright corruption and abuse of government loan schemes and an incapacity to set and enforce rigorous performance targets (Balassa 1991).

The developmental capacity of the state was further questioned when the ethnically based NEP was found to have failed to tackle the long-term underlying structural weaknesses of the Malaysian economy, such as low productivity, low skill and poor linkage between the highly protected and largely state-owned ISI sector and the export sector (Jesudason 1989; Bowie 1991; Lubeck 1992). Critics argued that, despite the official rhetoric of 'Look East' in Malaysia, the Malay-dominated state was simply more interested in seeking to control Chinese business development than to facilitate a well-integrated Malaysia Inc. along the lines of the NIC model. Instead of aligning with the domestic business class, i.e. the Chinese, the Malay state elites aligned themselves with foreign capital in exchange for directorships, joint ventures and other passive, essentially rentier, rewards (Lubeck 1992: 184).

Despite these problems, the NEP can be said to have played an important role in providing social and political stability through inter-ethnic wealth redistribution (Islam and Chowdhury 1997: 235). In this respect, it served a similar, albeit less effective, social function to that of land reforms in South Korea and Taiwan. Since Malaysia's average GDP growth rate of 6.5 per cent during the NEP years was similar to that of Indonesia, although lower than Thailand's, it can be argued that, contrary to the criticism

(Bowie 1988: 53), the redistributive imperative of the NEP did not compromise economic growth. The importance of this achievement is more significant in the comparative context of the Indonesian and Thai development experiences, in which no similar policies aimed at redressing ethnic imbalances were attempted. While Thailand had the worst record of income distribution during its period of rapid growth, Indonesia often saw anti-Chinese violence erupt, the most recent being the killings carried out during the 1997–8 financial crisis.

The 'semi-democratic' political context in which development took place in Malaysia also ensured a relatively large measure of legitimacy for the NEP (Case 1993). Although national politics was effectively dominated by the UMNO, the consociational-style elite representation in the UMNO-dominated national parliament nevertheless provided channels of influence on policy for other ethnic groups (see Chapter 7). The partial suspension in the late 1980s of the NEP's corporate restructuring element, which favoured the Malays, was an example of the government's relative responsiveness to changing social demands (Khoo 2000: 217–18).

In 1991, the NEP was replaced by the New Development Policy (NDP), which shifted policy priority from increasing *bumiputra* corporate ownership to tackling the structural weaknesses of the economy (Islam and Chowdhury 1997: 236–7). The NDP has been the basis of the government's 'Vision 2020' programme, 2020 being the year set for Malaysia to achieve developed status. However, in the absence of a fundamental shake-up of the 'administocratic' power structure of the Malaysian political economy, measures of liberalisation and privatisation introduced under the NDP ultimately led Malaysia to the 1997–8 financial crisis, revealing the continuing weakness of the Malaysian-style developmental state (see Chapter 9).

Indonesia: crony capitalism

Being the world's largest archipelagic state, spanning over 13,000 islands and covering more than 5,000 kilometres from east to west, Indonesia is the most diverse of all societies in Pacific Asia in terms of ethnicity, culture, religion and language. Yet in parallel with this enormous spatial and cultural diversity is an astonishing degree of concentration of economic and political power. While 60 per cent of the population lives on the central island of Java, traditionally the economic, political and cultural centre of Indonesia, about 70–80 per cent of private business corporations, especially large firms, are controlled by around 4 per cent of Indonesian Chinese (Lubeck 1998: 293, 295).

Since the late 1960s, the Indonesian economy has grown sixfold, with the average income per capita quadrupled (Hill 1997: 256). This achievement no doubt raised the living standards of the world's fourth largest population and contributed to poverty reduction. However, despite the rise of export-oriented manufacturing, about two-thirds of Indonesians still live in rural areas, and official statistics on poverty – a reduction from 55 per cent of the population living below the poverty line in the mid-1960s to 14 per cent in 1993 (Hill 1997: 261) – are widely believed to have grossly underestimated the incidence of poverty (Booth 1993; Rigg 1997: Chapter 3, especially Box 3.1). In parallel with rapid industrialisation since the mid-1980s, income inequality between the business and military bureaucratic elite and the masses, between rural peasants and urban workers, between Java and the outer islands, has been widening (Jones 1998: 185).

During the 1997–8 Asian financial crisis, the term 'crony capitalism' became widely publicised, referring essentially to the murky business world dominated by the close interpenetration of political and economic power in Pacific Asia. In the Southeast Asian context, while this could be taken as an alternative and more vivid expression of Jomo's 'administocracy', the Indonesian political economy under Suharto was perhaps the closest to the perfection of cronyism. As in Malaysia, the state sector featured prominently in the Indonesian economy, effectively monopolising the production of capital and intermediate goods (Islam and Chowdury 1997: 21). However, instead of being an effective instrument of either technological upgrading, which is what the state is good at in the NICs, or ethnic wealth redistribution, which is what the Malaysian state aspires to, the Indonesian state was a huge reservoir of patronage and privilege. Rent seeking, corruption and the appropriation of public resources to shore up support for the repressive military regime and for blatant private gain has been common. *Patrimonialism*, rather than developmentalism, has often been the over-riding concern of the administocrats based in military and civil bureaucracy.

Economic development in Indonesia did not take off until the inauguration of the 'New Order' in 1967 by President Suharto, who had come to power through a 2-year 'incremental coup', during which about a million allegedly communist members, most of whom were Chinese, were slaughtered. Under Suharto's New Order, state capitalism and extensive government intervention in the economy, in the form of a large state sector, was justified partly in terms of preventing the excessive concentration of economic power in the hands of the Chinese (Mackerras 1992: 438). However, in the first decade of Suharto's rule, the Indonesian economy relied heavily on foreign support; its economic technocrats were trained in the United States, and its ISI was financed mostly by US and Japanese investment and aid (Berger 1997: 177). Thanks to its abundant primary resources, especially oil and gas, manufacturing industry in Indonesia developed mainly in the primary sector. Until the mid-1980s, oil and gas dominated Indonesia's export trade, accounting for nearly three-quarters of its total export revenue (Islam and Chowdhury 1997: 213–14). The state apparatus, dominated by the Javanese *priyayi* military officers, whose aristocratic ancestors had dominated the Dutch colonial bureaucracy, did little to transform the economic structure from commodity-based to manufacturing-based exporting. Instead, it either entered into a parasitic relationship with the Chinese or dominated the 'indigenous' business monopolies by supplying company presidents, directors and managers (Schwarz 1994). Their direct command of state power was the key determinant of their business success.

During the 1970s and early 1980s, sharp rises in primary commodity prices, oil in particular, dramatically increased state revenue, which in turn gave the state enormous financial clout to create an indigenous, or *pribumi,* class of entrepreneurs, whose business success depended on privileged access to state-controlled networks of credit, contracts, distribution and trade. Prominent among these entrepreneurs were members of the Suharto family, whose business empires began with equity holdings in the companies of the large Chinese conglomerates that dominated the private sector (Robison 1997: 33). With the expansion of state patronage, the Suharto children soon began to build and expand their own corporate empires, the business dealings of which straddled the public and private sectors and which owned the only indigenous conglomerates of substance (Robison 1986). As Macintyre (1994: 254) noted, 'the business careers of Suharto's children highlight the fundamental importance of clientelistic connections as the key to gaining access to state generated rent taking opportunities and thence to commercial success.'

The slump in the oil price in the world market in the 1980s and the resultant decline in government revenue forced Indonesia to diversify its industrial production through EOI to reduce its dependence on the oil sector. From the mid-1980s, a series of reform packages were introduced with the aim of liberalising the economy and attracting foreign investment. Trade and financial sectors were substantially deregulated, which significantly brought down average tariff barriers and enabled a freer mobilisation of savings and investments, both domestically and from international sources (Robison 1997: 34–5). However, the opening of state monopolies to private sector ownership did not lead to a weakening of the state's power in determining the market, because public monopoly was simply transferred to politically connected private monopoly (ibid: 35–41). The Suharto family and a few other politico-bureaucratic family companies turned out to be the major beneficiaries of privatisation and liberalisation. As most of them were not involved in the competitive export manufacturing sectors, they continued to rely overwhelmingly on state patronage for market operations. The notorious 'national car' scandal was but one of the best-known examples of crony capitalism in Indonesia (ibid: 55–6).

The Indonesian political economy under Suharto was a good example of a weak and predatory state incapable of building transformative institutional capacities to address the structural weaknesses of the Indonesian economy. Economic nationalism sanctioned official exclusion of the Chinese from Indonesian politics but did not prevent the political class from entering into covert patron–client relations with the Chinese for mutual gains. Because the relationship was for mutual gain rather than national development, there never developed in Indonesia the NIC-style institutional framework for systematic government–business cooperation. The economy thus developed a dual structure: the heavily protected domestic sector, monopolised by the Chinese and indigenous politico-bureaucratic families, and the dynamic exporting sector, dominated by MNCs. This policy fuelled public resentment not only of the Chinese, but also of the corrupt regime, culminating in violent attacks against the Chinese and the collapse of the Suharto regime during the 1997–8 financial crisis.

Thailand: laissez-faire capitalism

Although Thailand escaped colonial rule, it was forced to open its economy to Western trade in 1855, when it signed the Bowring Treaty with Britain. A bureaucrat-led bloodless coup in 1932 resulted in a constitutional monarchy but failed to establish democracy. Instead, it ushered in at least four decades of bureaucratic–authoritarian rule dominated by the military. During the first two decades after the 1932 coup, anti-Chinese economic nationalism provided the rallying point for the various military and civilian factions engaged in an incessant power struggle. In seeking to promote indigenous business through state investment, politicians and bureaucrats also sought to keep local Chinese capitalists as social and political outsiders, 'pariah entrepreneurs'. Meanwhile, military and civilian leaders sat on the boards of many Chinese enterprises to reap benefits both for personal gains and for political funding (Girling 1981: 75–6), a situation similar to New Order Indonesia.

The twin coups of 1957–8, led by General Sarit Thanarat, marked the reversal of anti-Chinese nationalism and the beginning of Thailand's ISI. The integrationist policy on the Chinese meant that most of the capital for Thailand's industrial development came from private, mainly Chinese, sources (Jansen 1997). The Thai state, therefore, unlike its counterparts in Malaysia and Indonesia, did not resort to large public ownership to lead development. State investment was confined largely to infrastructural development, particularly in agriculture, during the 1960s (Doner and Unger 1993).

Integration of, rather than discrimination against, the Chinese in the Thai political economy made Thailand the only Southeast Asian NEC to approximate the NIC-style government–business cooperation. By the 1980s, economic growth had given rise to a more open political environment in which substantial numbers of Chinese business people had become not only Thai citizens but also parliamentarians and cabinet members. At the same time, a significant number of independent business associations had emerged, openly seeking to influence economic policy-making processes. These developments helped Thailand to gradually break free from its bureaucratic polity and develop into a liberal corporatist polity (Anek 1992; Hewison 1997). The steady transition to democracy, which began in 1992, has enabled the regime to weather the storm of the 1997 crisis, unlike the Suharto regime, which was brought down by nationwide violence.

Of the three NECs, Thailand had the fastest economic growth rate between the early 1970s and the mid-1990s. However, a relatively laissez-faire state also meant that Thailand had a relatively unfavourable record in terms of wealth distribution. The extreme concentration of economic activity in the capital city, Bangkok, and its surrounding areas meant that poverty reduction was regionally unbalanced. In 1990, whereas only 7 per cent of the urban population was officially counted as living under the poverty line, the figure for the rural population was 29 per cent, making Thailand the most unequal among the NECs in terms of rural–urban disparity (Lubeck 1998: 285, Table 11.2). As in Indonesia, but for different reasons, poverty reduction in Thailand was primarily a function of rapid economic growth rather than any positive government policy.

The state played a similarly limited role in human capital investment, providing only 6 years of compulsory education. Even in the late 1990s, only 20 per cent of the labour force had completed secondary education (Islam and Chowdhury 1997: 260). Not surprisingly, the Thai economy, like the Indonesian economy, became increasingly trapped in the lower technological end of production (Yoshihara 1988: 117; Asian Development Bank 1998: 208, Box 3.8). The two economies' loss of their competitiveness to the new tiger economies such as China in the 1990s was one of the reasons that rendered them the hardest hit in the 1997–8 financial crisis.

The patron–client relationship between political and economic power is also a serious problem in the Thai political economy. Both the arrival of liberal corporatism and the expansion of electoral politics, in which political funding became crucial for success, seemed to have exacerbated the problem. As over two-thirds of the Thai population still lives in the countryside, electoral politics remains primarily the game of the urban rich.

The resultant lack of policy transparency, the deleterious effects of which on the Thai economy were magnified by Thailand's move towards financial liberalisation in the late 1980s, was a key factor in causing Thailand's financial meltdown in 1997–8.

What the Thai political economy of development has shown is thus a state that is the most successful in Southeast Asia in breaking down the ethnic barrier but perhaps the least effective in combining rapid growth with equity. Meanwhile, Thailand shared with Malaysia and Indonesia many structural weaknesses in its economy, which arose mainly from the predatory nature of the state. The relative lack of competence and discipline of the state apparatus in all three economies was partly to do with historical continuity with the power structure in these societies and partly to do with the lack of the survival imperative brought on by geopolitical rivalry. The abundance of primary resources in these societies also did little to create the sense of survival crisis seen in the NICs.

CONCLUSION

In this chapter I have examined the divergent approaches to economic development of the three Southeast Asian NECs, Malaysia, Indonesia and Thailand. All the NECs have shown a weaker transformative state capacity for economic development than the NICs, largely due to the dominance of the traditional aristocratic class in the post-colonial (or post-monarchical) state apparatus. The patron–client relationship is common across Southeast Asia, which compromises state discipline. However, within this pattern of broad similarity, the three states have adopted very different approaches to a major historical problem facing their societies, namely the Chinese problem. While Thailand has virtually eliminated the problem through social and political integration, the Malaysian political economy is still based on an explicit ethnic division of labour, managed by elite-level cooperation within a quasi-parliamentary politics. In contrast, New Order Indonesia resorted to the same tactic employed by pre-Sarit Thailand, which was based on overt discrimination and covert predatory exploitation. The consequences of these policies have been evident: while Thailand is moving closest to the NIC-style government–business corporatism, Malaysia finds itself trapped in the ethnicity-based political economy. Finally, the Chinese community in Indonesia has borne the brunt of the violent backlash against that economy during the 1997–8 economic crisis, and the post-Suharto government is still grappling with the effect of over a century of ethnic hostility.

5 Political development in Japan

A model of 'illiberal democracy'?

In the last two chapters on the economic development of Pacific Asia, we have discovered wide variations both between the NICs and the NECs and among the individual national economies in terms of their political–institutional context of development. These variations, which took place despite the perceived cultural similarities, not only belied the New Orientalist prediction of the emergence of 'Asian capitalism' but also pointed to the centrality of politics in economic development.

The influence of the culturalist perspective is not restricted to the study of economic development in Pacific Asia; it extends into the study of political development in the region. Just as economic Orientalism predicts the emergence of Japanese-style 'Asian capitalism' in Pacific Asia, political Orientalism predicts the arrival of Japanese-style 'Asian democracy' (Fukuyama 1992; 1995a; Roy 1994; Pye 1985; Bell *et al.* 1995). Asian democracy is construed as essentially an illiberal democracy, typified by Japan, whereby Western democratic institutions are copied for the purpose of advancing illiberal Asian values said to put a premium on community and consensus at the expense of individual rights and freedoms (Huntington 1993b; Bell *et al.* 1995). Japan's one-party dominance has been seen as the symbol of illiberal democracy.

In this chapter, I will scrutinise the culturalist claim that post-war Japan has pioneered the illiberal form of democracy for Pacific Asia by examining the historical evolution of the Japanese political system and the reasons for the weaknesses of its democracy. In so doing, I will seek to argue that these weaknesses, which form the basis of the culturalist claim, are better understood in terms of the political configuration of power in Japanese society than in terms of Japan's Confucian heritage. The implication of our argument for the study of political development in the rest of Pacific Asia will also be considered.

I will argue my case in two parts. In the first part of the chapter, I will discuss briefly the meaning and conditions of democracy, focusing on its relationship with ideology and culture. In the second part, I will examine the trajectory of political development in Japan, focusing on the factors shaping the origin, evolution and unique characteristics of democracy in Japan. Finally, I will conclude by noting the historical–political factors that moulded Japanese political development.

DEMOCRACY: ITS MEANING AND CULTURAL CONDITIONS

The meaning of democracy

The word 'democracy' is as controversial as it is old. However, it can be argued that the controversy is less about its meaning than about the object to which the concept is applied. In other words, while the meaning of democracy can be seen to remain fairly consistent over the centuries, the conceptions of it – the differing ideas about how to achieve it and the resultant differing judgements about a real political system – have been contested. So, in practice, what appear to be theoretical disagreements on the meaning of democracy often turn out to be ideological differences on the democratic credentials of an actual or potential political system (Holden 1993: Chapter 1). In most cases, the controversy centres on the conditions necessary for a polity to qualify as a democracy.

The meaning of democracy, 'rule by the people', had its origin in the fifth century BC, when the Greek historian Herodotus combined the two Greek words *demos*, meaning 'the people', and *kratein*, meaning 'to rule'. Since then, democracy has basically been conceptualised as a political system constructed on the principle of rule by the people. The desirability of such rule was not universally accepted until after the end of World War I. Even since then, what constitutes 'true' democracy has been a matter of fierce ideological debate, featuring prominently in the Cold War, which dominated much of the twentieth century.

The collapse of communist regimes worldwide and the accompanying end of the Cold War in the 1989 'democratic revolution' marked the discrediting of the communist conception of democracy, the contention that only a communist one-party state embodies genuine democracy. However, the universal embrace of the liberal conception of democracy, the idea that rule by the people is best achieved by limiting the power of the state, does not necessarily spell the end of ideological rivalry on democracy. The continuation of the rivalry is guaranteed by what Beetham (1992) rightly sees as the 'deeply ambiguous' relationship between liberalism, the belief in the paramount importance of individual rights and freedoms, and democracy (Holden 1993: 15–43). In other words, it is theoretically conceivable that disagreements even among liberal democrats will continue over the actual mix between elements of liberalism and democracy.

The tension between liberalism and democracy is an intrinsic feature of modern representative democracy, which emerged in Western Europe during the formative period of the nation-state and capitalism. Unlike classic Greek democracy, which was based on direct rule by the people (i.e. free adult males), modern democracy relies on the mediating mechanism of election to realise rule by the people largely due to issues to do with the size of 'the people' and the complexity of governing an industrial society. This inevitable creation of the distinction between the ruler and the ruled thus raises a whole range of issues concerning primarily the gap between the democratic entitlement of political participation and the reality of participation. An institutionalist/formalist/ minimalist theorist will, for example, feel less disturbed by the gap than a substantive/maximalist theorist, whose conception of liberal democracy involves conditions more than democratic institutions such as universal suffrage, regular and fair elections underpinned by civil and political liberties, multi-party electoral competition, etc. It sees redistributive socioeconomic policy as a vital condition for narrowing the participative gap and broadening popular participation. In short, one does not have to be a communist to mount a meaningful ideological challenge to certain conceptions of liberal democracy.

In the real world of democracy, there exists an amazing array of institutional configurations in terms of the mix between political equality and socioeconomic equality, all embodying differing conceptions of liberal democracy. Different welfare systems and frameworks of industrial democracy in the West are but two of the examples illustrating the point. Therefore, whereas institutionalist criteria provide us with a helpful framework for identifying democracy from non-democracy, substantive criteria are essential in helping us compare democracies to find out how much progress they have made towards the constantly evolving 'daring vision' called democracy (Dahl 1989: 312). This is the approach I will adopt in studying Japanese democracy.

Culture and democracy

A key controversy about the Japanese democracy concerns the cultural milieu in which it is situated. This stems from the unique phenomenon of unbroken one-party dominance in post-war Japanese politics. For culturalists, this can only be explained in terms of Japan's unique Confucian culture because Japan is the only non-Western capitalist democracy. The apparent effort to emulate Japan in the NICs and the similar phenomenon in Southeast Asia has further stimulated the 'Asian/illiberal democracy' discourse in the study of political development in Pacific Asia. The thrust of the discourse is essentially the argument that a Japanese/Asian-style illiberal democracy is emerging in Pacific Asia because of similar cultural values.

The Asian democracy discourse is, of course, the modern version of the age-old Orientalist view, dating back to ancient Greece, which portrays the European culture as essentially democratic and the Oriental as despotic (Friedman 1994: 1; Bouchlaka 1999–2000). In the context of modern liberal democracy, which is rooted in an ideology of individualism, Asian cultures are considered anti-democratic because they are said to be profoundly against individual rights and freedoms. '"Confucian democracy"', as Huntington (1993b: 18) puts it, 'is a contradiction in terms'. Confucianism, he argues,

> lacked a tradition of rights against the state ... Harmony and cooperation were preferred over disagreement and competition. The maintenance of order and respect for hierarchy were central values. The conflict of ideas, groups, and parties was viewed as dangerous and illegitimate. Most important, Confucianism merged society and the state and provided no legitimacy for autonomous social institutions at the national level
>
> (ibid.: 15).

Because of the influence of Confucianism, Pye argued, Japan's long-ruling party, the LDP, governed the country by consensus and gained the monopoly of power by doing so. Pye (1985: 65) wrote:

> It is impossible to understand the reluctance of a parliamentary majority in democratic Japan to crush a minority unless one can see it as an extension of the attitude of the Japanese father toward the rest of the family, an attitude that stresses consensus and treats minority views cautiously.

In what follows, I will seek to show how misleading this analysis actually is. But, at this stage, a few comments will suffice. A major problem with this culturalist argument is its apolitical conception of political development. In the context of Japanese and Pacific Asian political development, this conception implies that 'Asian democracy' enjoys widespread social support in Pacific Asia, whereas in reality it is but an ideological construct serving the interest of the authoritarian regime. In the context of political development in Europe, this conception leads to cultural determinism as it sees Christianity as the cultural fount of democracy. Fukuyama (1995b: 30) exposes this intellectual weakness when he observes that 'democracy [in Europe] emerged only after a long succession of incarnations of Christianity that were inimical to liberal tolerance and democratic contestation.'

That politics played a crucial role in reconciling Christianity with liberal democracy can be seen from both the uneven history of democratic development in Europe and the long time it took for democracy to consolidate. With regard to the former, Friedman (1994: 5) points out that historically both Roman Catholicism and Orthodox Christianity were considered to be cultural barriers to democracy because of the difficulties southern European countries experienced in consolidating democracy. With regard to this last, contrary to the Eurocentric claim about the culturally programmed smooth birth of democracy in Western Europe, democracy had both a long gestation and a painful birth. Even after birth, it nearly lost its life in its childhood during the two world wars (Mazower 1998). 'It is only for the period after World War II that one can talk about extended, stable democratic rule in the industrialised countries of Western Europe and North America', as Sorensen (1998: 20) helpfully reminds us.

Now that we are familiar with some of the key controversies regarding the meaning and conditions of democracy, we will move on to analyse post-war Japanese democracy.

POST-WAR POLITICAL DEVELOPMENT IN JAPAN

The historical roots of Japanese democracy

Democracy in Japan began only after World War II. But like most other European democracies, pre-war Japan saw democratic agitation, which sowed the seeds for Japan's democratisation. Constitutional government was introduced in the 1889 Meiji Constitution, under which the first Japanese parliament, the Diet, was elected by limited suffrage in 1890. Increasing urbanisation and the influence of political ideas from the West led to growing desires for political reform during the 'Taisho democracy' period, the first two decades or so of the twentieth century. Despite heavy government repression, this period saw the emergence of Marxist-influenced political parties and counter-governmental organisations such as trade unions. Universal male suffrage was introduced in 1925, although women had to wait until 1947. The rise of militarism in the late 1920s led to the crushing of the green shoots of democracy and ultimately to Japan's own military defeat in World War II.

American Occupation and the reverse course

The American Occupation of Japan at the end of the war had started with high hopes for radical changes in the Japanese polity. Following the adoption of the US-written constitution in 1946, Japan continued with a radical reform programme designed to 'democratise, demilitarise and decentralise' the polity. Left-wing political parties, which had been banned during the war, were legalised, war personnel were purged from the state, and education, which had been a key institution of imperial indoctrination, was decentralised. In addition, land reform and the breaking-up of the *zaibatsu* were carried out to disperse economic power.

However, all these were reversed during the 1947–8 period with the onset of the Cold War, a development which was to have a profound impact on post-war Japanese political development. Concerned with the spread of communism in Asia, the Occupation now shifted its policy priority from transforming Japan to preserving stability in Japan, seen as an indispensable ally in containing communism in Asia. As a result, most of the reform programmes were either cut short or reversed; while most right-wing military personnel were allowed to remain in government, the rights of public sector workers to organise and strike were severely restricted. The *zaibatsu* were also allowed to re-emerge.

The reverse course profoundly shaped the configuration of power for the first two decades of post-war Japanese politics. Prior to its introduction, Japanese political forces had been divided into two camps on the issue of the US-written constitution. On the right, various conservative parties openly expressed their opposition, disparagingly calling it the 'MacArthur Constitution', after General Douglas MacArthur, who was the Supreme Commander for the Allied Powers. Well into the late 1950s, after the end of the Occupation in 1952, the newly formed LDP, an umbrella organisation for all the conservatives, vowed to reverse many of the democratic reforms introduced during the Occupation, denouncing them as too radical and 'un-Japanese'. The left, however, consisting mainly of the Japan Socialist Party (JSP) and allied labour unions, had been an enthusiastic ally of the American Occupation and its reform programmes for Japan.

All this changed with the reverse course. While the left remained committed to the democratic and pacifist vision embodied in the constitution, they became fierce critics of the United States and its foreign policy. The conservatives, on the other hand, now supported both the United States and all the new policies it had introduced or acquiesced to (Ishida and Krauss 1989: 10–11). In the international climate of the deepening Cold War, Japan's foreign policy towards the United States became a crucial factor determining the electoral fortune of political parties. Therefore, the

US reverse course sowed the seeds for what Stockwin (1999) aptly calls the 'divided politics' of post-war Japan, which, paradoxically, contributed to the long LDP-dominated 'consensus politics' (Curtis 1997).

The politics of confrontation and the emergence of LDP dominance

As mentioned earlier, culturalists see the LDP dominance of post-war Japanese politics as the quintessential symbol of Japanese Confucian culture. But this facile view ignores the highly confrontational circumstances in which the LDP emerged as the dominant party. In the first decade after the war, Japanese politics was divided by bitter ideological and policy polarisation between the radicals and the conservatives. Relative calm was not achieved until the early 1960s, and even well into the decade the LDP was concerned more with its political survival than with dominating Japanese politics (Stockwin 1999: 45–53). As Curtis (1997: 24, 26) rightly argues, one-party dominance emerged in Japan 'precisely because of the absence of consensus and harmony in Japanese society'.

Until 1955, electoral politics was highly volatile; multi-party competition resulted in successive coalition governments, including one headed by the JSP during the 1947–8 period (Pempel 1992). Supported by the intellectual community, the Marxist-leaning JSP inspired a radical and militant labour and student movement, actively engaged in sometimes violent protests against the United States and the reverse course. In October 1955, the JSP consolidated itself by amalgamating its two factions in the hope of strengthening its electoral position. In response, several conservative parties merged a month later, creating the LDP. This was the beginning of what is now known as the '55 system', a term originally coined to describe the two-party system widely anticipated in the wake of the reorganisation on both sides of the political spectrum. However, very few knew during the time that the term would come to refer to LDP dominance.

The deepening of the Cold War – communist China was founded in 1949 and barely a year later joined North Korea to invade South Korea, triggering the tragic 3-year Korean War – elevated the importance of Japan's defence and security policy in domestic politics and thus effectively killed off any hope of a two-party system. Being the only party committed to strengthening Japan's defence and to the 1951 Japan–US Security Treaty, which provided for continued US military presence in Japan, the LDP appeared to be a more realistic choice for Japanese voters, despite its commitment to the reverse course (Flanagan *et al.* 1991). The JSP, on the other hand, by calling for both 'unarmed neutrality' and immediate abrogation of the Security Treaty, made the majority of the voters worry that its accession to power might jeopardise Japan–US relations and destabilise Japanese security. Conflict on defence and foreign policy was thus made almost irreconcilable by the logic of the US geopolitical concern about containing communism in Asia. As a result, the LDP won the first post-1955 election in 1958.

However, political crisis was soon to follow. In the same year, the JSP succeeded in forcing the defeat in the Diet of the Police Duties Law Amendment Bill, designed to increase the powers of the police to control demonstrations. Encouraged by its success, the JSP in 1960 launched a bitter opposition campaign, both inside and outside the Diet, to the Kishi government's attempt to negotiate with the United States a revision of the 1951 Security Treaty. The month-long opposition triggered the most serious political crisis in Japan since the end of the Occupation, with widespread demonstrations, strikes and riots on an unprecedented scale. Prime Minister Kishi eventually succeeded in ramming through the Diet, within 15 minutes of the opening of its session, the revised Security Treaty, by calling in the police to physically remove the obstructive JSP members of parliament (MPs). (So much for Pye's Confucian father figure here.) However, his heavy-handed tactics sparked widespread fears about the survival of the fragile Japanese democracy, which forced him to resign 4 days later. And this episode was to turn out to be an important turning point in post-war Japanese politics.

'Creative conservatism' and the consolidation of LDP dominance

If the LDP was greatly helped by the Cold War logic in winning its first election, its subsequently uninterrupted dominance of Japanese politics must be attributed to what Pempel (1982) calls the party's flexible brand of 'creative conservatism'. Central to this was the party's ability to adapt to social changes, to broaden its social interest coalition by opening up various channels of influence to the opposition social coalition.

The 1960 crisis on the revised Security Treaty led to a fundamental change in the LDP's policy thinking. For the next decade, the LDP followed what is known as the pragmatic 'Yoshida doctrine', which shifted government priority from reversal of the Occupation reform to an ambitious 'double-your-income' economic development programme. The Japan–US security alliance was portrayed as helpful because it enabled the LDP government to single-mindedly pursue economic growth by keeping low its defence spending. This strategy was so successful that by 1964 Japan had completed its post-war economic reconstruction, and 4 years later it became the second largest economy in the capitalist world. Economic achievement undoubtedly contributed to the LDP's electoral success. In addition, the moderation of its policy moved the party to the centrist position, which also helped to consolidate its popular support (Curtis 1988). For the next three decades, the LDP's electoral dominance was a result of a combination of political co-option, blatant manipulation and corruption.

The ability of the LDP to co-opt social interests was perhaps best captured in the term 'patterned pluralism', coined by Krauss and Muramatsu (1988: 208–10). What this refers to is the 'iron triangle' of LDP politicians, bureaucrats and businessmen who have formed the elite ruling class of Japanese society at the expense of popular participation. However, despite the close and often corrupt relationship between the LDP and big corporations, policy making in Japan is not always dominated by big businesses. In his study, Nakano (1997) found two types of policy process: elite accommodation, in which big business is a key player, and client-oriented, in which small businesses and other interest groups are allowed access to various channels of influence to maximise their benefit. The farmers' union Nokyo, the Japan Medical Association and various environmental and consumer groups are but some of the best-known examples of interests routinely consulted by the LDP government. The co-option of opposition groups into loyal supporters by offering them benefits in exchange for their support has been an important factor in ensuring the LDP's long reign (Calder 1993).

But LDP dominance has rarely derived from an overwhelming electoral mandate. In fact, during the 1955–93 period of its dominance, the LDP won over 50 per cent of the votes in only three elections (1958, 1960 and 1963), and for the rest of that period over half of the population did not vote for the LDP. In addition, the party actually lost votes at every Lower House general election between 1958 and 1976 (see Stockwin 1999: 158, Table 9.8) for election results). What saved the party from falling from power was the fragmentation of the opposition, resulting partly from Japan's multi-member single non-transferable vote (SNTV) electoral system.

The SNTV tended to work in favour of the LDP, not only because it fragmented the opposition but also because the LDP was the only party with sufficient financial resources to put several candidates in a single constituency. Furthermore, the LDP also manipulated the system in its favour by deliberately failing to adjust electoral boundaries to reflect demographic changes, resulting in severe malapportionment in favour of the rural areas, the LDP's traditional stronghold. In the worst cases, it took four to five times more votes to elect a representative in an urban district than in a rural district (Krauss 1989: 42). The LDP also used other tactics, such as its claimed preference for a single-member electoral system, to stall major electoral reforms, as opposition parties were similarly worried that reform would lead to the demise of smaller parties and increase the LDP's dominance.

'Money politics' and the LDP's downfall

The electoral system, with its encouragement of intra-party factionalism, also led to expensive candidate-centred election campaigning. Dependency on big business finance was thus essential for individual electoral victory. This is partly why political corruption, or 'money politics', as the Japanese prefer to call it, has been such a widespread phenomenon in post-war Japanese politics. Corruption usually takes two forms: large-scale business donation mainly, but not exclusively, to the LDP; and LDP government ministers taking kickbacks from public works contracts, especially from the infamous construction industry (van Wolferen 1989: 132–8; Woodall 1996; Schlesinger 1997). Once in power, the LDP pursued both pro-business policies and lax anti-corruption laws, further reinforcing 'money politics' (Stockwin 1999: 98–9). One of the major reforms carried out after the LDP lost the 1993 general election was the long overdue electoral reform followed by a tightening of anti-corruption laws (Stockwin 1999: 122–9).

Corruption in post-war Japanese politics was public knowledge, and the apparently high threshold of public tolerance of it can be largely accounted for by two factors. The first was the LDP's remarkable record of rapid economic growth with equity. Second, the generally low public opinion of politicians was somewhat counterbalanced by the high prestige and authority enjoyed by bureaucrats, who were widely regarded as paragons of rectitude. However, these conditions began to crumble in the years running up to the 1993 general election for two reasons. First, since the 1980s, financial scandals had increasingly involved civil servants, demonstrating the political limits to maintaining a 'clean island' of the civil service surrounded by a polluted sea of corrupt politicians. And second, public confidence in the bureaucracy was further weakened when Japan's economic bubble burst in the early 1990s. The Tokyo stock market crash in 1990 brought to an end nearly 5 years of the 'most extreme financial mania seen this century' (Wood 1992: 8), leading to unprecedented bankruptcies, lay-offs and unemployment. It also revealed the spectacular extent of government mismanagement of the economy, stemming largely from the corrupt collusion between bureaucrats, politicians and big businesses (Gibney 1998: 74–6). Increasing public discontent, together with the LDP's continuing resistance to electoral reform, led to a split within the LDP in 1993 shortly before the July general election, which ultimately brought to an end the party's near four-decade monopoly of power.

The politics of reform

Admittedly, little has changed in Japanese politics since 1993, when the LDP lost its parliamentary dominance for the first time since World War II. The much expected electoral reform, which replaced the expensive SNTV system with a mixed system combining plurality voting and proportional representation, proved inconsequential in either depriving the LDP of its electoral majority or reducing money politics. Having won the largest proportion of the vote, the LDP returned to power in the 1996 Lower House election, the first election held under the new electoral system. Since then, not only has the LDP been firmly in charge, albeit with various coalition partners, but there has been little sign of money politics receding, showing that money and special interest groups have maintained their grip on the party (Kruger 2001). In the past decade, a massive amount of public investment has been made in an attempt to spend Japan's way out of recession. However, the spending still favours the infamous construction industry, the financial backbone of the LDP, at the expense of private consumption, despite low consumer confidence (Buckley 1998: 186). All in all, this lack of political reform has become a major obstacle to Japan's economic revival.

The question to raise, however, is whether these difficulties have shown Japan to be constrained by its culture from adopting genuine 'Western'-style democracy, based on open debate rather than backroom machination. In line with our analysis so far, which has shown the salience of both domestic political issues and geopolitical factors in shaping pre-1993 Japanese politics, I will continue to argue for a politics-based approach to future developments in Japanese politics. In this view, the lack of a radical political shake-up in post-1993 Japanese politics can be accounted for primarily by the entrenched vested interests that constitute the LDP support base. As has been observed, the LDP 'spent the decades of rapid growth distributing the country's hard-won wealth to a plethora of interest groups, building a diverse support base that, while gradually being eroded, remains extremely effective in holding power' (Kruger 2001; see also Calder 1993). In addition, the support base is both diverse and to some extent well justified, as it consists of people who 'really need political help', such as those in declining industries (for example agriculture), old people and shop-owners, according to a Japanese political scientist (Kruger 2001). Therefore, as in most other Western democracies, it is entrenched special interests, justified or otherwise, not culture, that is stopping Japanese democracy from moving forward.

As in many Western democracies, deficiencies in Japanese democracy are also generating increasing disillusionment in Japanese politics. Consequently, the electoral turnout has been declining, especially among young voters (McCargo 2000: 124). In the last Lower House election of 1996, turnout dropped to a record low of 59.65 per cent, and well over 50 per cent of voters in their twenties and thirties did not vote (Mikuriya 1996). Therefore, contrary to what the culturalist would have us believe, there is hardly any widespread societal support for the deficient Japanese democratic political system. Reform of Japanese politics into a more open and liberal system is widely desired (Ezrati 1999).

CONCLUSION

Few aspects of post-war Japanese politics generate so much controversy as its party politics. In this respect Japan is indeed unique among liberal democracies in having a 38-year-long, unbroken, one-party-dominated political system. However, from our historical analysis of the various structural and political factors that have contributed to the dominance of the LDP, it can safely be concluded that there is little in Japanese culture that preordained this situation. Consensus politics in Japan emerged from a bitter ideological and policy divide, which was exacerbated by Cold War geopolitics. Its subsequent consolidation was a result of a combination of good policy performance, judicious political co-option and blatant manipulation and corruption. Therefore, the difficulty Japan is undergoing in making a radical break with its past is best seen as a drawn-out political struggle rather than a cultural eternity.

This interpretation of Japanese politics also holds analytical lessons for the study of political development in other parts of Asia. Since Japanese democracy is politically, not culturally, deficient, it follows that any expectation of similar political developments in other Pacific Asian countries, based on the assumption of similar cultural values, is bound to be disappointed. To test this judgement, we need to study political development in other Pacific Asian countries, a task to which I will now turn.

6 Political development in Taiwan, South Korea and Thailand

The triumph of democratisation

Decades of rapid economic development in Pacific Asia have led to a diverse pattern of political development. Instead of moving towards the so-called Japanese-style illiberal democracy, countries such as Taiwan, South Korea and Thailand have all made great strides towards liberal democracy. Furthermore, the Confucian rhetoric, which was once used by authoritarian regimes in Taiwan and South Korea to justify their method of ruling, has also been discarded by new generations of politicians committed to democratic values (D. J. Kim 1994; Klintworth 1995). At the same time, however, there has been little progress in democratisation in Singapore and Malaysia. If anything, authoritarianism in these two countries has actually increased rather than decreased over the decades of rapid economic development. Finally, democratic transition in Indonesia, precipitated by the 1997–8 financial crisis that brought down the Suharto regime, has been marred by the eruption of ethnic strife that has gripped the country since. So why such a varied pattern of political development in the region?

I seek to address this question in two chapters, this one and the next. In this chapter, I will focus on the three countries that have travelled far on the road to democracy. We are interested in why these countries have made a successful transition from authoritarian rule to democracy. In other words, what led to the rise of democracy in these countries?

I approach this question from a theoretical and comparative-historical perspective. In the first part of the chapter, I will provide a brief overview of the four major theoretical perspectives on democratisation, namely the socioeconomic perspective, the strategic perspective, the structural perspective and the cultural perspective. The object of this is to spell out a dynamic theoretical framework within which to carry out my comparative study. In the second part of the chapter, I will compare the process of democratisation of the three countries by situating each national experience in its historical and political context. Finally, I will conclude by noting the common factors that led to these countries' successful democratisation and by commenting on the impact of those factors on the future democratic development of the countries' different transition trajectories.

CONDITIONS FOR DEMOCRATISATION

Between 1974 and 1997, more than thirty countries sought to move away from authoritarian rule to democracy, although not all of them were successful in their transition (Sorensen 1998: 30). This latest upsurge, or third wave , of worldwide spread of democracy (Huntington 1993b) has led to a revival of academic interest in the conditions for democratisation and the emergence of four major theoretical perspectives on the issue, namely socioeconomic, strategic, structural and cultural. In what follows, I will examine briefly the core ideas of each perspective before formulating an integrated approach to democratisation in Pacific Asia.

Socioeconomic perspective

The socioeconomic perspective on democratisation is what lies at the heart of modernisation theory (see Chapter 1). Essentially, it sees a nation's affluence as a condition favouring the emergence of democracy. Following Lipset's lead, Dahl (1971), for example, considered it pretty much beyond dispute that the higher the socioeconomic level of a country, the more likely that it would be a democracy.

National wealth helps the cause of democracy mainly in two ways. First, it leads to the general rise of literacy and education in society, which both enables the people to participate in political decision making and fosters the values of tolerance (Lipset 1960: 39). Second, it provides the resources needed to mitigate the tensions produced by political conflict (Huntington 1984: 199).

This perspective has sometimes been wrongly criticised for alleged economic determinism, i.e. for seeing economic development as the single most important cause of democracy. The criticism is based on two observations: that not all wealthy societies are democracies (such as many Middle East sheikdoms) and that some poor countries, such as India, have maintained a relatively stable democratic system. Although these observations are undoubtedly true, they do not invalidate the socioeconomic thesis because it does not depict a causal relationship between socioeconomic development and democracy. Rather, by drawing researchers' attention to the strong correlation between the level of economic development and democracy, this perspective sees richer countries as offering better opportunities for democracy without specifying why some countries fail to take up this opportunity. This explanatory gap is filled by the strategic perspective, which emphasises human agency or action.

Strategic perspective

The key point of this perspective is that democracy does not fall from heaven; it is a product of social conflict, the resolution of which requires human initiatives. As Rustow (1970: 362) argues, a people who are not in conflict about some rather fundamental matters would have little need to devise democracy's elaborate rules for conflict resolution. In this view, the crucial role of capitalist development in stimulating democracy is not the creation of wealth but the triggering of serious and prolonged social conflicts, which force social actors to negotiate with each other for their peaceful solution (Przeworski 1988).

As the negotiation involves primarily two sides, the ruling elite and the powerless, who have been barred from political influence during authoritarian rule, strategic calculation by both sides is crucial in determining the transition to democracy. Very rarely is the beginning of a democracy possible if the envisaged new system is likely to lead to the complete defeat of the ruling elites. Democratisation is only possible if there exist institutions that provide a reasonable expectation that interests of major political forces would not be affected very adversely under democratic competition (ibid.: 79). In other words, ingenuity and compromises on both sides of the conflict are required for a successful transition to democracy (O'Donnell and Schmitter 1986; Shain and Linz 1995).

The strength of the strategic perspective on democratisation is mainly twofold: its emphasis on human choice in bringing about democracy and its highlighting of the almost necessarily limited nature of the initial transition to democracy resulting from strategic conservative agreement. These insights point to the contingent nature of the democratisation process as a function of conflict rather than wealth.

Structural perspective

However, the strategic perspective has been rightly criticised for its overemphasis on human agency at the expense of due regard for the structural changes in society that either restrict or enhance the decision choices available to social actors (Karl 1991). According to the structural perspective, actors cannot make any kind of choice in a given situation; they are constrained by the structures, social groups or classes that have been formed over a long period of the country's history (Moore 1966). Capitalist development brings about changes in the relations among these classes, and a society's prospect for democracy is fundamentally shaped by the balance of class power (Rueschemeyer *et al.* 1992: 47).

Five structures of power or classes are identified as the main protagonists in the struggle for democracy in a capitalist society. These are: the large landlords, the peasantry (including rural workers and independent farmers), the urban working class, the urban bourgeoisie (owners or employers of enterprises engaged in industry, trade and commerce) and the salaried and professional middle class. Of the five classes, only two have been historically known for their unambiguous orientation towards democracy. While the large landlords are fiercely anti-democratic for fear of losing large profits derived from cheap labour, the urban working class is consistently pro-democratic in its push for the extension of suffrage, unions and other democratic rights. The position of the remaining three classes, however, is less clear and often varies from country to country, depending on the alignment of other classes, the position and power of the state and external factors. Two general points sum up the structural perspective. First, no single class is strong enough on its own to either prevent or push for democracy. Second, because class alliance is crucial for political development, different class alliances can occur in different countries, which can be more or less favourable to democratisation.

The structural perspective is also the only perspective that examines the role of the state in democratisation by arguing that a state that enjoys some degree of autonomy from all social classes is the most congenial to democratisation. Historically, capitalist development has led to the emergence of a denser civil society, the independent public space in which voluntary social organisations make regular collective attempts to influence the exercise of state power (Bernhard 1993: 308), as a counterweight to state power. By empowering the previously excluded classes, civil society thus improves the chance of democratisation (Rueschemeyer *et al.* 1992: 50).

Finally, the structural perspective also shows the way in which external factors can affect class alignments and the nature and form of state power. For example, the economic dependence of a country on another can delay industrialisation and thus prevent the small working class from exerting a powerful pro-democratisation influence. Similarly, geopolitical dependence can also delay democratisation as massive military and economic aid strengthens the state apparatus vis-à-vis the social classes. So, the relaxation of international tensions may improve prospects for democracy.

The strength of the structural perspective on democratisation is obvious. By emphasising the structured choice available to social actors in different countries with different histories and international positions, structuralists bring out the dynamic process of democratisation whereby structure and choice both shape and are shaped by each other. From this perspective, neither economic wealth nor strategic human initiatives alone are sufficient conditions for democracy; rather, it is a product of the interplay between the two sets of factors. This is effectively the approach I will adopt in my study of democratisation in the three countries of Taiwan, South Korea and Thailand. But before I move on to the next part of the chapter, it is necessary to examine briefly the cultural perspective on democratisation.

Cultural perspective

As noted in Chapter 5, the cultural perspective is particularly influential on political development in Pacific Asia. The central point of this perspective is the view that some cultures are a barrier to democracy while others are an important precondition for it. Examples of the former include Confucianism and Islam and of the latter, Christianity. Although it may appear plausible to treat the cultural thesis in the same way as the socioeconomic thesis, namely to see both perspectives as no more than identifying structural conditions for democracy, there is in fact little intellectual case for the cultural perspective. This is mainly due to the problem arising from what Keesing (1991: 44) describes as the 'coral reef' conception of culture, which assumes 'a substantial degree of sharedness, boundedness and coherence of a locally cumulated way of life'. Such a static and insular conception of culture inevitably sees the impact of culture on political development in deterministic rather than probable terms.

This is why the cultural perspective is rejected by both strategic and structural perspectives. The challenge of democratisation, as Schmitter and Karl (1991: 82) contend, 'is not so much to find a set of goals that command widespread consensus as to find a set of rules that embody contingent consent'. Such consensus can appear only after a long period of the functioning of democratic institutions, which 'habituate' society to their rules and underlying values (Rustow 1970). In short, the values supporting democracy are a consequence and not a cause of the practice of democracy itself.

Having critically reviewed the various theoretical perspectives on democratisation and spelled out our approach to political development in Pacific Asia, I will now move to the next part of the chapter in which I seek to locate the democratisation experiences of Taiwan, South Korea and Thailand in both theoretical and historical contexts.

DEMOCRATISATION COMPARED

Democratisation in the three countries of Taiwan, South Korea and Thailand took very different trajectories. While it was relatively smooth in Taiwan and South Korea, it was long and tortuous in Thailand, which, until 1992, saw seemingly endless swings between military rule and parliamentary democracy (Sukatipan 1995: 193). Capitalist development in all three countries generated similar structures and forces seeking to influence state power. However, different national history, political institutions and geopolitical dynamics mediated these forces, resulting in distinct patterns of democratisation.

Of the three countries, Taiwan and South Korea share more similarities with each other than with Thailand. Historically, both countries were influenced by Confucian culture and fell under Japanese colonial rule until the end of World War II. Cold War politics also saw both countries divided, which fostered their geopolitical dependence on the United States (South Korea still accommodates US troops today). These two factors of Japanese colonial rule and geopolitical dependence on the United States have both served to strengthen the state apparatus of the two countries, especially in the early years of their economic development (see Chapter 3). In addition, the common threat of communism from their 'brother enemies' served as a powerful disincentive for democratisation. This would partly explain why democratisation in both countries, which started in the late 1980s, coincided with the relaxation of international tensions.

Elite-led transition in Taiwan

Democratisation in Taiwan, like that in South Korea and Thailand, although helped by capitalist development, was never a simple outgrowth of economic wealth. Its driving force long preceded Taiwan's economic development, and its unfolding at every crucial historical stage reflected the ingenuity of key social actors, keenly aware of the changing structural constraints and opportunities both at home and abroad. Specifically, Taiwan's transition to democracy was profoundly influenced by one overarching context: its unique international status as a de facto state for the previous half-century, whose sovereignty was (and still is) disputed by the People's Republic of China (PRC) in Beijing. Seeing it as a 'renegade' province of the PRC, the Beijing regime vowed to retake Taiwan into the 'motherland', by force if necessary. This uncertainty about Taiwan's political identity has been both the source of Taiwan's driving force for democracy and its largest structural constraint. Managing 'Strait relations' is thus an important part of Taiwan's democratisation.

Taiwan's struggle for democracy started almost immediately after the KMT landed on the island at the end of World War II. Inept rule sparked widespread resentment towards the mainland 'outsiders' on the part of the native Taiwanese and helped to forge the incipient Taiwan nationalism (Watchman 1994: 96). The brutal suppression of the 'Taiwan Uprising' of 28 February 1947, followed by the imposition of martial law, which was to last until 1987, drove the nationalist movement underground but also marked the beginning of the nationalist-cum-democratic struggle in Taiwan.

The KMT's loss of mainland China to the Communist Party in the civil war, which forced its followers to flee to Taiwan in 1949, fundamentally shaped its ruling practice in Taiwan. Although authoritarian rule was deemed vital in a situation of external threats to security and internal instability, the KMT practised a new brand of authoritarianism described by Rigger (1996) as 'mobilisational authoritarianism'. Based on *Sanminzhuyi*, the Three Principles of the People, mobilisational authoritarianism had three key policy ingredients to it: economic development, social equality (achieved partly through the widely admired land reform) and controlled and limited political participation (Tien 1989). These policies were designed to mobilise the entire Taiwanese population behind the KMT in its drive to eventually launch a military campaign to reunify and rule China.

The KMT's highly centralised party structure, with its hierarchy paralleling all levels of state institution and educational establishments, was the ideal instrument for such authoritarian mobilisation. The combination of corporatist co-option of independent social interests with the controlled opening of local politics to political contestation greatly boosted the regime's legitimacy as well as pre-empting the emergence of an independent civil society. As social interests began to proliferate from the 1950s, an array of government-affiliated interest groups were set up. Ambitious local elites and citizens, mostly Taiwanese, were also channelled into the KMT-dominated local electoral politics.

In comparison with South Korea, mobilisational authoritarianism rendered Taiwan's politics far more stable and under control; the systematic application of army and police coercion was thus not necessary. With the help of rapid economic success, the regime encountered little political opposition until the 1970s.

All this began to change in the early 1970s, when Taiwan lost its United Nations (UN) membership to mainland China following a US diplomatic rapprochement with the latter. This event called into question the legitimacy not only of a regime that claimed to represent all China but also of the entire project of reunification, which had hitherto been used as a major justification for authoritarian rule. So, from the early 1970s, as the military project of reunification became increasingly unrealistic, opposition forces began to mobilise for an alternative vision of politics, which would put the interest of the majority Taiwanese above that of the KMT-led minority mainlanders. Popular demand for abandoning the pretence of sovereignty over mainland China to enable Taiwan to pursue an independent course of democratic development thus became the rallying cry for the democracy movement in Taiwan.

During the 1970s, the opposition movement to the regime was led mainly by Taiwanese nationalist intellectuals, who, through political journals and contestation of local and provincial elections, called for political reforms and ethnic justice, i.e. equal political rights for the majority of native Taiwanese. Specifically, they called for an end to such official policies as forcing opposition groups to stand in elections as 'independents' or *dangwai* (Party outsiders) rather than opposition party members, and the practice of freezing Taiwan-wide direct elections to national legislative bodies, which were last constituted in 1947 on mainland China. In 1977, *dangwai* candidates stunned the KMT by winning twenty-one of the seventy-seven seats in the Taiwan Provincial Assembly election. Two years later, the Kaohsiung incident occurred when opposition rallies in the city of Kaohsiung erupted into violence that led to the arrest of dozens of opposition activists.

As Taiwan entered the 1980s, a confluence of domestic and international changes helped to speed up its move to democracy. With an annual growth rate averaging 9.2 per cent between 1950 and 1980, Taiwan was quickly becoming a well-educated, industrialised and urbanised society. By the late 1980s, three out of four adults viewed themselves as middle class (Metzger and Myers 1989: 301). With *dangwai* capturing an increasing share of electoral positions and with the proliferation of social movements, covering such issues as women's rights, workers' rights, and environmental conservation, all demanding the opening up of civil society, mobilisational authoritarianism found it increasingly difficult to co-opt these social forces into the state fold (Gold 1990; Hsiao 1992; Chu 1994).

Since the late 1970s, the increasing 'Taiwanisation' of politics has also boosted the nationalist–democratic movement. Partly as a result of the passing away of the mainland old guard and partly because of the government policy of Taiwanisation in response to pressure from the *dangwai*, both party and state positions were increasingly occupied by Taiwanese. By the late 1980s, a majority of KMT members and state officials were Taiwanese (Chu 1993). In 1988, Lee Tenghui became the first Taiwanese to hold both the KMT chair and the state presidency following the death of Chiang Chingkuo, his mainland predecessor. As many of the

Taiwanese had never set foot on mainland China, they had far less sympathy and commitment to the KMT state's official 'one-China' policy.

An opening for democracy in Taiwan occurred in 1986, when the *dangwai* defied martial law by forming the first opposition party, the Democratic Progressive Party (DPP). This led to the subsequent lifting of martial law and a series of legislation guaranteeing the people's political rights to association, opposition and a free press. Political liberalisation set Taiwan firmly on the road to democracy as more political parties emerged and social movements proliferated.

The initial period of democratisation was greatly overshadowed by the issue of Taiwan's political identity, which restricted the full-blown development of civil and political rights. The KMT made it clear that any advocacy of violence, communism and Taiwan 'independence' from China would not be tolerated. However, since Taiwan nationalism was the soul of its democracy movement, the KMT gradually began to adopt a more pragmatic approach to it, embodied in President Chiang's claim that 'I am Chinese and I am also Taiwanese'. This indicated the KMT's readiness to admit to Taiwan's political distinctness, while acknowledging its cultural affinity with mainland China (Moody: 1995: 274). This pragmatism on the part of the KMT ensured Taiwan's orderly transition to democracy.

Following President Chiang Chingkuo's death in 1988, democratisation made rapid progress. As part of the post-Chiang political reforms, the KMT, under Lee Tenghui, followed a largely electoral route to democracy. Taiwan-wide direct elections were held not only for the legislative bodies, the National Assembly and the Legislative Yuan, ending the resented 'Long Parliament', but also for the provincial governorship and the mayoralties of Taipei and Kaohsiung, two of the largest cities in Taiwan. The process was completed by the first direct election of the president, held in 1996. These elections, promoted by the KMT as an expression of the emerging 'new Taiwanese' identity, based on unity between native Taiwanese and the mainlanders, marked not only the beginning of the Taipei regime's democratic politics, but also its tacit renunciation of any claim to the sovereignty of the whole of China. They gave expression to the consensus that Taiwan needs to move on from its undemocratic frozen past to a new kind of politics that expresses the collective choice of Taiwan's population. The determination of the Taiwanese people to defend their hard-won democratic rights was demonstrated in the 1996 presidential election, which was held amid grave military threats being made by Beijing (*The Economist*, 10 February 2000).

Beijing's territorial claim on Taiwan continues to cast a shadow on the island's democracy. Otherwise, there is little doubt that Taiwan today is one of the most vibrant democracies in Pacific Asia. The year 2000 marked yet another landmark in Taiwan's democratic transition. In the second presidential election held in March, the ruling KMT finally lost the presidency to its long-time opponent, the DPP. Although the DPP was born out of the Taiwan independence movement, its leadership has shrewdly moved to a pragmatic China policy based on continuing dialogue and negotiation (*The Economist*, 23 May 2000), showing the party's growing political maturity in steering Taiwan's new democracy.

Taiwan's successful democratisation has shattered the culturalist myth of the alleged incompatibility of Confucianism with liberal democracy. Democratisation in Taiwan is a product of the dynamic interaction between changing structures of power – at both national and international level – with the political courage and ingenuity of individuals, key figures among whom were the *dangwai*/DPP activists Presidents Chiang Chingkuo and Li Tenghui (Chang 1986; Cohen 1988; Watchman 1994). In short, all the following factors helped Taiwan's struggle for democracy: capitalist development, the diversification of social structure, the emergence of civil society, the demise of large landlords in the wake of land reform and the relaxation of cross-Strait tensions during the 1980s, brought on partly by mainland China's shift towards market reform, which required a peaceful international and regional environment.

Protest-driven democratisation in South Korea

In contrast to Taiwan's relatively peaceful transition in which the elites – intellectuals and political leaders – played a large role, democratisation in South Korea was driven by popular protest led by students, industrial workers and, later, the urban middle class. The highly visible 'vicious cycle of opposition and suppression' (Jeon, quoted in Cheng and Kim 1994: 134) was something unseen in authoritarian Taiwan. This bottom-up pattern of democratisation was a result of very different domestic class alliances and geopolitical dynamics.

Unlike Taiwan, the initial period after the creation of South Korea (in 1948) was marked by rule by a democratically elected government. However, the division of the Korean peninsula, followed by the tragic Korean War, was soon to have a devastating effect on South Korean political development. Because of the well-justified perception of a much graver threat from communist North Korea, the first democratically elected government under President Syngman Rhee quickly turned to authoritarianism. The army and the police were built up as major state institutions. Rhee's rule (1948–60) was characterised by heavy-handed political repression, assassination, widespread corruption and economic mismanagement.

In 1960, after Rhee won the fourth election through blatant vote rigging, massive student demonstrations and riots broke out and they were quickly joined by society at large. Rhee was forced to step down. For the next 26 years, Korea was effectively ruled by two military men, Park Chung Hee (1961–79) and Chun Doo Hwan (1980–7), both of whom came to power through coups. During these authoritarian years, the state relied on an extensive security and police apparatus to quell any perceived challenge to its authority. Under draconian laws, such as the National Security Law of 1948, agents of control, ranging from riot troops to undercover intelligence agents, were deployed to destabilise and weaken the organisational ability of existing groups such as trade unions (Choi 1989). In the meantime, close government–*chaebol* relations meant that financial scandals and corruptions involving top government officials were commonplace, fanning increasing popular discontent.

Throughout the 1960s and 1970s, popular protests for democratisation were led mainly by students and workers, more often in isolation from each other because of the highly repressive state apparatus (Choi 1989; Cheng and Kim 1994). In the 1980s, however, several events converged to bring the two forces closer together. These included the suicide of a factory worker in 1970 in protest at the regime's denial of workers' rights (Dong 1993) and the Kwangju Massacre of May 1980, in which about 200 people involved in violent demonstrations against the regime were killed by the police (Koo 1993).

As in Taiwan, rapid industrialisation also created an articulate middle class, which comprised mainly white-collar workers in the public and private sectors of the economy, including urban professionals, intellectuals and people in the media and the self-employed (Koo 1991). Since the early 1980s, the middle class had increasingly joined the students and workers as part of the rapidly developing broad protest alliance known as the *minjung* movement (Wells 1995). The Chun regime, while appearing to tolerate a degree of open political competition by allowing some minor opposition parties to compete with its dominant Democratic Justice Party (DJP), strengthened the security and surveillance apparatus and tightened controls on the press and the increasingly organised and militant labour movement.

The struggle for democracy gained added momentum in 1985, when all the opposition parties came together to form the New Korea Democratic Party (NKDP) and won sixty-seven of the elective 187 seats in parliament. The party immediately went to battle with the government in parliament by calling for constitutional reform to provide for direct presidential elections for the coming election in early 1988. On the streets and campuses, the struggle was picked up by workers, students and the middle class, whose alliance was precipitated by the torture and death of a student activist at the hands of the police in January 1987 (Cotton 1989).

The first few months of 1987 saw in South Korea 'some of the largest mass rallies for democracy in world history' (Borthwick 1992: 351), a result of the Chun government's announcement of the temporary suspension of the debate on constitutional reform. By June 1987, violence was both widespread and escalating, with areas of Seoul, the capital city, looking like war zones. Faced with the choice between complete suppression and substantial concession, the regime was divided, and the impasse was broken only when General Rho Tae Woo, the ruling party's official presidential candidate, declared in June 1987 his intention to hold direct presidential elections and initiate all the democratic reforms demanded by the public. This marked the end of the violent 'spring of discontent' and the beginning of the democratic process in South Korea.

The immediate results of the start of democracy in Korea were the lifting of restrictions on political activities and the release of opposition political prisoners, among whom were Mr Kim Dae Jung, the veteran opposition leader and present Korean president. In October 1987 a new constitution was approved by a national referendum, which provided for direct election for the president for a 5-year non-renewable term and also for a mixed political system combining presidential and parliamentary elements. Two months later, the first presidential election was held under the new constitution. Rho won with only 36.6 per cent of the total vote cast because of a split between the opposition parties. In the National Assembly elections, held in April 1988, President Rho's party failed to achieve an overall majority for the first time since the party's formation in 1980 (Cheng and Kim 1994: 138). Subsequent efforts to emulate the Japanese-style one-party dominance by constructing a 'grand conservative coalition', in the form of the Democratic Liberal Party, failed, largely because of public suspicion of the undemocratic intentions of the politicians involved (Lee 1994: 155). Instead, a US-style 'split government', in which different parties control the presidency and parliament, has become somewhat the norm in Korean politics since the 1990s.

Probably more so than Taiwan, the young Korean democracy has yet to overcome many of the legacies of authoritarian rule. As in Taiwan, relaxation of the tension between the two Koreas will also be an important factor for the deepening of Korean democracy. Since its transition, South Korea has also seen a flourishing of civil society, concerned about issues relating to social justice, such as government favours to the *chaebol*, the inequitable tax system, the underprovision of social welfare, gender inequality, and environmental protection (Dalton and Cotton 1996).

However, with the arrival of democracy, the solidarity between the working and middle classes, which was central to Korea's democratic beginning, has largely dissipated. Instead, the explosion of working-class radicalism that followed democratisation (Ogle 1990; Choi 1993) has made the middle class increasingly worried about its potentially negative impact on South Korea's economic health. So, there is a far wider policy agenda open to public contestation in South Korean politics today.

The capitalist revolution in Thailand

Of the three countries that have successfully moved to democracy, Thailand started democratisation in the mid-1970s at a much lower level of socioeconomic development and with a greater degree of socioeconomic inequality. Even today, over two-thirds of its population still lives in the countryside and over half of its workforce is engaged in agriculture. Most of the country's industrial and commercial activity is also concentrated in Bangkok and its surrounding areas. This much lower level and very unequal pattern of socioeconomic development, therefore, has greatly undermined the quality of Thai democracy and constrained its further development.

The limited nature of Thai democracy is largely a product of the dominant role of the capitalist class in bringing about democracy. More than in Taiwan and South Korea, democratisation in Thailand was shaped by the capitalist revolution, which began in the late 1950s and accelerated in the 1980s. The Thai business class, which was the agent of the Thai economic miracle, first by collaborating with the military-dominated bureaucratic–authoritarian state, then by penetrating the state itself during Thailand's transition to liberal corporatism, was also the key force behind Thailand's move to democracy. This, however, does not suggest a stronger normative commitment to democracy on the part of the Thai capitalist class. Far from it; its largely instrumental support for democracy, a support motivated by vested interest, is both a result of Thailand's laissez-faire pattern of economic development and a major constraint on the deepening of democracy in Thailand.

The first attempt to bring about democracy in Thailand began with the 1932 military coup, which, however, failed to meet its objectives but ushered in a military-dominated bureaucratic polity instead. Two decades of economic and political drift led to the rise of the military strong man Sarit Thannarat in the late 1950s, who launched Thailand's industrialisation, based on productive, albeit corrupt, collaboration between the military government and the Chinese capitalists. During the next two decades, military rule was consolidated and the economy flourished. The emergence of a threatening communist insurgency in the country's north and northeast and the US support of the state's robust anti-communist stance both helped to keep at bay occasional popular demands for democracy.

The 1970s marked an important watershed in Thai political development. The year 1973 witnessed the biggest demonstrations by workers and students demanding democratic reform. The ensuing return to civilian rule produced the hitherto most democratic constitution in Thai history, which enabled ordinary citizens to participate in politics for the first time. However, ideological and social polarisation, partly accentuated by the perception of the growing communist threat from neighbouring countries, led to another military seizure of power in 1976 through the bloodiest coup in Thai history.

But politics after 1976 was not to be the same again. Democratic participation, albeit for a brief period, raised public expectations, and for the next two decades Thai politics was dominated by the struggle for power between bureaucrats and officers, on the one hand, and politicians, on the other. Partly due to dissension within the military, and partly due to the opposition to military rule expressed by the monarchy, a revered Thai institution, Thailand embarked on a move to *semi-democracy* during the 1976–91 period (Chai-Anan 1989; Neher and Marlay 1995: Chapter 3). During this period, the press was freed and regular elections held. Under the prime ministership of Prem Tinsulanond (1980–8), a former general, the military was constrained and the civilian-led legislature was given greater responsibility for domestic policies. When Prem refused to serve another term in 1988 despite his popularity, for the first time since 1976 Thailand elected a civilian member of parliament as prime minister.

A major characteristic of this period of semi-democracy was the Thai state's evolution from bureaucratic authoritarianism to liberal corporatism dominated by businesses (Anek 1992). While labour remained politically weak, businesses became increasingly well organised and involved in politics. It became common for wealthy business leaders to win parliamentary elections and go on to become cabinet members. The increasing penetration of the state by the capitalist class was later to prove a crucial factor for Thailand's limited democracy, characterised by 'money politics' and rampant vote buying (Callahan and McCargo 1996; Neher 1999: Chapter 3; Hewison 2000: 200).

When the 1991 military coup toppled the civilian government, there was little objection from the capitalist and middle classes, hitherto staunch allies in their push for democratisation. However, as Hewison (1997: 81–5) explains, their silence was understandable for two reasons. First, the coup was not an attempt to attack the capitalist state; rather, it intended to curb democracy – 'parliamentary dictatorship' – by limiting the political space that had been opened up to civilian politicians and social movement. In other words, it merely represented a reconfiguration of state power by wresting it from the hands of civilian politicians into the hands of military and bureaucratic officers. Second, the business and middle classes both shared with the military its concern about corruption and money politics, issues that the military claimed to warrant limited democracy.

But a year later the most massive popular revolt against the military in Thai history broke out, leading to the tragic events of 'Black May', in which hundreds of civilians were killed or injured. This, however, turned out to be a turning point in Thailand's move towards democracy, and since then major constitutional reforms have been implemented and the military appears to have been firmly subordinated to civilian rule. So how do we account for this dramatic turn of events?

What triggered the demonstrations was the military-sponsored election of March 1992 in which the 'devil' (pro-military) parties won and the 1991 coup leader Suchinda Kraprayoon became prime minister. The demonstrations escalated following Suchinda's appointment to his cabinet of many 'unusually wealthy' politicians, who had been investigated by an anti-corruption panel, established by himself after the coup. This move belied the coup leaders' claim that their purpose in overthrowing the civilian government was to curtail corruption. It also dawned upon the business and middle classes that the military was no better than civilian politicians when it came to expanding its own economic base. Military rule was seen to be a particular danger to the new business class, whose success depended less on political patronage than on access to international opportunities. With the critical intervention of the King, Suchinda was forced to resign in May and in another general election held 4 months later, the 'devil parties' were eventually defeated by the 'angel (anti-military) parties'. A five-party coalition government was then formed under the prime ministership of Chuan Leekpai, a long-time leader of the Democrat Party, Thailand's oldest political party, and a man famous for his honesty and moderate approach to politics.

Since 1992, democratisation in Thailand has made great strides, and the role of the military in politics is increasingly moving from one of direct control to one of influence. The democratic base of Thailand was expanded in January 1995, when Chuan succeeded in obtaining the approval of the National Assembly for a series of constitutional reforms (*EWYB* 1998: 3293). Democratic reforms reached a high point in September 1997, when the National Assembly approved a new constitution designed to set Thai democracy on a more stable and clearer path (*EWYB* 1998: 3295).

The new democratic reforms met their first crucial test during the 1997–8 financial crisis, which started in Thailand. Following the IMF-imposed austerity programmes, mass demonstrations broke out against the government, which was believed to be corrupt and inept. In the end, speculation over another 1992-style suppression turned out to be unfounded and the government resigned, effecting the first peaceful transfer of power under the terms of the new constitution (*The Economist*, 15 November 1997, p. 86).

Democracy in Thailand still faces many problems, chief among which is that of vote buying, which takes many forms and plagues all elections, including the first two elections held under the 1997 constitution. These were the election to the Upper House, the Senate, held in March 2000 (*The Economist*, 29 July 2000, p. 67), and the first election to the Lower House, the House of Representatives, held in January 2001 (Crispin and Tasker 2001). Vote buying is particularly rampant in rural areas, where over 65 per cent of the population still lives and the patron–client relationship remains important. Against the background of growing inequality between the urban and rural populations, vote buying became a perverse means by which income was transferred to the Thai peasantry, if only during the formal campaigning period! Government campaigns urging the people not to 'sell your freedom' must sound hollow at best and sinister at worst in a country in which big business and politics are so entwined.

More so than in Japan, structural interpenetration between big business and politics is the major cause of money politics, a feature which, unfortunately, is likely to get even more entrenched with the election as prime minister of Thaksin Shinawatra, a former tycoon and the richest man in Thailand. Thaksin's coming to power is widely seen to augur ill for Thailand's future democracy as it is likely to lead to a full-blown merger between politics and big business (ibid.). Having won the latest Lower House election, many candidates from his party, including himself, have been under investigation for corruption by the National Counter Corruption Commission and the Election Commission. The Thai experience of democratisation has thus illustrated the way in which democracy is limited by a state captured by the capitalist class and by a low level of socioeconomic development.

CONCLUSION

In this chapter I have analysed the different trajectories of democratisation in Taiwan, South Korea and Thailand, three of the newly democratised countries (NDCs) in Pacific Asia. Contrary to the culturalist prediction, none of the countries has adopted a dominant-party system similar to that of Japan despite their broad cultural similarities. Nor is it likely that they will develop one in the future, given the very different political institutions and practices established. While South Korea failed in its explicit attempt to emulate Japan in this respect, Taiwan's long-ruling KMT lost its grip on power in the country's second direct presidential election in March 2000. Thailand, on the other hand, has never experienced a one-party dominant system since its move to democracy in the late 1970s. The diversified pattern of democratic development suggests that culture is a far less influential factor on democratisation.

In terms of the other theoretical perspectives on democratisation that I reviewed briefly at the beginning of the chapter, the experiences of the three countries appear to provide overwhelming support for a dynamic approach to democratisation that emphasises the interplay between structural changes in society brought on by capitalist development and human choices made in response to those changes, their opportunities and constraints. As I have noted, capitalist development in all three countries generated pressures for democratic change, but that change came about at different levels of national wealth, under different configurations of class alliance, and with different consequences for the deepening of democracy. At key historical junctures, dominant personalities in all three countries – Chiang Chingkuo of Taiwan, Rho Tae Woo of South Korea and the Thai King Bhumibol Adulyadej – also played a critical role in shaping events. In short, the successful move to democracy in these three countries has shown that the struggle for democracy is ultimately won by people actively taking initiatives in a particular time and space rather than being predetermined by static precepts of culture.

7 Political development in Malaysia, Singapore and Indonesia
Democratisation blocked

Having analysed the various forces that converged to bring about democracy in Taiwan, South Korea and Thailand, I will shift the focus in this chapter to the other side of the coin, namely the forces that have succeeded so far in blocking democratisation in Malaysia, Singapore and Indonesia. Using a similar approach, namely the comparative-historical, I will nevertheless organise this study on the theme of legitimacy. By projecting our concern through the conceptual lens of regime legitimacy, I will seek to compare the dynamic relationship between the social challenge of regime legitimacy and the state attempts to manage the challenge. In so doing, I will show that while all the three Southeast Asian societies have been subject to similar structural pressures for democracy, unleashed by capitalist development, failure to democratise can be largely accounted for by more or less successful political manoeuvres by the state that blunted the edge of the impulse for democracy.

I will advance this argument in two parts. In the first part of the chapter, I will outline the concept of legitimacy and its relationship with democratisation. Then, in the second part, I will compare the ways in which the three regimes managed to maintain legitimacy and thus to block democratisation. I will argue that, although they all employed the rhetoric of culture and the practice of electoralism and developmentalism to maintain legitimacy, they have nevertheless produced different degrees of political success and outcomes. I will conclude by discussing the prospects for democracy in these countries.

DEMOCRATISATION AND REGIME LEGITIMACY

As all students of political change know, *legitimacy*, namely 'the degree to which [a political system] is generally accepted by its citizens' (Lipset 1960: 22), is fundamental to the survival of a regime. A regime that loses its legitimacy loses the citizen's consent to its 'right to rule', triggering crisis of state power and paving the way for political change. From an empirical point of view, a regime can enjoy different degrees of legitimacy, ranging from moral to pragmatic. While moral legitimacy refers to active support of the citizens based on its belief in a set of coherent normative principles, such as rights or justice, pragmatic legitimacy refers to the citizen's passive acquiescence to the state's exercise of power based on some instrumental or pragmatic reasons (i.e. the belief that to obey the state may be the best way of achieving stability and social harmony or that there may be no realistic chance of a successful challenge to state power). Undoubtedly, a regime is most stable when it enjoys moral legitimacy, whereas its collapse indicates the state's loss of even the minimal level of popular consent to its right to rule.

Seen in this light, democratisation marks the collapse of authoritarian regimes and the transformation of the basis of state power from what Max Weber (1957) identified as tradition and personal charisma to uniformly applied rules and procedures, i.e. democratic rule of law. The question we face now is why democratisation in these three Southeast Asian countries has yet to happen. In other words, what is blocking their move to democracy? Furthermore, we need also to contemplate whether the experiences of these countries have invalidated our conclusion about democratisation, namely that it is a result of the interplay of structural changes and human initiatives, not a culturally determined phenomenon. It is these questions to which I now turn.

MANAGING FAÇADE DEMOCRACY: A COMPARISON

In comparison with authoritarian Taiwan, South Korea and Thailand, Malaysia, Singapore and Indonesia had one thing in common, which was their façade democratic apparatus, a legacy of their colonial past. Although they operated different forms and degrees of authoritarian rule, ranging from Malaysia's ethnic-based 'semi-democracy' (Case 1993; Crouch 1993), to Singapore's highly centralised Leninist-style party state, and Indonesia's ruthless military rule, all three Southeast Asian regimes went to great lengths to maintain a parliamentary front. In these regimes, political parties were allowed to set up only to be tightly regulated and controlled; elections were regularly held and votes fairly counted but only the ruling party was allowed to win (Taylor 1996). No wonder parliament was in the hands of the government rather than an articulator of social interests. However, I will argue that façade democracy, with its focus on *electoralism*, the practice of using elections as no more than a symbol of regime legitimacy, nevertheless generated its own dynamics of regime legitimation by simultaneously holding out the promise of and marginalising popular participation. I will show the different mechanisms by which this 'useful fiction' of electoralism (Liddle 1996) was maintained in the three societies and its growing limits in the context of capitalist development.

Abortive democracy and the rise of electoralism

Like most post-colonial states, Malaysia, Singapore and Indonesia experimented with democracy after national independence. National crises however sooner or later led to the failure of the experiments and the rise of authoritarian rule. As a result, all three states kept the institutional shell of parliamentary democracy, especially the trappings of elections, while adopting authoritarian practices in different degrees and forms. Whereas Malaysia managed to maintain its reputation as a 'semi-democracy', Indonesia and Singapore were at best pseudo-democracies dominated respectively by the military and a Leninist-style political party. Over the years, economic development and political stability have not only sustained Malaysia's relatively 'soft' ethnic authoritarianism and Singapore's legalistic, meritocratic authoritarianism, but have also enabled leaders of both regimes to claim their own system to be the exemplar of 'Asian democracy'.

On the other hand, however, the highly repressive military regime in Indonesia was brought down by popular revolt during the 1997–8 financial crisis. Two years after its collapse and the establishment of a democratically elected government, the world is still holding its breath over the future of a country gripped by ethnic violence (Napier 2000; BBC World Monitoring, 27 Feb 2001). Therefore, although Malaysia and Singapore are facing increasing challenges to their legitimacy, their relative stability vis-à-vis Indonesia suggests different dynamics of authoritarian rule.

The retrenchment of democracy was triggered by different national crises, which also had a lasting effect on subsequent political development in the three countries. Of the three societies, democracy in Indonesia was the most short lived because of a confluence of economic, ethnic and political crises, many of which were legacies of Dutch colonial rule. After a brief experience with federalism, foisted on it by the Dutch, Indonesia adopted a parliamentary system in 1950 but it failed to consolidate its authority over the immense archipelago for the next seven years. Small parties representing competing religious, class, and regional interests formed fleeting coalition governments while the economy continued to be dominated by Dutch and Chinese capital. Meanwhile, the emergence of 'politicoeconomic empires' built by Javanese aristocrats turned bureaucrats and politicians (Robison

1986: 48–9) worsened economic inequality and fuelled separatist feelings and revolts in west Java and Aceh in the north of Sumatra.

Against deteriorating economic, social and political crises, the nationalist President Sukarno replaced constitutional democracy with his authoritarian 'guided democracy' in 1957, wherein parliament was suspended, opposition parties dissolved and elections banned. Western democracy, spurned as 'fifty plus one democracy', was bitterly attacked for bringing division and conflict, rather than harmony, to Indonesia. Guided democracy, formulated on the 'five principles' of *pancasila* (belief in one God, national unity, humanitarianism, people's sovereignty, and social justice and prosperity) (Mackerras 1992: 238), was promoted as an indigenous form of democracy best suited to bring 'unity in diversity' to Indonesia.

But guided democracy proved no better than parliamentary democracy in nation building and achieving economic development. The tacit deal struck between Sukarno and the military in holding together a geographically and politically fractious Indonesia became increasingly strained as Sukarno veered towards the Indonesian Communist Party (PKI) by adopting an economic policy of nationalisation and a foreign policy of 'confrontation' with the newly formed Federation of Malaysia. Talks of a Beijing–Jakarta axis against Western 'neo-imperialism' also prompted the United States to channel its financial assistance to the military, police and large Islamic parties in an attempt to undermine the influence of the PKI (Kolko 1988). In the end, soaring inflation and growing social disturbances led to the demise of Sukarno and the coming to power of General Suharto's New Order military regime in 1968, which was erected on the lives of hundreds of thousands of actual or suspected PKI members. The social chaos and economic stagnation associated with this period of democratic and semi-democratic experimentation was, for a long time, to condition the nation in favour of development and stability, both of which featured prominently in New Order ideology.

By contrast, the immediate period of post-colonial democracy in Malaysia saw little such upheaval. The peacefully negotiated transition from British colonial rule to national independence in 1957 created two important conditions for political stability, both of which were absent from Indonesia, which was forced to wage a 4-year war of independence. These two conditions were the defeat of the communist movement before independence and the agreement between the Malay political elite and the departing British government over the importance of preserving the ethnic division of labour as a means of maintaining Malay political dominance. The latter aspect amounted to an effective curtailment of universal suffrage, portending the centrality of ethnicity in post-independence Malaysian politics. The establishment in 1946 of the Malay political party the UMNO was not only a reflection of the relative cohesiveness of the Malay political elite, again a contrast to the divided Indonesian political elite at the time of its independence, but also laid the foundation for Malaysia's ethnic-based 'statist democracy' (Jesudason 1995: 337).

Until 1969, 'statist democracy' served Malaysia reasonably well. While the Malays dominated national politics through the UMNO, the Chinese were left with a monopoly on the economy. With the setting up of the Alliance Party (AP), consisting of the UMNO, the Malaysian Chinese Association (MCA) and the Malaysian Indian Congress (MIC), with the last two representing the 30 per cent or so of Malaysian Chinese and 10 per cent or so of Malaysian Indians respectively, ethnic accommodation was formally institutionalised in Malaysian politics. Until 1969 the Alliance Party won every free election with a two-thirds majority in parliament. But the loss of its majority in the 1969 election provoked a communal riot, which resulted in nearly two hundred deaths and ushered in the period of 'ethnic authoritarianism' that persists today (Simone and Feraru 1995: 106).

Strictly speaking, Singapore did not experience political disruptions similar to those seen in post-colonial Malaysia and Indonesia. The nationalist PAP, which won the first parliamentary election 1 year after Singapore gained home rule from Britain in 1958, has always maintained the need to adapt Western democratic practice to indigenous culture (Rodan 1996: 61). However, the forced independence of Singapore in 1965, which engendered a real sense of a crisis of national survival, gave the PAP both a good opportunity to put its views into practice and a large measure of legitimacy in curtailing democracy in the name of nation building. Therefore, as in Malaysia and Indonesia, the stripping of democracy to bare electoralism formed an important part of the formative years of Singapore's political development.

Developmentalism and consolidation of authoritarian rule

Electoralism was but one of the ingredients of the regime stability enjoyed by Malaysia, Singapore and New Order Indonesia. As in authoritarian Taiwan, South Korea and Thailand, *developmentalism*, namely official commitment to economic development, formed another pillar of regime legitimacy in Southeast Asia. Rapid economic growth not only reduced absolute poverty but also made it easier for the government to co-opt potentially disruptive social interests into its fold. In Malaysia and Indonesia, where the patron–client relationship was common, especially in rural areas, economic growth also greatly enhanced the government's ability to buy electoral support. Governments in both Malaysia and

Singapore were used to making thinly veiled threats about withdrawing development funds or certain public services from constituencies that voted 'the wrong way' (Rodan 1992; Crouch 1996: 118). Developmentalism thus reinforced electoralism, making elections a means of political co-option for the government and a means of reaping material rewards for government supporters. Both tendencies worked to prevent the emergence of grass-roots popular participation, helping the three regimes to consolidate their authoritarian rule.

Upon seizing power, Suharto launched a 'New Order' that was to remain the official vision for Indonesia until his ignominious downfall in May 1998. A combination of Western political thought and indigenous culture, New Order ideology contained the following five principles:

1   adherence to *pancasila*;
2   anti-communism;
3   the dual function of the military, i.e. the military is responsible for both defence and 'supervising domestic politics and administration';
4   the 'floating mass' principle, whereby the people must be 'freed' from the burden of participating in organised politics except during elections;
5   striving for economic development to achieve self-reliance and international prominence.

(Anderson 1992: 311–22)

All organisations in Indonesia, including the civil service and the opposition parties, were required to pledge allegiance to this ideology, especially '*pancasila* democracy', which recognises no conflict of interest between state and society or between different groups within society.

For 32 years under Suharto, direct elections were held every 5 years for the parliament, the People's Representative Council (DPR), which consisted of 400 elected members and 100 military appointees. The DPR met annually and had to approve all proposed legislation, including the government's budget. The president was elected, also every 5 years, by a superparliament, the People's Consultative Assembly (MPR), which consisted of all members of the DPR plus an additional 500 appointees, most of whom were selected by the military, the ABRI, and the government's party, Golkar. Not surprisingly therefore, Suharto 'won' every presidential election after 1968, including his seventh term in March 1998. As discussion and consensus were said to be the essence of Indonesian culture, both the complete domination of the parliament by the executive and the MPR's 5-yearly 'unanimous' approval of the presidency were portrayed as the triumph of *pancasila* democracy.

Like Suharto, who was guaranteed to win the presidency, Suharto's party, Golkar, was also guaranteed to win every parliamentary election, taking well over two-thirds of the vote in every election. Instead of being a political party, Golkar was 'the electoral face of the civilian bureaucracy and the armed forces, mobilized every five years to get out the vote for the ruling group led by Suharto' (Liddle 1996: 44–5). In the phoney party system, opposition activities were so severely restricted both before and during the campaign period that they could hardly challenge the government. Since 1973, only two political parties had been allowed to compete with Golkar, and both of them had been created and effectively sustained by the government as part of the trappings of democracy. Not only were their leaders approved and sometimes hand picked by the government, most of their party finance also came from the government (ibid.: 45; Vatikiotis 1998).

Behind Indonesia's show democracy was an elaborate system of patronage with Suharto standing at its apex. While few people probably believed in the democratic legitimacy of the regime, economic development nevertheless both accorded the regime performance legitimacy and made it materially rewarding for the majority of rural voters, who voted through powerful local patrons such as village heads.

The consolidation of authoritarian rule in post-1969 Malaysia centred on two major political innovations – the introduction of the New Economic Policy (NEP) and the broadening of the ruling coalition of parties – both of which were aimed at entrenching ethnic authoritarianism. Because of the NEP's institutionalised discrimination against the non-Malay population, especially the Chinese, the government relied heavily on three pieces of legislation to curtail civil liberties in the name of racial harmony in addition to its nearly complete control of the media (newspapers and TV and radio stations). These were the Internal Security Act, the Societies Act and the Official Secrets Act, all of which were intended to ban or severely restrict any form of public discussion or mobilisation on issues relating to Malay special rights, the pre-eminence of the Malay language and the status of Islam and of Malay rulers (Crouch 1992: 25; Jesudason 1995: 339).

In parallel with these coercive measures was the broadening of government co-option, mainly in the form of the Barisan National (BN) or National Front, which was a revamped version of the AP. Dominated by the UMNO, like the AP, the BN now contained several other parties, including the old MCA and MIC. The broadened coalition was mainly aimed at increasing the influence of Islamic groups at the expense of non-Malay groups, especially the MCA. By supporting each other's candidates in different constituencies, the BN has, since the early 1970s, won every election with a two-thirds majority in parliament. This Malaysian-style democracy, based on careful ethnic balancing and restriction of civil rights, was justified in terms of maintaining a consensus rooted in Malaysian/Asian cultural values.

Although elections in Malaysia allowed a larger degree of public participation and political contestation than in Indonesia, curtailment of civil and political liberties meant that elections often served to 'measure and re-energise UMNO's levels of mass support' (Case 1993: 187) rather than presenting real opportunites to dislodge the government. However, as Crouch (1996) argues, because the government sets itself the task of not just winning elections but also winning at least two-thirds of the parliamentary seats, a position that would enable it to amend the constitution, elections do play an important role in Malaysia in making the government responsive to social pressures.

In Singapore, the consolidation of authoritarian rule after 1965 bore many similarities to both New Order Indonesia and post-1969 Malaysia. Over the years, a combination of a culture-based national ideology emphasising collectivism and consensus (Chua 1995: 32), a restriction on civil liberties and extensive political co-option under the umbrella of the Leninist-style PAP, together with rapid economic development, has made PAP rule virtually unassailable. Until 1980, the PAP was the only party in parliament.

Like Indonesia and Malaysia, the PAP leadership is profoundly suspicious of Western-style democracy, believing that the liberal notion of the opposition being an important force for keeping government accountable is at best irrelevant and at worst harmful in the Singaporean – and hence Asian – social context (Rodan 1992: 4). Consequently, political opposition in Singapore is tightly controlled by an extensive array of means, often with legalistic pretensions. Opposition political leaders are often kept under close surveillance, threatened with lawsuits, harassed and sometimes arrested. Except during the run-up to elections, little political activity is allowed. At the same time, supporters of the opposition are often intimidated by government warnings of cuts in public expenditure and services in districts that vote 'the wrong way' (Rodan 1992). Lee Kuan Yew describes this linking of public service with the outcome of voting as a 'political loyalty test' (*FEER*, 14 May 1992: 15). Therefore, as in Indonesia, the existence of opposition parties in Singapore indicates little genuine political competition.

A typical Singapore way of silencing vocal opposition leaders and critics of the government is to bring legal charges against them for 'abusing free speech'. The PAP routinely won multimillion-dollar libel awards against political opponents (Neher 1999: 143). The conviction, fining and banning from politics during the 1980s and 1990s of B. J. Jeyaretnam and Tang Liang

Hong, two of the leaders of the Workers' Party (WP), are but two of the best-known cases in point (*KRWE*, November 1997: 41918; *KRWE*, February 1998: 42073). This method was also extended to non-Singaporeans, as shown in the well-publicised 'Lingle affair' of 1994, in which Professor Christopher Lingle, an American economist, then teaching at the National University of Singapore, was charged with 'criminal defamation' in the Singapore courts for an article he had written in the *International Herald Tribune* (*New York Times*, 10 January, 1995, p. A5).

What emerged in the three Southeast Asian nations was thus a common pattern of authoritarian rule masquerading as democracy. In the immediate aftermath of national crises, authoritarian rule was consolidated with wide public acquiescence, if not active support. The subsequent flourishing of the economy in all three societies further enhanced regime legitimacy. Over the years, however, capitalist development has also generated similar structural changes in the three societies, gradually undermining the same authoritarian power structure. Yet unlike the Asian NDCs, both Malaysia and Singapore have managed to maintain their authoritarian semi- or pseudo-democracy, whereas Indonesia was forced to abandon its military rule in 1998. So what was the reason behind the relative stability of authoritarianism in the three Southeast Asian countries? What prospects are there for democracy in the region?

Challenges to authoritarian rule

In all three regimes, developmentalism was a double-edged sword; it helped at once to consolidate authoritarian rule and to undermine the basis of that rule. An important mechanism by which challenges to authoritarianism arose with development was the emergence of new social issues and classes wishing to have a bigger say in government decision making. However, the way in which this challenge was managed differed a great deal in the three countries, leading to different consequences for regime stability.

In Indonesia, the coalition of social interests that brought to power Suharto's New Order regime was from the beginning an uneasy partnership despite its common support for the regime's anti-communist stance and promise of economic development and political stability, all those things that the disliked Sukarno regime had failed to deliver. The alliance began to fray in the early 1970s when local, especially Islamic, businesses protested against their increasing marginalisation by the influx of foreign capital and growing inequality despite economic growth. Throughout the decade, students led the protest against abuse of power by the military and the corrupt alliance between foreign capital, Chinese business tycoons and government bureaucrats. In 1980, fifty prominent intellectuals joined the students in their call for greater social justice, fair distribution of the fruits of economic growth, and a more open political system. They drafted the famous 'Petition of the Fifty', criticising *pancasila* and the government policy of 'simply increasing GNP [gross national product] only'. Although the government responded by firing all fifty signatories from their jobs and by more stringent curbing of freedom of speech, Islam began to develop rapidly as a vocal voice against the military regime.

Indonesia's move to EOI and economic liberalisation in the 1980s led to a surge of patrimonialism; Suharto increasingly ruled the country as if it was his own personal property, always available for patronage distribution. The resultant growth of rampant nepotism and corruption, as seen in the growing prominence of notable politico-business families, added urgency to the call for the democratic control of government.

In the 1990s, social transformation, a result of capitalist development, greatly broadened the social base of opposition and strengthened its organisation (Aspinall 1996: 228–37). The simultaneous growth of the urban middle and working classes led to mass mobilisation for workers' rights and democratic reform. The early 1990s witnessed both an explosion of middle-class-supported strike actions and a proliferation of middle-class-based non-governmental organisations (NGOs) working on a wide range of issues, including human rights, income generation for the poor, and the environment. In the absence of any meaningful opposition from political parties, the NGOs became the most important vehicles for middle-class opponents of the regime and constituted a nascent civil society of Indonesia, constantly pushing at the boundaries of opposition.

The Suharto regime responded to increasing social protest with a brutal crackdown and extended co-option. The arrest and harassment of workers, students and journalists was paralleled by the appointment of an increasing number of middle-class Muslims into the government and the military. Until the 1997–8 financial crisis, which hit Indonesia hard, this two-pronged strategy had sustained the regime primarily because of the fragmentation of the opposition movement. For the growing rise of Islamic influence had caused serious concerns shared by the military and the secular and liberal critics of the regime alike, enabling the corrupt regime to hang on to power. However, the crisis, especially the president's handling of it, swept away any veneer of legitimacy that the regime may have enjoyed up to that point and the public could no longer tolerate a dictator who was determined to put his family wealth before the nation's fate. The ensuing popular wrath not only brought down the New Order regime but also left little on which the new regime could build. Continuing ethnic violence, rising separatist tendencies, the dominant role of the military, Islamic radicalism, the emergence of the new poor in the wake of the financial crisis – all these put a serious strain on the Wahid government, formed in November 1999, casting a long shadow over Indonesia's prospects for democratisation (*The Economist*, 10 February 2000; 6 July 2000; 30 September 2000; 9 December 2000).

In Malaysia, three decades of economic growth have also created a large middle class as well as the working class (Crouch 1985; Kahn 1996). As in Indonesia, the concern about the 'spiritual dimension of development' has led to a revival of radical Islam, represented by the Pan-Malaysia Islamic Party (PAS). At the same time, a number of social movements have begun the struggle to influence government on issues ranging from workers' rights and consumers rights to environmental protection. However, class alliance for greater democracy has been significantly weakened by both the continuing centrality of ethnicity and the statist manner in which economic development was achieved (Girling 1988; Crouch 1993). Divided along ethnic lines, the working class is both structurally and organisationally weak in its struggle with the state for workers' rights (Jesudason 1996: 143–4; Majstorovic 1997). The middle class, on the other hand, although similarly divided, finds its discontent either channelled by the fairly effective electoral mechanism (for both Malays and non-Malays) or insufficiently strong – in the case of the Muslim middle class – to rock the boat of a regime that, after all, created it by means of the NEP. As Jesudason (1996: 145) observes, 'when members of this class are given a semblance of participation or are entrapped in electoral mechanisms, their capacity and desire for further democratisation are limited.'

The structural weakness of the Malaysian middle class is perhaps best illustrated by the electoral rise and fall of the party Semangat '46, which was created as a result of the split within the UMNO in 1987, against the background of a severe economic downturn and growing criticism of corruption and Prime Minister Mahathir's authoritarian leadership style. In the 1990 general election, despite high hopes of the party breaking the mould of Malaysia's ethnic authoritarianism, Semangat's strategy of forming a multi-ethnic electoral alliance with other opposition parties stumbled badly on the issue of an Islamic state, which divided two other parties, the PAS and the largely Chinese-based secular Democratic Action Party. In the event, the BN easily won its two-thirds majority in parliament. With the economy recovered, which strengthened the ruling party's ability to offer patronage, a steady flow of Semangat members were lured back into the UMNO, precipitating its demise. A year before the fateful 1995 election, Semangat decided to abandon its multi-ethnic stance and mobilise on sectional Malay issues. This move, however, only made the party appear extremist vis-à-vis the multicultural BN and thus led to its electoral demise (Jesudason 1996: 136–9). The episode of Semangat thus demonstrates how pressure for democratic reform in Malaysia was diluted by channels of ethnic representation and by the dynamic combination of coercion and co-option.

Having won the 1995 election, however, Dr Mahathir's government was quick to respond to some of the concerns voiced by the opposition in an attempt to further co-opt the Malay middle class. The privatisation programme of 1994–5 was launched partly with this objective in mind. The government also showed some willingness to work with moderate civil society organisations, which were less threatening to its dominance. Since the 1990s, a new nationalist agenda has been pursued in the form of Dr Mahathir's strong rhetoric against the 'Western' record of democracy and human rights, which has diverted some social organisations' attention to West bashing (Jesudason 1996: 154–5). Partly reflecting this anti-Western mood, which increased during the 1997–8 financial crisis, the BN once again won the last general election, held in November 1999, albeit with a reduced share of the vote, down to 56 per cent from 65 per cent in 1995 (*The Economist*, 4 December 1999: 79). A major challenge facing the BN is the increasing electoral appeal of the Islamic PAS, which has since the 1990s emerged as a leading opposition party competing with the UMNO for the vote of the Malay middle classes.

In Singapore, the first visible sign of challenge to the PAP state came in 1981, when the Workers' Party won a by-election, breaking for the first time since 1959 the PAP monopoly on parliamentary seats. As Beng-Huat Chua (1995: 173) observes, this election was also the first psychological breakthrough in Singapore politics, whereby the population realised that it was possible to vote for opposition parties without endangering the nation's prospects for survival. Three years later, the PAP support dropped to its lowest since independence, from 84 per cent of the national vote in 1968 to 62 per cent, a trend aided by the receding communist threat both internationally and in the region.

Although hardly an electoral debacle by most international standards, the PAP's loss of the popular vote in 1984 triggered an avalanche of political reforms designed to make the party more responsive to popular concerns without moving the country in the direction of liberal democracy. To pre-empt the emergence of an autonomous civil society, the PAP state expanded its network of government institutions by both parliamentary and extra-parliamentary means, leading to tighter social control and management. At the same time, all the reforms were legitimated by 'an elaborate ideology of elitism', which, argues Rodan (1996: 62), has become so deeply embedded in the social structure of Singapore and so dominant in its political culture that it has effectively depoliticised politics and turned it into a mere administrative affair.

Within the parliamentary arena, three co-optive measures have been adopted to broaden public representation without endangering PAP dominance. These involve sending non-voting MPs to parliament from opposition parties, appointing nominated MPs from business, labour, women's and ethnic organisations to help the PAP make 'better' policies, and creating 'group representation constituencies', in which voters choose a team of candidates, at least one of whom must be an Indian or a Malay (Neher and Marlay 1995: 135; Rodan 1996: 103–4). The emphasis on formal education and technical qualifications for these appointments means that the institutional reforms are less about making politics more representative than about making it more meritocratic.

Outside parliament, greater public participation is encouraged by opening government-sponsored 'feedback' channels. These include residents' committees, citizens' consultative committees and the Feedback Unit in the Ministry of Community Development, which holds regular closed-door discussions with invited members of the public. In addition, the government also set up a number of ethnically based institutions as a way of addressing increasing inequality in society. By confining the issue of inequality within each ethnic community, the government seeks to prevent it from developing into a class issue (Rodan 1996: 105).

These political reforms, by obstructing the formation of interest groups and hence cutting off the potential social bases of opposition parties, have hitherto succeeded in preventing Singapore from moving beyond electoralism into a liberal democracy. They have reinforced PAP dominance by providing institutional channels through which it can closely monitor public opinion, shape its formation, and restrict the expression of political dissent to the formal political process. In short, the extended network of co-option has shaped the form and character of opposition politics in Singapore in favour of the PAP (Khong 1995; Rodan 1996).

In the last general election held in January 1997, the PAP increased its share of the vote from 61 per cent to 65 per cent and took eighty-one parliamentary seats out of a total of eighty-three. Immediately after the victory, Prime Minister Goh Chok Tong claimed that the result demonstrated that Singapore's voters had rejected 'Western-style liberalism' in favour of Asian democracy (*KRWE*, January 1997: 41449–50). The reality, however, is more complex than what he suggested. While many Singaporeans undoubtedly support the PAP, given its relatively benign authoritarian character and competent and clean image, many others, especially the well-educated professionals, find it intolerable to live in a paternalistic regime seeking to regulate every aspect of its citizens' life. By 'voting with their feet', i.e. emigrating, they have contributed to the serious problem of the 'brain drain' facing Singapore. Many Singaporeans living overseas voice outspoken criticisms of the regime (Seow 1994).

CONCLUSION

Like Pacific Asia's NDCs, such as Taiwan, South Korea and Thailand, the three yet-to-democratise Southeast Asian countries differ both in their levels of socioeconomic development and in their historical–cultural heritages. Their lack of progress in moving towards democracy, therefore, is as much a vindication of a dynamic approach to democratisation as the successful democratisation of the NDCs. For what blocks or moves democratisation, is neither history/culture or economy nor any single historical group or class; rather, it is the dynamic interplay of all these factors at a particular point in time. Capitalist development, although vital in generating social conflicts that provide the context for the human struggle for democracy, is not determinant of a smooth or linear transition to democracy. Electoralism, a façade commitment to democracy, as we have seen in Southeast Asia, has for a long time been more or less successfully employed to prevent the full-blown development of democracy. The kind of legitimacy these regimes enjoyed (and continue to enjoy in Malaysia and Singapore), therefore, is more conditional on their development performance than on their threadbare claim to procedural fairness, a minimum requirement of democracy. In other words, these façade democracies are intrinsically vulnerable to performance setbacks that could endanger their fragile legitimacy, the collapse of New Order Indonesia being a good example. While this is by no means suggesting that democratisation in Southeast Asia could only be brought about by performance disasters, it does indicate the great difficulties of maintaining authoritarian rule in modern diverse societies.

8 'Welfare Orientalism' and social development in Pacific Asia

Having examined the politics of economic and political development in Pacific Asia in the previous chapters, I now turn to the social development of the region. In the West, social development is closely associated with the establishment of the welfare state, which took place after World War II. The term 'welfare state' does not have a precise meaning and is often ideologically charged. However, it broadly refers to a liberal democratic state, the role of which expands markedly in a capitalist economy with the objective of providing its citizens with a more or less generous but guaranteed standard of living, encompassing aspects such as health, education, housing and income maintenance. Such a pattern of social development in the West, underpinned by the notion of *social entitlement*, is widely interpreted as an almost inevitable culmination of more than two centuries of civil and political rights (Marshall 1963). Hence the currency of the convergence view, which sees industrialisation and democracy as the key factors likely to lead to the emergence of the Western-style welfare state in other parts of the world.

Social development in Pacific Asia, although it differed a great deal across nations, as in the West, in terms of both policies and outcomes, has nevertheless displayed some common differences vis-à-vis the West. These differences, first identified in Japan and later in the NICs, have informed the cultural perspective on social development, which emphasises the key role of local cultures in shaping social policy. In singling out Confucianism as the key determinant of social policy in Japan and the NICs, 'welfare Orientalism', as White and Goodman (1998) describe this perspective, not only claims to explain such differences, but also seeks to assert the superiority of the 'Asian' model of social provision over the 'Western' model.

In this chapter, I will examine the patterns of social policy in Pacific Asia with a view to identifying and explaining similarities and differences. By situating social policy in its national–historical context, and by showing the trend towards increasing cross-national divergence in social policy in the region, I will seek to highlight the centrality of the dynamics of national politics rather than culture. In particular, I will argue that while the political logic of the developmental state, i.e. the twin need to promote economic growth and legitimate the regime, was the driving force behind social policy evolution in all the states in Pacific Asia, divergent cross-national political development is beginning to generate different approaches to social policy. The more or less keenly expressed rhetorical commitment to 'welfare Orientalism' across the region, however, I will further argue, is a reflection more of the global ascent of neo-liberalism than of 'Asian values'.

I will divide the chapter into three parts. In part 1, I will introduce the political–ideological circumstances in which welfare Orientalism emerged by outlining some of the common features of social policy in Pacific Asia that inform the Orientalist discourse. In part 2, I will carry out a detailed profiling of social policies in the region by situating them within their respective historical–national context. Major social programmes in each country will be identified. In part 3, I will seek to explain the cross-national similarities and increasing differences by highlighting the changing political context within which social policy is made. I will conclude by noting the ideological nature of welfare Orientalism.

WELFARE ORIENTALISM AND POLICY SIMILARITIES

Social policy in Pacific Asia did not arouse much research interest in the West until the 1980s, when the region emerged as an economic rival. Until then, Western literature on social policy had been dominated by two broad theoretical perspectives, the socioeconomic and the political, emphasising respectively levels of socioeconomic development and an array of political factors as key determinants of social policy (Heidenheimer *et al.* 1990: Chapter 1; Mabbett and Bolderson 1999). However, the economic rise of Pacific Asia, and the realisation of the region's apparently different approach to welfare provision vis-à-vis the West, has led to a third perspective, welfare Orientalism, which sees Confucianism/Asian values as the key determinant of the region's social development.

Welfare Orientalism gained currency at a time when the Western welfare state was coming under severe attack from mainly *neo-liberal* intellectuals and politicians for allegedly undermining economic efficiency, the work ethic, the family and community. The contrasting economic dynamism and ostensible social cohesion exhibited in Pacific Asia was thus portrayed as the product of a region blessed with the unique Confucian/Asian virtues of individual responsibility, family solidarity and group support

(Rozman 1991; Jones 1993). By promoting social provision as the primary responsibility of the individual, family and community, argues the welfare Orientalist, the states in Pacific Asia have helped their societies escape the 'Western disease' of welfare dependency and social decay.

The basis of welfare Orientalism comes from three identifiable, similar patterns of social development across Pacific Asia. First is the comparatively high level of social development in the region, from Japan to Indonesia. As I have shown, international organisations such as the World Bank have singled out these high-performing economies for their remarkable record in achieving 'shared growth'. Moreover, these countries have consistently ranked highly in the *Human Development Report*, which has been published annually since 1990 by the UN Development Programme. The Human Development Index, a key indicator of a country's social development used by the Report, is compiled by measuring three areas: longevity, knowledge and standard of living. It includes such indicators as life expectancy at birth, adult literacy rate, enrolment ratios for primary, secondary, and tertiary education, and GDP per capita adjusted for local cost of living.

The second common characteristic of social development in Pacific Asia concerns government spending patterns, reflected in two aspects. First, the region is well known for its comparatively small public expenditure on social policy. While Japan and the NICs all spend considerably less of their GDP on social programmes than their industrial counterparts in the West, the NECs also display a similar pattern compared with countries in the developing world, i.e. in Latin America, with similar levels of economic development (World Bank 1998). Furthermore, the spending priority also appears to differ between Pacific Asia and the West. Whereas social security takes the lion's share of public expenditure in all Western societies, education is the top government spending priority in all Pacific Asian societies (except Japan), followed by health or housing, with social security receiving the smallest or second smallest share of public spending (Ramesh 2000; Tang 2000). This pattern has given rise to the major welfare Orientalist claim that Pacific Asia offers a cheaper and more effective alternative method of welfare provision to the Western-style welfare state.

And, finally, the underlying philosophy of social policy appears very different between Pacific Asia and the West. The high-sounding rhetoric of social rights is prominent only by its absence in Pacific Asia, where individual responsibility and community cooperation are the catchwords, even in societies that have moved some way towards Western-style social provision. In the next section, therefore, I will make a more detailed examination of the evolution of social policy in the region with a view to identifying the historical–national factors that have contributed to these similarities as well as to the emerging divergences.

WELFARE SYSTEMS IN PACIFIC ASIA:
A NATIONAL–HISTORICAL PROFILE

Any study of social development in Pacific Asia must start from the fundamentally different political–institutional context in which social policy was/is made. Unlike the post-World War II West, in which social policy is mainly a democratic response to societal pressures organised around class, gender and race, Pacific Asia saw the initiation of most social policies by an authoritarian developmental state. The dominant position of the state in social policy meant that it was conceived less for social protection than for economic development and regime legitimation. Hence the widely noted 'productivist' orientation of social policy in the region, namely the tendency to use social policy as an instrument of economic development on which the regime staked its legitimacy (Deyo 1992; Ramesh 2000). But, as we will see, democratisation in the region is already beginning to transform social policy despite the official rhetoric of Asian values. This is particularly evident in the region's NDCs of South Korea, Taiwan and Thailand, which, like Japan, have moved towards social insurance schemes as major instruments of income maintenance or service provision. The less than fully democratised countries, on the other hand, such as Singapore, Malaysia and Indonesia, have tended to rely on provident fund schemes, which operate no mechanism of financial sharing.

Japan: founder of the 'Confucian welfare society'

As the first country to industrialise in Asia, Japan was naturally the first to construct a welfare regime to cater to the social needs of its population. The discovery in the late 1970s, when comparative social policy began to emerge as an academic field of enquiry in the wake of the oil crisis-induced 'fiscal crisis' facing the Western welfare states, that Japan was operating no Western-style, high-taxation, high-spending welfare system, despite its huge national wealth, led to its characterisation as a 'Confucian' welfare state. This marked the beginning of the welfare Orientalist discourse on social development in Pacific Asia and beyond. The essence of Japan's Confucian welfare system was famously described as having the ability to offer 'security without entitlement' (Vogel 1980). Japanese writers and politicians, on the other hand, preferred to call it either 'welfare society' or 'welfare superpower' (Nakagawa 1979; Gould 1993: 75), indicating both its distinction from and its superiority to the Western system.

As revealed in the Japanese government's social policy discourse, the emphasis on 'society' as opposed to 'state' expresses the government's belief in a society-centred approach to welfare provision. The general unwillingness of the state to shoulder responsibility, especially financial, for social provision means that Japan has enjoyed the reputation within the OECD of a nation producing 'prosperity without the amenities', because of the poor quality of housing, roads and public leisure facilities enjoyed by its people (Inoguchi 1987: 126). Within the OECD, Japan has consistently been one of the least-taxed and lowest-spending industrial societies (OECD 2000). Social provisions in areas such as personal social services, unemployment benefit and public assistance for the poor are particularly inadequate (Maruro 1986; Soeda 1990; Goodman 1998). Often, family members and the community are expected to take up the responsibilities.

However, despite official rhetoric against 'too much Westernisation' in social provision, Japan, in comparison with other late-coming 'Oriental' welfare regimes such as Singapore, Malaysia and Indonesia, still looks far more 'Westernised' than it cares to admit. This is not only because Japan's social spending as a percentage of GDP is by far the largest in the region (see Table 8.1), which is somewhat expected given its far more advanced economy. (However, as Table 8.1 also shows, Singapore, whose GDP per capita is not far from Japan's, spends less than half of Japan's expenditure on social policy). More importantly, the overall ethos of the Japanese welfare system, as embodied in the social programmes operated, appears different.

Rather than being based on provident fund schemes, as in Singapore, Malaysia and Indonesia (more to follow), Japan's welfare regime is centred on the social insurance principle for both health care and pensions. Unlike the provident fund, which is effectively a compulsory savings scheme with no inbuilt mechanism of financial redistribution between members and no

Table 8.1 Economic development and social spending in Pacific Asia, 1997

Economy	GNP per capita (US$)*	Social spending as % of GNP	Social spending as % of total government spending
Japan	34,500 (1999)	14.0	–
Singapore	32,810	6.6	37.8
Taiwan	13,470	4.4	32.0
South Korea	10,550	7.7	28.3
Malaysia	4,530	9.8	36.8
Thailand	2,740	5.0	35.4
Indonesia	1,110	3.8	25.6

*Asian Development Bank, *Annual Report 1998*, Table 1, www.adb.org/Documents/Reports/
Annual_Report/1998/statanx1.pdf.
  Based on World Bank (1998) *World Development Indicators 1998*.
  All data for Japan based on OECD (2000) *Social Expenditure Database: 1980/1997*.

basic guarantee of benefit level, social security is a predefined benefits scheme designed to pool financial contributions. While the state plays a limited role in provident fund schemes, functioning mainly as a financial administrator and regulator, it invariably functions as a more or less substantial financial contributor in social insurance schemes. This is why since 1970, despite sustained government efforts to control social spending, Japan, like other Western welfare states, has seen its health spending as a proportion of GDP double and social security spending treble, prompting an article in *The Economist* (12 May 2001: 76) pointing out the grave policy dilemma facing Japan. To finance its 'European standards of welfare', the article argues, Japan must raise its 'American levels of taxes', which the government has been trying to avoid for fear of hurting Japan's economic competitiveness. Changing demographic trends in Japan, such as ageing, the increase in single-person and elderly households and a decline in fertility rates, coupled with rising unemployment, will only exert more pressure on the state to expand welfare provision (Ministry of Health, Labour and Welfare 2000).

The Japanese welfare system today is perhaps best characterised as 'conservative corporatist', similar to the likes of Germany but with lower levels of social spending (Jones-Finer 1999: 30). Like Germany, or indeed most other continental European welfare regimes, Japan's social security system preserves social inequality based on employment status. This is particularly true of its health care system, which, unlike the universal state pension, is organised into several separate schemes offering different qualities of benefits to different categories of employees (Hiwatari 1993; Kwon 1998). In short, Japan's welfare system is less 'Confucian' than its official rhetoric suggests.

South Korea and Taiwan: democratisation and welfare expansion

Japan's move, albeit reluctantly, from a Confucian welfare system to a social security system is being followed in South Korea and Taiwan. In both societies, democratisation has opened the road leading in the direction of a social security-based welfare system, in which the state extends its role from a financial regulator to a partial contributor. The changed political–institutional context of social policy is thus transforming the productivist nature of welfare politics in the two societies, putting the state under increasing pressure to expand and universalise social provision. Furthermore, democratic politics has also made social policy an increasingly contested issue, susceptible to public opinion and pressure. Social groups such as women have begun to question both the adequacy and fairness of welfare systems in both societies (Chen 2000; Tang 2000: 163).

Of the three NICs, Korea is the least wealthy, in terms of GDP per head, but has the highest level of social spending in terms of its share of GDP (see Table 8.1). Most of the social programmes in operation today evolved from those established by the military regime, seeking to legitimate its unpopular rule and to stimulate economic development. These include Industrial Accident Insurance, funded by employers only, National Health Insurance (NHI), the National Pension Programme (NPP), and the means-tested Public Assistance Programme for the poor. The latest addition to the welfare system is Employment Insurance, which was introduced in 1995 to provide unemployment benefit.

As in Japan, social services in Korea, such as those for the elderly, are basic and inadequate; the family and the community are expected to provide them rather than the state (Palley 1992; Goodman and Peng 1996; *The Economist*, 18 December 1999: 132). Similarly, the Confucian-informed welfare discourse, which stigmatises state-provided poor relief, has led to very low take-up of public assistance. It is believed that nearly half of those living in poverty receive no social assistance benefits at all as a result of stringent eligibility criteria (Adema *et al.* 2000).

NHI became a compulsory programme in 1977 after an unsuccessful 10-year trial period as a voluntary scheme. It started first with large companies, then moved to include public employees and private school teachers. By 1987, most employees in the industrial sectors had access to health care through the NHI schemes. The coverage became universal in 1989, when the state took financial responsibility for the farmers and the self-employed by paying half of their contribution and provided a non-contributory Health Assistance Programme for the poor. This move means that the state has now become a partial financier, as opposed to a mere regulator, of health care. In the period 1990–7, the state spent 2 per cent of GDP on health, a figure lower than Taiwan but higher than Singapore (Tang 2000: 51). However, like its Japanese counterpart, the Korean NHI suffers a similar problem of fragmentation and financial inequality, as separate insurance funds for different groups of people prevents risk sharing and financial redistribution between them (Kwon 1998: 56). Fear of losing middle-class support has prevented the democratically elected governments from integrating the NHI schemes.

The NPP constitutes the other pillar of the Korean social security system. Like the NHI, it is mainly financed from contributions paid by employees and their employers. The government is responsible for the administrative costs only. Set up in 1989 as a single fund, the NPP currently covers only a quarter of people of retirement age (Adema *et al.* 2000). However, the programme does not cover civil servants, private school teachers or the military, all of whom have their own separate occupational pension schemes funded by the state. Largely because of its early stage of development, in which more people are contributing than are claiming benefit, the NPP fund is currently running a huge surplus, amounting to nearly 8 per cent of GDP. Most of the reserve provides the state with cheap capital for public sector projects (Tang 2000: 103). However, the publicly funded pension schemes are rapidly approaching fiscal imbalance; the World Bank (quoted ibid.) projects them to run into deficit some time in the next decade.

The divided nature of Korea's public pension schemes reflects the legacy of the productivist welfare system set up in the authoritarian era. Indeed, the NPP evolved from the pension schemes for civil servants, professors and teachers that were introduced in the 1960s and 1970s as part of the military regime's commitment to economic development. These groups of personnel, together with the military, were deemed vital to the government's development drive. As we will see, this clear distinction between the public and private sectors is still a dominant feature of the welfare systems in the Southeast Asian NECs.

The outbreak of the 1997–8 financial crisis, which led to soaring unemployment in Korea, has seen both an expansion of state welfare and an explicit embrace of social rights by the newly elected government under President Kim Dae Jung (Adema *et al.* 2000; Tang 2000: 103–4). Based on the idea of 'productive welfare', both Employment Insurance and the Public Assistance Programme were expanded as part of the government's obligation to facilitate 'self-reliance' by providing welfare to which access is a matter of individual rights.

Like Korea, Taiwan's early welfare system was typically statist and productivist, providing social protection only to selected groups of the population deemed vital for Taiwan's economic development and military security. As late as 1991, 74.9 per cent of the total social welfare expenditure by central government was on military servicemen, government employees, teachers, veterans and retired MPs, reflecting a strong bias in favour of the privileged social groups (Kwon 1998: 47–8). The KMT government's strategic decision to economically enrich and militarily strengthen the island for the purpose of retaking mainland China meant that a large part of the society was left to provide for its own welfare.

However, the nationalist-led democratic movement changed the context of social policy. Rising social movements, representing issues ranging from the environment to the rights of the disadvantaged, began to demand an extension of social protection from the already privileged groups to women, labourers, farmers, the handicapped and the homeless. They called for an end to using reunification as an excuse for neglecting Taiwan's social development. Social policy came to be politicised, becoming an integral part of the identity politics contested between the pro-reunification KMT and the pro-Taiwan independence DPP. In other words, pro-welfare came to be seen as both pro-democracy and pro-Taiwan.

This popular pressure for welfare expansion scored an important victory in 1995 when the state-run National Health Insurance (NHI) programme was introduced, guaranteeing for the first time universal access to health care. By integrating all the health insurance programmes into one scheme in which the state makes part of the financial contributions, the NHI marked a clear break from past social policy orientations (Ku 1998: 125). Not only does the state play an important financial role in the nation's health care, but there is no discrimination in the level of service received regardless of the amount of contribution paid by the insured. Health care in Taiwan is thus more equal than that in either Japan or South Korea, although all three countries offer universal coverage.

Although great strides have been made towards equal citizenship in health care, Taiwan has yet to extend the same principle to other social welfare areas. In comparison with South Korea, Taiwan remains a limited welfare state in terms of both policy orientations and programmes. 'Family values', 'private resources' and 'economic vitality' are the key emphases of the Department of Social Affairs (see its official website at vol.moi.gov.tw/sowf3w/eng/) in its policy thinking. Consequently, crucial social programmes are absent, including national pension, unemployment insurance and family allowance. Social services are particularly inadequate in Taiwan, leaving the family, especially women, to shoulder the main responsibility of care with little state help (Chen 2000). In addition, the means-tested Public Assistance Programme is both limited and stigmatising. Being the highest public spender on education among the NICs (Tang 2000: 71), Taiwan maintains its policy priority for education as a means of maintaining its economic vitality.

The election of a DPP president in March 2001 seems to have injected new impetus into social policy as a result of the party's historical identification with Taiwanese nationalism and social development. The discussion of a National Pension Programme, which was started in 1994 by the then KMT government but subsequently lost its momentum partly due to the increasing financial difficulty facing the NHI programme (Tang 2000: 76), has now been revived (see the Department of Social Affairs website). One of the first priorities of the new administration under President Chen Shui-bian will be to implement its so-called '333' social welfare policy (NT$3,000-per-month pensions for senior citizens, free medical treatment for children under the age of 3, and low-interest loans of 3 per cent for first-time home-buyers), to which the president committed himself during his election campaign (*Economic Daily News*, 23 May 2000).

Singapore: rugged individuals in a controlled society

Being the second richest country in Pacific Asia, with a per capita income second only to Japan, Singapore was and is a 'Confucian' welfare system par excellence. Unlike South Korea and Taiwan, where democratic pressure is increasingly forcing the state to play a larger and more equal role in welfare provision, Singapore's uninterrupted one-party state is facing little such pressure. Although dominant in Singapore's social development, the PAP state has no intention of moving Singapore in the direction of South Korea and Taiwan. By regularly resorting to welfare Orientalism, the PAP state continues to use social policy as an instrument of economic development and political and social control.

Singapore's welfare system centres on one umbrella institution, the Central Provident Fund (CPF). First created in 1953 by the British colonial government as a compulsory savings plan for retirement for private sector workers, the CPF has evolved into an elaborate welfare regime covering areas such as housing, medical care, education and pensions. Civil servants, who had long enjoyed publicly funded pension schemes before the CPF was introduced, now also contribute to the CPF at a reduced rate. Only the top officials in the civil service, the armed forces, the judiciary and the legislature are eligible for public pension (Ramesh 2000: 58). It is estimated that around 75 per cent of the workforce is covered under the CPF, with foreign, casual, part-time and some contract workers excluded.

Unlike social insurance, which pools risks to a greater or lesser extent among the insured and offers predefined benefits as a matter of entitlement, the CPF does neither. As a compulsory savings scheme, it is financed entirely by employees and their employers; the state finances the administrative cost only. Instead of paying into a pooled fund, all contributors pay into their individual accounts, from which they subsequently draw benefits. Therefore, there is no mechanism of financial redistribution between CPF members. The level of benefits varies between individuals, depending on the amount of contribution they have paid throughout their working life. A person who has made only a small contribution because of a long period of unemployment or sickness has to make do with a low level of benefits.

At present, each CPF member has three personal accounts for different purposes: the Ordinary account for purchasing housing and approved investment; the Medisave account for hospitalisation expenses; and the Special account for old-age pensions and contingencies. Since 1992, most of the self-employed have been incorporated under the Medisave account of the CPF. Just as there is no financial transfer between individual CPF members, neither is there any financial sharing between the different accounts. With the bulk of the contributions channelled to the Ordinary account, which is in turn mostly used for house purchase, Singapore has secured one of the world's highest rates of home ownership (Ramesh 2000: 56). Nearly 90 per cent of Singaporeans live in and own public flats provided by the government (Tremewan 1998: 83).

Over the past decades, the self-financed CPF has been a powerful instrument in the hands of the state for both welfare provision and economic, social and political regulation. Economically, the Fund serves two important functions: it is a source of cheap capital for development-related investment, such as the country's infrastructure, and a macroeconomic management tool (ibid.: 85). In 1996, the CPF had a membership of 2.74 million, with a total saving of S$73.8 billion, equivalent to 55.6 per cent of that year's GDP (Ramesh 2000: 57). Politically, the progressive expansion of the programme into other social areas, a kind of privatisation in effect, such as health (Medisave) and education (Edusave) reinforces the government's explicit commitment to 'anti-welfarism' (Tang 2000: 53). Singapore consistently spends less of its GDP than South Korea and Taiwan on education and health, and considerably less on health (ibid.: 51).

As a major plank of the Singapore-style welfare system, public housing is a key instrument of social and political control as well as social provision. By involving itself directly in allocating public flats, the state, through its statutory board, the Housing Development Board (HDB), uses the scheme to prevent the concentration of ethnic enclaves and, in so doing, also prevents any politicians, especially those of Malay and Indian origin, from taking electoral advantage of otherwise ethnically concentrated constituencies (Chua 1995; Kwon 1998: 37–8). Furthermore, public housing is also an effective vehicle for promoting 'Asian values' and the associated acceptable social behaviour. Fear of losing one's major asset and savings compels all residents of public housing to conform with the detailed regulations on acceptable social behaviour set by the HDB, which is empowered to evict non-conforming residents without compensation (Tremewan 1994). Meanwhile, the state offers special housing schemes to encourage middle-income families to have more children and subsidies to multi-generation households as a way of supporting family care for the elderly.

Since the early 1980s, declining electoral support has led the PAP state to increasingly use public housing as a weapon to threaten potential dissident voters. Explicit threat is often made of withdrawing government services in upgrading HDB flats from opposition voting constituencies, accompanied by promises of 'asset enhancement' measures for 'loyal' constituencies (Tremewan 1998: 93–4).

What we have seen in Singapore is a welfare system that is unashamedly non-distributive, paternalistic and authoritarian. It is as much about economic regulation and social and political control as about social protection. Over the years, the CPF has generated high rates of national savings and economic investment, which served as a powerful ideological launch pad for rugged individualism in social policy and provided an effective arena in which social morality has been moulded by officially defined values. The state's ideological adherence to welfare Orientalism has raised major issues concerning the adequacy, accessibility and equity of the welfare system. The working poor, the unemployed, women and the disabled are the major losers in the system.

The NECs: choosing between social security and welfare privatisation

Western interest in the welfare systems of the three Southeast Asian NECs is at an early stage as a result of their recent development history. The work by Ramesh (2000) is the only in-depth comparative study of social policy in the region. Therefore, the following discussion on the region is based primarily on that study.

The reason for studying the three countries as a group is mainly because of their similar levels of economic development. Yet beyond that, the NECs have little in common in their approaches to social policy except in two aspects: their shared emphasis on education, a policy area that receives by far the largest proportion of GDP in all three countries; and the division in their welfare systems between public and private sector workers. All three governments rely on general revenues to fund generous income maintenance benefits for their civilian and military employees while resorting to a plethora of compulsory and optional social programmes to cover private sector workers.

The differences between the three NECs' welfare systems are twofold: quantitative and qualitative. While the level of economic development, as measured by GDP per capita, corresponds better in the NECs than in the NICs with the level of public spending on social policy as a proportion of GDP – Malaysia being the largest spender, followed by Thailand and Indonesia – Malaysia's high spending far exceeds what is expected of a developing country. In fact, Malaysia is the second largest social spender in Pacific Asia, second only to Japan, spending more than twice as much as Taiwan with a GDP per capita just over a third of Taiwan's (see Table 8.1). However, the major difference between the three NECs lies in their underlying social policy orientations. Whereas Malaysia and Indonesia both prefer provident fund schemes for social provision, Thailand is the only country in the region that has set up a comprehensive social security scheme covering a number of contingencies.

Both Malaysia and Indonesia started their welfare programmes for private sector workers earlier than Thailand. In Malaysia, the Employee Provident Fund (EPF), set up in 1951, is the major social programme for the workforce. Originally a compulsory savings plan for retirement, it has been expanded over the years to fulfil a range of objectives, though not as much as its counterpart in Singapore. Currently there are three individual accounts, covering pension (60 per cent of contribution), house purchase or upgrade (30 per cent), and part of medical costs (10 per cent). All workers, except domestic servants, casual and agricultural workers and some groups of government employees, are included compulsorily in the scheme. In 1996, the total savings of the Fund stood at 5.5 per cent of GDP (Ramesh 2000: 46). Despite growth in membership, the scheme still covers only about half of the labour force. Given the non-distributive nature of the scheme, low-income contributors, mainly Malays and Indians, and those with higher than average life expectancy, especially women, are likely to have inadequate benefits upon retirement (Ramesh 2000: 45–7).

In addition to the provident fund, Malaysia also provides employment injury and invalidity benefit under the Employees' Social Security Act 1969, popularly known as SOCSO. It consists of two separate schemes: the Employment Injury Scheme, financed entirely by employers, and the Invalidity Pension Scheme, jointly financed by employees and employers. Voluntary occupational pension schemes are also encouraged by the government.

In Indonesia, private sector workers are covered by a compulsory provident fund, JAMSOSTEK, and voluntary employer-sponsored pension plans. Established in 1992, JAMSOSTEK provides employment accident insurance, a provident fund for pensions, death insurance, and health insurance. Employers are entirely responsible for contributions to employment accident and death benefits. Other components are jointly funded by employees and employers. Contribution rates are low due to political opposition from employers. Consequently, benefits are small and totally inadequate; an average retiree under the plan will receive only a 10 per cent salary replacement based on his or her current contributions and past investment performance. High administration costs and poor returns are also important reasons for low benefits. Total savings accounted for a mere 0.2 per cent of GDP in 1996. According to Ramesh (2000: 39–42), members would probably do better by simply depositing their contributions in a normal savings account with a bank. In any case, the scheme covers only 10 per cent of the Indonesian workforce.

In addition to JAMSOSTEK, many large, state-owned enterprises also run employer-sponsored, provident fund-type pension schemes for their employees on a voluntary basis but they receive tax concessions on their contributions.

Although a late starter, Thailand has moved rapidly since the early 1990s in establishing a welfare system, based on the social insurance rather than the provident fund principle for private sector workers. The Social Security Act (SSA), enacted in September 1990 and amended in 1994, covers health care, maternity, disability, pension and child allowance, and is financed by three parties: employees, employers and the state. It is a pay-as-you-go (PAYG) scheme, in which annual revenues from contributions and investments must be sufficient to meet current expenditures. The government argues that current contribution rates are sufficient to cover current benefits for the next 50 years. The SSA now covers all employees in private firms employing at least ten, but in 2001 the scheme will be expanded to cover all employees in firms employing at least five. The self-employed were included on a voluntary basis in 1995. In 1997, the Act covered about 18 per cent of the labour force; the figure is projected to rise to 21 per cent by 2025 (Ramesh 2000: 60–1).

The retirement pension component was implemented in January 1999, and the requirement for a minimum 15-year contribution period means that no-one will be entitled to a full pension until 2014. Under the benefit formula, after 35 years of contribution, a member will receive a monthly pension equivalent to 35 per cent of the average wage during the last 5 years of employment.

In addition to social security, the government has also set up provident fund schemes for private sector workers and, since 1997, state enterprise workers. The accumulated fund in a member's account may be withdrawn only at the time of retirement or termination of employment. While participation in the scheme is optional for employees, employers are required at least to match employees' contributions. In 1996, the scheme covered about 13 per cent of the labour force (ibid: 63).

What has emerged in the incipient Southeast Asian welfare systems is thus a clear choice between two very different approaches to social provision: one based on the provident fund principle of rugged individualism and the other on the social insurance principle of risk sharing. However, as Ramesh (ibid.: 69) rightly argues, the low coverage of the social programmes in the NECs suggests that neither approach may be the most appropriate to these societies. As a large proportion of the labour force in these societies works in the informal or non-wage sector – 38.1 per cent in Malaysia, 69.2 per cent in Indonesia, and 74.9 per cent in Thailand – neither provident fund nor social insurance can protect these people because such arrangements rely on the payroll for the collection of contributions. The lack of social protection for non-wage labourers, especially those in rural areas, is a major reason for the disproportionate distribution of poverty in this section of the population. The way forward may lie partly in continuing industrialisation and urbanisation.

One of the reasons the region stands out as a success story in both economic and social development is government effort in education and health (Ramesh 2000: Chapters 4 and 5). However, in recent years, there has been a trend in all three countries to move towards private provision in both areas, a trend that is likely to exacerbate social inequality, which is already on the increase since the move towards economic liberalisation in the late 1980s.

The outbreak of the 1997–8 financial crisis hit the NECs the hardest, reversing decades of hard-won social achievements and imposing considerable financial constraints on the state despite the international organisations' relaxation on social spending rules in the region (Lee and Rhee 1998). Although all governments have implemented measures to tackle rising unemployment and poverty, with Thailand leading the way by passing a bill in the parliament in January 1998 to establish an unemployment insurance scheme (Ramesh 2000: 183–9), social policy in the region is in a state of flux. Many factors could shape its future development – economic, demographic and social, as well as political.

SOCIAL POLICY IN PACIFIC ASIA: A COMPARATIVE EXPLANATION

Until recently, social policy in Pacific Asia differed in detail, a function of the domestic political contingencies, rather than underlying philosophies, which emphasised individual responsibility, family solidarity and community support. This can be explained largely by the common context of the authoritarian developmental state in which social policy was made. However, democratisation is transforming the context of social policy, leading to increasingly divergent approaches to social development. Broadly speaking, social policy in the NDCs of Taiwan, South Korea and Thailand, like that in Japan, is increasingly driven by pragmatism as opposed to welfare Orientalism, despite strong official rhetoric against welfare expansion, especially in areas such as social services and public assistance. As a result, these countries are increasingly relying on the social insurance principle to organise their welfare system. In the authoritarian or semi-authoritarian regimes such as Singapore, Malaysia and Indonesia, however, social policy remains the prerogative of the state, which continues to resort to welfare Orientalism to move the countries towards privatisation rather than socialisation of welfare. Consequently, provident fund schemes are the preferred way of welfare provision.

The trajectories of social development in Pacific Asia demonstrate the importance of national politics and international influence. In terms of the former, the logic of the authoritarian developmental state was the key determinant of the productivist origin of the Pacific Asian welfare regime, which emerged in political circumstances very different from those surrounding the creation of the welfare state in the West. The absence of powerful working class politics, in the forms of independent trade union movements and social democratic political parties, meant that unlike in the West, the welfare system was initiated by the authoritarian developmental state both as a pre-emptive strike to compensate for its legitimacy deficit and as an instrument of economic development. Therefore, they were an integral part of the developmental state in its drive for economic growth and social stability. Social policy in Pacific Asia, in other words, was an indispensable state instrument in creating the pro-business *developmental* welfare system (White *et al.* 1998: 214).

Although social policy was driven by the political logic of the developmental state, this tendency was reinforced by the wider global environment. Two particular factors stood out. One was the Cold War factor, which severely restricted the development of union/left-wing politics in all societies, giving the authoritarian developmental state a large measure of autonomy to implement its productivist social policy. The second factor was the growing influence of neo-liberal anti-state welfarism, which began to emerge in the West in the 1970s. By attacking the welfare state for the alleged economic inefficiency and social ills of the West, neo-liberalism also reinforced the innate conservatism of Pacific Asia's developmental welfarism, serving as a convenient warning against 'Westernisation'.

Nowhere was this more vividly illustrated than in Japan. Before its embrace of 'welfare Orientalism', the LDP government, worried by its sagging electoral support and facing increasing popular demands for improving the citizens' quality of life, declared the year 1973 as 'Year One of the Welfare Era' in Japan. The intention was to expand Japan's welfare state to catch up with the Western welfare state. The unfortunate coincidence of this policy with the oil crisis, which pushed up Japan's social spending in the wake of global recession, triggered a political backlash against the idea of the welfare state, leading to a policy reversal. To justify the change, Prime Minister Ohira developed the idea of the 'Japanese-style welfare society' in which individuals, the family and the community, and not the state, should take primary responsibility for social welfare (Lee 1987; Tabata 1990).

The impact of neo-liberalism on social policy in Southeast Asia is equally evident. This is not only reflected in the strategic targeting of social protection, whereby public spending is limited to the privileged sections of the population and to the productive areas such as education and health. It is also reflected in the region's move towards privatisation in education and health. Furthermore, during the period of authoritarian rule, while both Malaysia and Indonesia relied mainly on provident fund schemes for social protection, Thailand adopted a virtual laissez-faire approach to social protection for its private sector workers.

The fact that welfare expansion in the NDCs is not equated with the automatic increase in state financial responsibility can be attributed to the global influence of neo-liberalism. In a global environment of welfare retrenchment and academic dissension on the relationship between the level of public spending and economic competitiveness (Rao 1995), intensified globalisation (see Chapter 9) has become a powerful justification, rightly or wrongly, for limited social spending. Therefore, it would be simplistic to equate democracy with welfare statism. Pragmatism, the need to appeal to the electorate, to win and stay in power, is perhaps the best predictor of social policy change in the future.

Finally, having argued that national politics, influenced by global factors, plays the key determining role in social policy in Pacific Asia, it is worth commenting briefly on the socioeconomic perspective on social policy that I introduced in the first part of the chapter. While the spending pattern in the region, as in the West, clearly militates against any facile equation between level of economic development and level of social spending, economic development nevertheless matters for the overall quality of social coverage. Singapore may not be spending as much of its GDP on social policy as Malaysia is of its GDP, but its much higher level of economic development means that social coverage is both more extensive and of higher quality. Indeed, as we have already seen, the NECs' lower level of economic development in comparison with the NICs is a major reason for their limited social coverage, be it social insurance or provident fund schemes. Therefore, economic development is a necessary but not sufficient condition for social development.

CONCLUSION

Social development in Pacific Asia is increasingly taking divergent paths, largely because of the changing domestic political dynamics. Democratisation, although not leading to a rapid increase in welfare statism, is nevertheless reducing the discourse of welfare Orientalism to mere rhetorical significance ready to give way to the logic of democratic contestation. In countries undergoing little democratic change, welfare Orientalism is reinforced by the global ascent of neo-liberalism, which advocates limited social spending. In both situations, welfare Orientalism is but an official ideology seeking to maintain the productivist orientation of social policy, a tendency easier to justify under economic globalisation and the dominant influence of neo-liberalism.

Although it is not easy to predict the future of social policy in Pacific Asia, the evolution of the Japanese welfare system may nevertheless point to some common challenges that sooner or later will face all societies in the region. Japan may be an instructive example because it still maintains its official rhetoric of welfare Orientalism while in practice moving towards a Western-style welfare system. Although democracy played a role, in that electoral competition forced the LDP government to respond to popular demand for welfare expansion, economic and demographic factors have been equally important in forcing the state to put official ideology on hold in search of practical solutions to social problems brought on by slower growth, which is inevitable as the economy matures, an ageing population and a declining birth rate. Already, similar problems such as ageing and declining birth rates are predicted for the NICs and the NECs at some point in future (Ramesh 2000: 32–3; Tang 2000: 62). In addition, the outbreak of the 1997–8 financial crisis has seen several of the worst-hit countries, including Japan, expand their welfare provisions. Therefore it is probably safe to say that the politics of legitimacy will continue to be the decisive factor shaping social development in Pacific Asia.

9   The changing context of development

Democratisation, globalisation and the 1997 crisis

The year 1997 was a turning point in the development history of Pacific Asia. That summer saw the outbreak of the now well-known Asian financial crisis, which brought to an end the 'Asian Miracle' that had dominated the international press and academic research for the previous two decades. What started out as a currency crisis in Thailand quickly turned into a financial and economic crisis and spread to other economies like a 'contagion'. Under sustained speculative attacks, all currencies in the region – except the New Taiwan dollar and the Singapore dollar – lost heavily against the US dollar, and as international capital sought to withdraw from these economies, the prices on their stock markets also plummeted. To avoid total financial meltdown, the worst-hit countries, Thailand, Indonesia and South Korea, were all forced to borrow from the IMF and accept in return stringent conditionalities on the structural reform of their economies.

Although all the economies have been on the road to recovery since 1999, following 2 years of contraction (World Bank 2000), the theoretical and political debate on the nature and cause of the crisis continues. The contention centres on two broad interpretations, encapsulated in the now well-publicised imagery of 'rogue speculators', on the one hand, and 'crony capitalism', on the other. From the latter perspective, represented mainly by neo-classical economists, the crisis not only spelled the end of the Pacific Asian developmental state, it also marked the beginning of the region's convergence with the West. A South Korean official was widely quoted (in Cumings 1998: 71) as saying that, 'The model is now clear. It's not Japan, it's the West.'

In this chapter I will examine closely the nature and cause of the crisis with a view to exploring its theoretical and policy implications for development. I will present the view that, while the historical form of the Pacific Asian developmental state has indeed come to an end because of the changing domestic and international context of development, the developmental state as a theoretical model of political economy nevertheless remains relevant in the contemporary world. In particular, I will argue that both perspectives on the crisis suffer blind spots deriving from their common oversight of the changing political context of development.

The chapter consists of two parts. Part 1 gives a brief historical account of the crisis and its two dominant interpretations. Part 2 seeks to explain the countries' different experiences of the crisis by examining the way in which financial globalisation affects the developmental role of the state in the economy. In contrast to the simplistic argument that liberalisation undermined the role of the state in these economies, the focus is to demonstrate how liberalisation magnified the detrimental effect of 'crony capitalism', an integral part of several developmental states in the region. Finally, the chapter concludes by reflecting on the role of the state and democracy in an era of economic liberalisation.

THE 1997 CRISIS AND ITS EXPLANATIONS

What is now conveniently known as the 1997 Asian financial crisis in practice consisted of a series of currency and financial crises, which affected a number of the region's tiger economies between mid-1997 and early 1998. (For the hitherto most comprehensive documentation of the crisis, see www.stern.nyu.edu/globalmacro/.) The crisis started in Thailand in May 1997, when its currency, the baht, came under several waves of sustained speculative attacks in the international financial markets. The government initially responded by seeking to defend its value with its foreign reserves. However, as the reserves were quickly exhausted, the government was forced to abandon the fixed exchange rate between the baht and the US dollar in July, leading to a sharp devaluation of the baht. The falling baht, in its turn, triggered the collapse of the Thai stock market as international capital investors scrambled to withdraw from the Thai economy in a 'herd reaction'. Between July 1997 and January 1998, the baht lost 54.6 per cent of its value against the US dollar, and the value of the Thai stock market in January 1998 had fallen by 59 per cent in comparison with the year before (Hirst 2000). The government was then forced to seek an IMF rescue plan, which was announced in August. In return for the US$17.2 billion loan from the IMF, the Thai authorities agreed to carry out both short-term and long-term reform programmes.

Immediately after the Thai devaluation, a similar crisis soon spread to other parts of the region like a 'contagion'. By January 1998, the Malaysian ringgit had fallen by 44.9 per cent against the US dollar, the Indonesian rupiah by 83.6 per cent, and the South Korean won by 49.1 per cent. These countries' financial systems were further weakened by the consequent fall in their respective equity markets. By January 1998, the value of the stock market compared with the previous year had fallen by 61 per cent in Malaysia, 53 per cent in Indonesia, 53 per cent in Singapore, and 42 per cent in South Korea (Hirst 2000). Whereas Indonesia and South Korea both resorted to IMF rescue packages worth $43 billion and $57 billion respectively, Malaysia introduced stringent controls on capital movement in an attempt to prevent the flight of capital from the country.

Despite its recent recovery from the crisis-induced economic slowdown, the region is still grappling with the social consequences, such as rising unemployment and increasing poverty, particularly prominent in the worst hit societies of Indonesia, Thailand and South Korea.

As the crisis unfolded, two opposing perspectives began to emerge seeking to explain it. The first was articulated by the Malaysian prime minister, Dr Mahathir, who put the blame squarely on international financiers disparagingly characterised as 'rogue speculators'. Although most others do not adopt Dr Mahathir's deliberately provocative tone, they share his basic analysis of the crisis, that is, it was largely a product of unbridled financial globalisation (Wade and Veneroso 1998a; Winters 2000). Higgot (2000a: 262) describes it as the 'first crisis of globalisation'.

Opposing this view, however, is the neo-classical economic analysis, as expressed by the IMF, that 'crony capitalism' lies at the heart of the crisis. Although first coined to describe the corruption-ridden Philippine economy under Ferdinand Marcos, this term is now applied to all the 'miracle' economies, including Japan, largely to refer to the lack of policy transparency in government intervention in the economy. According to this view, as all the economies in the world are faced with similar external environments, differences in their performance can only be explained in terms of domestic policies and the way in which external factors are handled. A factsheet issued by the IMF on 17 January 1999, entitled *The IMF's Response to the Asian Crisis*, states that although private sector overborrowing triggered the crisis, it 'was made worse by governance issues, notably government involvement in the private sector and lack of transparency in corporate and fiscal accounting and the provision of financial and economic data' (www.stern.nyu.edu/globalmacro/).

While both perspectives contain some truth, neither provides a whole picture of the events. For the crisis-of-globalisation perspective, the major difficulty is its inability to account for the different degrees of disruption that the crisis brought to individual economies. As we have seen, not all the economies were affected in the same manner and with the same degree of severity. Although Malaysia was as badly hit as South Korea in terms of the loss it sustained of its currency and stock market values, it nevertheless escaped the humiliation of begging for the IMF's medicine. At the same time, Singapore and Taiwan were virtually unaffected by the crisis, apart from suffering economic slowdown due to the contraction of other Asian economies. Neither society experienced the widespread bankruptcies and job layoffs seen in other economies. Therefore, to account for this wide variation in the national experience, there is a need to explore the domestic dimension of the crisis.

The crony capitalism explanation appears to fill this gap by focusing on the domestic 'fundamentals' in relation to governance issues. However, it suffers its own omissions. Many critics of the neo-classical analysis have rightly pointed out the abrupt manner in which the IMF changed its discourse on Pacific Asian development during the crisis. The overnight shift from 'miracle' Asia to 'crony' Asia was made as if these economies had never before been branded a success let alone a model of development (Wade 1998; Dixon 1999: 449). As Jeffrey Sachs (quoted in Bullard *et al.* 1998: 507) commented, 'the IMF arrived in Thailand in July with ostentatious declarations that all was wrong and that fundamental surgery was needed' when, in fact, 'the ink was not even dry on the IMF's 1997 annual report, which gave Thailand and its neighbours high marks on economic management'!

According to Sachs (1997), in September 1997 the IMF had the following to say about Thailand in its annual report: 'Directors strongly praised Thailand's remarkable economic performance and the authorities' consistent record of sound macroeconomic policies.' On Korea, it said: 'Directors welcomed Korea's continued impressive macroeconomic performance [and] praised the authorities for their enviable fiscal record.' Similarly, Bullard *et al.* (1998: 512) quoted the World Bank a few months before Indonesia's crisis broke out as saying that much of its economic dynamism 'can be traced to the government's reform programme which liberalised trade and finance and encouraged foreign investment and deregulation'. The question that needs to be asked about the neo-liberal analysis is thus why no alarm was raised even on the eve of the crisis whereas the entire tone of the post-crisis analysis became one of 'I told you so'.

In the next part of the chapter, I will seek to address the questions raised about both perspectives by locating the cause of the crisis in the context of the international and national politics of globalisation and financial liberalisation. The *timing* of the crisis, I will argue, suggests that systemic cronyism and liberalisation are ultimately incompatible and detrimental to the economy. However, I will go further by arguing that the international (i.e. Western) neo-liberal advisers on development are also responsible for allowing the two to develop in tandem through their decidedly technocratic approach to economic development.

Explaining the crisis

In all the affected economies, the financial crisis manifested itself as a liquidity problem, i.e. insufficient credit to pay back foreign debt, resulting from overborrowing by private sector institutions, largely banks in Thailand and Indonesia and *chaebols* in South Korea. Most of the debt was short-term loans from foreign commercial banks to be paid within less than 12 months. Before the crisis, the ratio of short-term debt to foreign reserves stood as follows: 203.23 per cent for South Korea, 176.59 per cent for Indonesia, 99.69 per cent for Thailand, 40.98 per cent for Malaysia, 21.3 per cent for Taiwan, and 2.6 per cent for Singapore (Corsetti *et al.* 1998: Table 26), with Malaysia, Taiwan and Singapore in progressively better positions.

The problem, however, was compounded by a number of economic weaknesses that preceded it, greatly restricting the policy options available to the governments. These included a marked slowdown in the rates of growth in exports in 1995–6, and the consequent fall in the economies' GDP growth rates (*The Economist*, 1 March 1999). Worsening export performance also contributed to a deepening current account deficit, only to be exacerbated by the large inflow of foreign funds. In Malaysia and Thailand, the economies of which were suffering considerable overheating, most of the foreign funds went to heavily protected sectors, such as real estate developments and construction, instead of to the dynamic export sector. Therefore, when currency speculations began, governments in these economies were faced with a difficult dilemma. On the one hand, they were forced to hold on to the pegged exchange rate against the US dollar knowing that devaluation could only increase their debt burden. On the other hand, however, an artificially maintained high exchange rate was only hurting their already deteriorating exporting industries, which would have liked a cut in their currency values.

Although it is clear that the crisis was a product of a combination of home-made and external factors, the central issue in need of explanation is this: what leads to overborrowing/overlending? The question concerning borrowing is all the more puzzling given that all the economies that embarked on reckless borrowing had high levels of domestic saving, averaging around 30 per cent of GDP (Corsetti *et al.* 1998: Table 12). The answer to this lies in financial globalisation, a process aided by both national and international politics.

There is little doubt that financial globalisation played a part in the Asian crisis; what is in contention is the nature of its role. While neo-liberals blame government incompetence in its handling, their critics blame the anarchic nature of the global financial system for causing overlending and panic withdrawing as a result of 'rational' individual behaviour. In other words, while neo-liberals see the crisis as being caused by the technical failure of the governments to establish an efficiently functioning financial market as a result of unwarranted and corrupt intervention, their critics tend to see these governments as being at the mercy of international financiers at the expense of downplaying the significance of cronyism. It is therefore obvious that both perspectives ignore the political initiatives that lay behind the crisis. In the following section, I will address the weakness of the neo-liberal perspective by examining the international politics of globalisation.

The 'Washington consensus' and the international politics of globalisation

Since the 1980s, there has been a fast-expanding body of literature on globalisation in the study of international political economy (IPE). *Globalisation* refers to the increasing integration of national economies into a single world capitalist system and the resultant consequences for the national economy, society and politics. Terms such as 'borderless economy', 'interdependence', and 'global village', to name but a few, have now become common descriptions of this process. Although writers disagree over the precise time during which globalisation took place, there is a general agreement that the trend has been gathering momentum since the 1970s, abetted by technological innovations in transport and communications (Robertson 1992). Bretherton (1996: 3) argues that world affairs today is characterised by 'a significant intensification of global connectedness and a consciousness of that intensification, with a corresponding diminution in the significance of territorial boundaries and state structures'.

Globalisation reduces the grip and impact of local circumstances over people's lives (Giddens 1990; Harvey 1990). In the economic sphere, not only is the production and consumption of commodities organised at the global level, with the primary aim of securing the maximum return on capital, financial transactions also transcend national boundaries and time limits, with the world's major financial centres – London, New York, Tokyo – taking over from one another around the clock. It is estimated that by now over one-half of the world's goods and services are generated in the context of global strategies and networks of production and marketing, coordinated by MNCs (Bretherton 1996).

However, to many observers, the real distinction of the late twentieth-century phase of globalisation is the global integration of the financial market, which presages the 'end of geography' (Bretherton 1996). By 1989, foreign exchange trading alone in the world's financial centres already averaged around US$500 billion a day, amounting to forty times the volume of actual trade for the same period. This technology-dependent rapid mobility of capital means that: 'Few countries or parts of the world can any longer remain insulated from financial shocks or changes, wherever they may occur.' (Held 1995: 129).

For quite some time, the study of the origin and consequences of globalisation has been dominated by economists and sociologists, who overemphasised economic and technological change at the expense of politics, what Susan Strange (1996: xiv) lucidly calls 'the power element'. Because it is seen to be driven by technology and the 'rational' desire of consumers for 'access to the best and least expensive products' (Ohmae 1995: inside front cover), globalisation is often portrayed as a process of convergence, a homogenising force that leads inexorably to the end of the nation-state and national economy. In place of the much weakened state is something vaguely called 'global governance', an evolving alternative to the existing inter-state global system that regulates global affairs (Strange 1996: xiii).

Such an apolitical depiction of globalisation is increasingly challenged by political scientists who are dissatisfied with the sense of economic and technological determinism permeating much of the analysis. 'Globalization', wrote Ruigrok and van Tulder (1993: 22), 'seems to be as much an overstatement as it is an ideology and an analytical concept.' The focus on the ideological basis of globalisation leads to the spotlighting of the hitherto missing 'power element' involved in the process of globalisation. Specifically, the pivotal role of the US government in promoting a *particular* vision of the global system, based on the 'Washington consensus' (Williamson 1994), is scrutinised.

The 'Washington consensus' refers to the largely US-originated ideology of neo-liberalism, which, since the 1980s, has been the driving force for globalisation. Although it originated in the United States, a combination of international factors and US government initiatives has helped its ascent at the global level. During the Cold War, the economic dynamism of pro-US Asian tiger economies was held up by the US-dominated international agencies as the best example of 'open' market economies outperforming the stagnating socialist economies. The subsequent collapse of the socialist regimes and their embrace of the market economy was portrayed as further evidence of the wisdom of neo-liberalism. However, as Ruggie (1982) pointed out, for much of the Cold War period, economic order in the capitalist world was underpinned by 'embedded liberalism' rather than laissez-faire liberalism. The states, instead of giving free rein to the market, reined in market competition in the interest of social stability and military security. Hence the emergence of the welfare state in Europe and the developmental state in Pacific Asia. Moreover, the United States played a crucial role in supporting embedded liberalism in both Europe and Pacific

Asia by keeping open its own market without demanding reciprocity and by supporting authoritarian regimes in Pacific Asia. By the mid-1980s, the relaxation of international tension between the two ideological camps and the relative decline of the US economy, due to the rise of Japan, West Germany and an emerging Europe, led the United States to demand a 'level playing field' in the global economy by pressuring these hitherto 'free-riding' economies to liberalise and open themselves up to US businesses. The US-dominated international organisations such as the IMF, the World Bank, and the General Agreement on Tariffs and Trade (GATT) and the World Trade Organization (WTO) became the vehicles by which this demand was made.

The entrenchment of the Washington consensus in the post-Cold War IPE undoubtedly marks the changing international context of development. But, as is shown, the move towards globalisation and liberalisation is as much fuelled by technological advance as driven by US national interest. Contrary to the end-of-state argument, the US state plays an instrumental role in shaping the emerging global liberal order. Similarly, the neo-liberal doctrine promoted by the international organisations, which equates liberalisation with the introduction of more market competition based on the reduction or elimination of government regulations (Vogel 1996: 3), is not only blinkered but also open to the charge of serving the US national interest. Wade and Veneroso (1998b), among others, have identified 'the Wall Street–Treasury–IMF complex' as the main culprit for the Asian crisis.

The politics of financial liberalisation in Pacific Asia

Within this political context of economic globalisation in general, nothing illustrates better than financial globalisation the insight of the realist perspective on IPE. In this view, the 'international organisation is above all a tool of national government, an instrument for the pursuit of national interest by other means' (Strange 1996: xiv). Seen from this perspective, the latest structural change in the economies of the industrial West (Japan included), the United States in particular, from manufacturing to service industry, has been a powerful drive for the West's concerted pressure, exercised through the IMF and the WTO, for global financial liberalisation which gives their capital free movement worldwide (Wade and Veneroso 1998b; Cumings 1998: 51). This partly explains why the tiger economies in Pacific Asia carried out liberalisation reforms after the late 1980s, which resulted in financial deregulation and the opening of their financial markets to foreign operations despite their high domestic savings rate. It also explains the international organisations' manifestly technocratic approach in their advice on liberalisation in Pacific Asia. The latter point is of particular importance because it suggests that this technocratic approach was no more than a pretence to mask their hidden agenda of serving the interest of Western governments and capital.

There is no shortage of evidence, historical or contemporary, to support the argument that the West has been an indispensable accomplice in Pacific Asia's 'crony capitalism'. Its support of authoritarian regimes in the region during the Cold War is well documented. As far back as the early 1990s, many problems associated with the region's financial liberalisation, which were later to be suddenly 'discovered' and lambasted as 'cronyism', had also been well known. These included lack of government supervision, bank failures, financial fraudulence, large-scale accumulation of non-performing loans and downright corruption (Islam and Chowdhury 1997: 81). In the early months of 1997, South Korea and Thailand had already seen several of their corporations and financial institutions threatened with liquidity problems due to overborrowing (Hirst 2000).

Therefore, to blame the region's fallen economies for causing overlending by not providing sufficient information about their economies was simply untrue. As Wade (1998: 703) argues, it was less a case of lack of relevant information than a case of unwillingness to see that led to the overlending. In the same way that the politically connected national capitalists in Pacific Asia had been benefiting from crony capitalism, foreign lenders expected the corrupt governments to bail them out in the event of problems. So given the West's long and deep involvement in sustaining crony capitalism in Pacific Asia under the pretence of neo-liberalism, it is hard to disagree with Dr Mahathir when he responded to the charge of cronyism by saying: 'We have been doing the same thing all this while' (Godement 1999: 55)!

So far I have exposed the disingenuousness with which the criticism of crony capitalism is levelled at Pacific Asian economies by the West. The argument is that the West had been knowingly part of the very system that they later attacked for the sake of their own national interest. While this is not a critique of the conduct of international relations based on the defence of national interest, a topic beyond the scope of this book, it is certainly an attempt to highlight the damaging global consequences of the West's attempt to separate economics from politics in its interaction with Pacific Asia. It is in this sense that I am arguing for the West's responsibility for the Asian crisis.

Cronyism and the national politics of globalisation

Although financial globalisation provided the common background against which the Asian crisis broke out, the different degrees of disruption sustained by different economies suggests the dynamics of domestic politics in determining its effect. In the previous section, I showed the *external* source of financial liberalisation in Pacific Asia, which comes from the financially developed West, the United States in particular. However, apart from showing the way in which the West should be blamed for the Asian crisis, I did not analyse the part played by domestic politics in the crisis. In this section, therefore, I seek to show both the *domestic* political source of financial liberalisation and its relationship with cronyism in triggering the crisis.

Among the critics of the neo-liberal perspective of the Asian crisis, there is a tendency either to underplay the significance of crony capitalism (Wade 1998; Wade and Veneroso 1998b) or to blame foolish and imprudent liberalisation reforms for undermining the state's capacity (Weiss and Hobson 2000). While the former has difficulty in explaining the divergent experiences of the crisis among the economies, the latter has problems in explaining why such policy mistakes were made. The fact is that neither cronyism nor policy mistakes took place in historical and political vacuums.

In the neo-liberal parlance, cronyism in Pacific Asia is a thinly disguised euphemism for government intervention in the economy. However, both before and after, and especially after, the crisis, it was evident that government intervention did not have any direct causal relationship with cronyism, in the sense of mutual private enrichment between economic and political power holders. Nor, for that matter, did economic liberalisation reduce cronyism, as was assumed by the neo-liberal ideologues. In fact, there was strong evidence to suggest that in Pacific Asia, cronyism expanded in scope with liberalisation, resulting in economic weaknesses and eventually the financial crisis.

On the whole, the Southeast Asian NECs suffered greater losses from the crisis than the East Asian NICs. This can be largely attributed to the persistence of the structural weaknesses of these economies due largely to their weaker state capacity in comparison with the NICs (see Chapter 4). Economic liberalisation, which accelerated after the mid-1980s as part of their concerted move to EOI, brought about impressive growth rates, averaging more than 8 per cent between the mid-1980s and mid-1990s. However, it brought little improvement in their economic structure. None of the well-known features of 'ersatz capitalism', such as the dual economic structure, predatory behaviour of the 'administocrats', skills shortage and infrastructure bottleneck, were tackled under liberalisation.

Chronic structural weaknesses were exacerbated by the expanded scope of cronyism made possible by liberalisation. Instead of bringing 'good governance', as expected by the World Bank and the IMF, liberalisation had turned out to be a wonderful means of rewarding political and family friends, who now had almost unrestricted access to foreign funds. At the same time, the appearance of the 'free for all' (it was of course more free for the politically connected who had insider information), generated by slack regulation of local financial markets, also contributed to a great sense of liberation on the part of many new business people, who saw an open economy rather than political connection as vital to their business success. To these new business people, who were largely a product of economic liberalisation rather than political connection, the unregulated financial market was an important means of escaping the financial stranglehold of the old economic elite, which consisted mainly of the Chinese and their political patrons. Therefore, it appeared that both cronyism and liberalisation appeased the key sections of the population on whose support governments relied for legitimacy.

A direct consequence of the combination of regulatory laxity and cronyism was a runaway economy in all NECs prior to the crisis. Large profits were made, not in the dynamic export sector, but in the highly protected domestic sector, fuelling imports and trade deficits, which in turn sucked in more short-term borrowing for their finance. Meanwhile, the already deteriorating export performance and trade deficits were dealt another blow by the devaluation of the Chinese yuan in 1994 and the appreciation of the US dollar against the Japanese yen from 1995 onwards. Whereas the former cut the international competitiveness of these economies' products, the latter reduced their competitiveness specifically in the Japanese and European markets as a result of the effective pegging of their currencies to the US dollar. In principle, these economies should have been able to recover from their temporary losses resulting from currency fluctuations. In reality, they had been losing competitiveness to rising economies such as China and Vietnam because of their long-term neglect of investment in human capital and physical infrastructure. In other words, their lack of competitiveness was cumulative and structural rather than temporary. Without sufficient exports to pay for the mounting foreign debts, the economic boom became unsustainable.

The crisis in Southeast Asia thus reveals that financial liberalisation in the NECs was marked less by the developmental objectives of improving economic performance and redressing structural weaknesses than by enriching the cronies and appeasing the rising new business class. Although the weak state regulatory institutions were a legacy of the weak state traditions characteristic of these economies, in an increasingly globalised economy, weak institutions undermined by cronyism simply magnify national vulnerabilities to a rapidly changing international environment. As Jomo (2000: 27) argues, 'The recent currency and financial crises suggest that Southeast Asia's economic boom had been built on some shaky and unsustainable foundations.'

As another direct victim of the 1997–8 crisis, South Korea shared with the NECs some similar pre-crisis economic problems, such as deteriorating export performance, a ballooning current account deficit and rising short-term borrowing. However, unlike the NECs, the weakening of state capacity in managing the liberalised phase of economic development was not a historical legacy. On the contrary, South Korea had been held up as the developmental state par excellence in the developmental state literature for its close government–business relations, which were dominated by the former. Admittedly, corruption was an integral component of the developmental state. However, South Korea stood apart from the Southeast Asian 'ersatz capitalism' by virtue of the strict performance discipline that government was able to impose on the *chaebols* targeted to receive state funds (see Chapter 3). So, what went wrong then?

Many writers traced the origin of South Korea's downfall to the early 1990s, when the government introduced a rushed programme of economic liberalisation partly because of US pressure and partly as an attempt to bid for the coveted OECD membership (Moon and Rhyu 2000; Weiss and Hobson 2000). It was argued that while the government was busy dismantling the erstwhile key state institutions such as the EPB, it failed to set up new supervisory and regulatory institutions to monitor effectively the powerful *chaebols,* which were allowed direct access to foreign capital through the liberalised financial market. As a result, the *chaebols* were given a free hand to embark on reckless borrowing and overexpansion as a means of compensating for their increasing loss of competitiveness in the global market. In 1996, the top twenty listed *chaebols* were earning a mere 3 per cent on assets, while the average cost of borrowing rose to 8.2 per cent. In November 1997, eight of South Korea's thirty largest *chaebols* either went bankrupt or were facing severe financial strains. Late that month, saddled with having to repay some $66 billion out of a total foreign debt of $120 billion within one year, South Korea was forced to seek an IMF bail-out (Bullard *et al.* 1998).

The key issue raised by the Korean case thus seems to be one of loss of state capacity under liberalisation. However, as in the NECs, the underlying cause of state weakness was largely political in origin, reflecting deeper shifts in political and social power brought on by decades of economic development and the arrival of democratic politics as well as external pressures. Specifically, two particular developments during the decade before the crisis played an instrumental role in the crisis. First, the *chaebols* were developed into MNCs after the late 1980s in response to the US trade offensive against Korea and the forced appreciation of the Korean won against the US dollar. The increasing autonomy of the *chaebols* thus reversed their relationship with government under the authoritarian period, giving them increasing political power to demand more liberalisation. Second, the government's position was further weakened by the arrival of democratic politics, in which the mounting anti-government disposition in the middle and working classes led to a deepening of government reliance on the capitalist class for political as well as economic support, which was given in exchange for further economic deregulation (Lee and Kim 2000: 127). Both of these developments meant that the old practice of cronyism, i.e. the allocation of credit based on political connections, generated disastrous consequences in an age of globalisation, for it led to a relaxation of government monitoring and supervision of the globally active *chaebols*, which increasingly resorted to business expansion and dubious investment rather than research and development to compensate for their declining profitability. Therefore, government failure in South Korea, like that in the NECs, was primarily a political failure rather than technical, i.e. a failure to set up competent monitoring and supervisory institutions. As in the NECs, the pressure for economic liberalisation came as much from outside as from inside the society.

The Korean experience of the crisis suggests the obsolescence of the authoritarian developmental state due to the changed international and domestic context of development. In an age of globalisation and democratisation, close government–business relations based on opaque dealings rather than the rule of law not only weaken the government's position vis-à-vis business but also strengthen wider anti-government social coalitions, further undermining governmental ability to coordinate policy.

The argument that Korean-style cronyism undermines state capacity in an age of globalisation and democratisation can be further made by comparing Korea with Taiwan and Singapore, two of the economies least affected by the crisis partly because of their sound 'economic fundamentals' at the time the crisis spread. They were the only two economies that had low levels of foreign debt, large foreign reserves and consistent trade surpluses (Corsetti *et al.* 1998). Furthermore, the fact that neither country ever instituted a Korean-style government–business relationship meant that there was less opportunity for institutional rigidity to develop in the new era of development.

However, as Cotton (2000) rightly points out, the good fortune, as it were, of Taiwan and Singapore was less to do with 'good governance', in the sense of accountable and transparent politics, than with historically determined policy choices. As I have noted in Chapter 3, Taiwan's Malaysian-style ethnic divide between mainlanders and Taiwanese prevented close government–business collaboration *à la* Korea, whereas the Singapore state opted for close alliance with FDI because of the limitations of the domestic market. Furthermore, the need to attract international business has led Singapore to enforce stringent anti-corruption laws, winning Singapore the reputation of being one of the world's cleanest governments (see the website of Transparency International, an NGO monitoring corruption worldwide, at www.transparency.org/).

The comparison may seem ironic as it appears to show little positive correlation between democracy and clean government. Indeed, if anything, money politics actually expanded in the NDCs of Thailand, South Korea and Taiwan (after the introduction of local elections in the 1950s) as well as in the authoritarian and semi-authoritarian regimes of Indonesia and Malaysia, perhaps with Singapore being the only exception (Godement 1999: 136–40). While this phenomenon certainly raises many important research questions about the relationship between democracy and public corruption, a topic that cannot be adequately dealt with here, two specific points concerning the conceptualisation of democracy may be worth considering in the context of Pacific Asian development.

The first is the need to distinguish between electoralism and democracy (see Chapter 7). Although elections are an essential part of a democratic process, they are by no means democracy per se. Indeed, comparative studies are littered with incidents of democratising regimes seeing elections go hand in hand with the money politics of vote buying and influence peddling, with the late nineteenth-century US 'machine politics' being perhaps the best known (Banfield and Wilson 1963: 115). In this respect, it is important to remember the relatively recent experience of democracy in Pacific Asia. The second point is the need to appreciate the rule of law as a key ingredient of democracy. This is, in effect, an advocacy of the *liberal* form of democracy against the so-called *Asian* form of democracy. Only by legally entrenching the rights of society over those of the state and, within the former, the rights of the individual over those of the collective, can responsibilities be identified and held to account. It is perhaps no coincidence that of the world's top twenty cleanest governments, all except Singapore are liberal democracies (www.worldaudit.org/corruption.htm). So, Singapore is the exception rather than the norm. Therefore, I share the judgement made by Phongpaichit and Piriyarangsan (1994: 21) that a parliamentary system with corrupt politicians is preferable to an 'honest' dictatorship, because '[a]t least under a democratic framework there is the possibility of developing a civil society with the will to control corruption.'

CONCLUSION

The 1997–8 Asian financial crisis broke out against the background of profound changes in both national and international politics. Financial liberalisation, which was the obvious trigger of the crisis, was nevertheless a product of both international pressure and changing social and political power relations at home. Broadly speaking, countries in which cronyism multiplied under economic liberalisation suffered the most severe losses during the crisis. The *timing* of the crisis, therefore, suggests the devastating consequences of combining economic liberalisation with systemic corruption. However, to the extent that this was allowed to develop under the aegis of the IMF and the World Bank, the crisis was also a damning indictment of the depoliticised approach to economic development adopted by the neo-liberal ideologue.

Democratisation in Pacific Asia, instead of being a check on corruption, was very much part of the problem because of the increasing demand for money necessitated by electoral politics. However, as I have suggested, this could well be a transitional phase of democratisation because of the underdevelopment of the rule of law in the NDCs. In the long run, democracy provides the best institutionalised check on public corruption through both a vibrant civil society and legal mechanisms of public accountability.

Pacific Asia has undoubtedly come to a historical juncture in its quest for development. What has become obsolete is the 'old way' of crony capitalism rather than state intervention in the economy. An increasingly globalised economy will not prosper under cronyism but must rely on the legitimating authority and legal infrastructure provided by the nation-state to function effectively (Heilbroner 1985). The challenge for the future is thus the move towards democratic governance and the rule of law.

10 The rise of regionalism in Pacific Asia

Contested visions, changing realities

Apart from calling into question the political systems of Pacific Asia's many hitherto successful economies, another major consequence of the 1997–8 crisis has been the rise of what is known as East Asian regionalism, namely, the growth of governmental initiatives aimed at promoting regional economic cooperation. Although there had long been calls from East Asian political leaders for closer economic cooperation in Pacific or East Asia, the idea did not seem to take off until after 1997, partly fuelled by what Higgott (2000a) described as 'the politics of resentment'. The handling of the financial crisis by the West, the United States in particular, was widely perceived as an example of the West seeking to take advantage of the region's vulnerabilities. Consequently, regional cooperation was promoted as an important way of counterbalancing the global dominance of the West.

The emergence of East Asian regionalism is both part of a wider global phenomenon of regionalisation, namely, the process of increasing regional economic integration, and a reflection of the region's Japan-led 'flying geese' pattern of development (see Chapter 2). This has resulted in a growing body of literature seeking to theorise the emergent post-Cold War IPE. The argument has been made that the growing prominence of East Asia as a region signals not only the arrival of a tripartite international system dominated by the evolving European Union, North America and East Asia but also the emergence of a Japan-led third form of capitalism competing with the other two regional forms in the global economy (Stubbs 1995; Stallings and Streeck 1995; Beeson and Jayasuriya 1998).

However, Japan is not the only dominant actor in Pacific Asian regional development. The United States' long involvement in the region's economic, political and security affairs both reflects the complex geopolitical motives driving regional cooperation and has led to contested visions of regionalism, typified by the ongoing debate on the region's geographical delineation: Asia-Pacific or East Asian? In addition, changes in national politics have also begun to subject some of the issues concerning regional development to political contestation.

Given the embryonic nature of East Asian regionalism, the purpose of this chapter is not to predict its future. Rather, I will seek to analyse the contested nature of regional development in East Asia by situating it in the context of the complex interplay between international geopolitics and changing national politics. In so doing, I will endeavour to highlight the intellectual and political problems of the notion of an East Asian regionalism underpinned by a Japanese-/Asian-style capitalism. Our main emphasis is on the politically contested and hence contingent nature of regional development in Pacific Asia.

The chapter is divided into three parts. Part 1 gives a brief introduction to the intellectual linkage between the concepts of regionalism, globalisation and forms of capitalism. Part 2 examines the historical origin and changing basis of political support for the two contending visions of regionalism in Pacific Asia, namely Asia-Pacific regionalism and East Asian regionalism. Part three is a critical assessment of the prospects for a Japan-led East Asian regionalism based on an analysis of the changing national politics and the intellectual and political problems associated with Japan's regional leadership role. I conclude by noting the changing normative basis of regional identification.

REGIONALISM, GLOBALISATION AND FORMS OF CAPITALISM

Since the late 1980s, there has been a dramatic upsurge in the number of regional economic blocs in the world economy, all aimed to liberalise trade between member states as a way to promote national economic development. The three 'mega-regions', Europe, North America, and East Asia, in which a disproportionate share of the world's production, trade and investment is concentrated, have been described as the 'global triad' dominating the world economy (Dicken 1998: 101–4). Unlike 'old regionalism', typified by the European Community (EC), which took place against the backdrop of Cold War-induced 'embedded liberalism' underwritten by active US economic and military support (Ruggie 1982), 'new regionalism' takes place in the post-Cold War era of intensified globalisation characterised by 'nonhegemonic interdependence' (Stallings and Streeck 1995: 67). It is primarily a product of new US foreign economic policy designed to foster a 'level playing field' in international trade and investment, namely an open global economy with minimum trade barriers.

However, the poorly regulated global economy, with a power to severely disrupt national economies, means that regionalism is promoted by national governments with mixed motives, as both a defence against globalisation and a way of taking advantage of it (Hveem 2000). Increasingly, regionalisation is seen as providing the optimum space in which national economies can combine to liberalise intra-regional economic transactions and mediate the destabilising effects of globalisation.

Many writers see in this ambiguity the potential for regional economic blocs to develop distinctive forms of capitalism based on the ideas of their respective regional leader(s). In other words, the regional leader's normative assumptions about capitalism and human development are expected to mould the characteristics of its neighbouring economies, leading to distinctive regional forms of capitalism and modes of regional integration (Stubbs 1995; Stallings and Streeck 1995; Beeson and Jayasuriya 1998). While Germany and the United States are said to be the leader of Europe and North America respectively, Japan is seen to be such a leader in East Asia because of the deep penetration of its industrial capital in the region (Thurow 1992; Hatch 2000). In short, post-Cold War IPE is increasingly seen to be characterised by a dynamic combination of cooperation and conflict between the three competing forms of capitalism embodied in the three mega-regional blocs. For our purpose, we need to examine both the nature of the emergent East Asian regionalism and the extent to which it is being underwritten by a supposedly distinctive Japan-led Asian capitalism, a topic to which I will now turn.

REGIONALISM IN PACIFIC ASIA

All three regions in the world economy are in the process of continuous evolution. While the European Union (EU) is engaged in its tumultuous eastward expansion, the talk in North America is to expand the North American Free Trade Agreement (NAFTA) to encompass the whole of the Americas. It has even been proposed that a Transatlantic Free Trade Agreement, a TAFTA, be established between NAFTA and the EU (Dicken 1998: 102).

However, compared with the other two regions, regional development in Pacific Asia suffers relative institutional deficit although the situation has been seen to be changing since 1997. Private sector actors rather than governmental initiatives have been the main driving force for regional economic integration. As a result, few regional institutions exist for inter-governmental collaboration (Ravenhill 1998: 247). The two exceptions are the loosely associated trans-Pacific Asia Pacific Economic Cooperation Forum (APEC), which was set up in 1989, and the ASEAN (Association of Southeast Asian Nations) Free Trade Area (AFTA), set up in 1992 by the six members of ASEAN, Malaysia, Singapore, Brunei, Indonesia, Thailand and the Philippines, and which now includes four other new members: Vietnam, Cambodia, the Lao People's Democratic Republic and Myanmar. However, in recent years, progress towards trade liberalisation has been painfully slow within the APEC forum, while that within AFTA has been accelerating (APEC 2000: Chapter 2). Moreover, there has been a move towards greater East Asian inter-governmental collaboration since 1997, a move that is yet to overcome many obstacles ahead. While history still casts a long shadow over East Asian regionalism, new geostrategic and political issues have also arisen due to the changing balance of power both between and within nations.

Competing visions: historical origin

Regional development in Pacific Asia has historically been shaped by the close interaction between the region's two dominant powers, the United States and Japan (Higgott and Stubbs 1995). Almost at the same time as a vague sense of 'Asianness' began to develop among the region's political and intellectual elites in the early twentieth century, a sensibility fed largely on the trauma of the Western incursions, a 'pan-Pacific' regionalist idea also began to emerge, based on interdependence and cultural exchange between Pacific Asia and North America. The latter saw the creation of such pre-war organisations as the non-governmental Institute of Pacific Relations in which many outstanding scholars and public figures from both sides of the Pacific participated (Borthwick 1992: 522; Woods 1993). Japan's attempt to create by military force a Greater East Asia Co-prosperity Sphere during World War II was the first time East Asian regionalism was invoked in an adversarial manner against trans-Pacific regionalism. As a result, it killed off both and sowed the seeds of the deep distrust of Japan felt by all the Asian nations that came under Japanese occupation.

The Cold War era saw the deepening of United States involvement in Pacific Asia in both military and economic affairs as it sought to contain communism in the region. Not only was it the region's largest market, but also its security linchpin, guaranteeing military security and political stability in both Northeast and Southeast Asia through a series of bilateral security treaties. While this tended to foster a trans-Pacific perspective in regional cooperation, economic and military cooperation was regarded by both sides of the Pacific as vital to the imperative of containing communism and promoting economic development.

However, the rise of Japan and the end of the Cold War led to a rapid integration of East Asian economies under the leadership of Japan. What Japan failed to do by military means began to look increasingly realisable by economic means. Both the 1985 US-initiated Plaza Accord, which forced a dramatic appreciation of the Japanese yen against the US dollar, and increasing US trade protectionism forced Japanese manufacturing industries to relocate, first to the NICs and then to the NECs, as they sought to maintain their manufacturing competitiveness in the world market. This large-scale inflow of Japanese FDI in Pacific Asia resulted in the establishment of close-knit production networks centred on Japanese capital, technology and management expertise, leading to de facto, as opposed to EU-style *de jure*, economic integration in the region. For their part, all East Asian governments showed willingness to let the pragmatic need for economic development over-ride historical animosities.

Herein lies the essence of the relationship between Japan and its neighbours in Pacific Asia: economic interdependence coexists with mutual distrust in other spheres, military in particular. Consequently, despite its towering economic presence in the region, Japan has never taken the political lead to promote inter-governmental cooperation. Furthermore, continuing economic reliance on the US market, by both Japan and its Asian neighbours, together with other geostrategic and political factors (to be discussed later), means that today both streams of regionalism have their adherents in Pacific Asia. Nothing was more instructive of this than the circumstances surrounding the creation of APEC.

APEC and Asia-Pacific regionalism

Although APEC is the only trans-Pacific institution, it was a product of Australian initiative. A major factor behind this initiative was Australia's worry about the tendency towards trade protectionism in the Pacific region, with which it increasingly identified itself. This concern stemmed from the faltering GATT negotiations on global trade and the apparent US move from GATT *multilateralism*, i.e. the implementation of trade liberalisation by all GATT members under GATT supervision, to regionalism in an attempt to exert greater pressure on the EU and East Asia to liberalise trade. In 1988, the United States signed with Canada the Canada–United States Free Trade Agreement, which later became a major building block for NAFTA. Clearly feeling the need for a fall-back position in the form of closer trans-Pacific cooperation, the Australian government invented the entire concept of Asia-Pacific regionalism in the institutional form of APEC.

The proposal won immediate support from both sides of the Pacific with the notable exception of Malaysia, whose prime minister, Dr Mahathir, came up with an exclusively 'Asian' institution he called the East Asian Economic Grouping (EAEG), to be separate from APEC. There were several reasons for APEC support, mostly to do with the region's economic and security realities. From the viewpoint of Japan, which was the main target of the Unites States' aggressive unilateral trade offensive, a loosely associated APEC suited its needs. Bringing the United States into regional issues helped keep it engaged in Asia and promoted the region's economy. It might even help constrain US behaviour by thwarting its resort to unilateralism, i.e. the demand that Japan carry out fundamental reforms to its economic system to remove 'structural impediments' to US exports. Moreover, the non-binding nature of APEC was thought to prevent the United States from imposing its own rules of economic behaviour on other members.

Other smaller East Asian countries shared Japan's views in addition to being fearful of dominance by any one of the region's three big powers: Japan, the United States and China. Given the region's precarious security situation, APEC also came to be seen as having the potential to play a positive role in the region's security. Most APEC members saw it as a good way to sustain an active US role in regional security matters by increasing its involvement in the regional economy under the auspices of APEC (Ravenhill 1998: 257–8).

Most importantly, the APEC initiative also enjoyed US support for two reasons. First, it gave the United States a foothold in the Pacific region from which it could stop it sliding towards 'fortress' regionalism, i.e. protectionist trade policies against non-members. Second, it gave the United States a regional forum in which to promote democratisation and civil and political rights. The United States saw it as an important part of its foreign policy to help construct a 'Pacific community of nations built on shared strength, prosperity, and commitment to democratic values as well as regional approaches to global problems' (US Congress 1993: 7). However, this is the area that has generated disharmony among some East Asian members, particularly those whose politicians are critical of 'Western' notions of democracy and human rights. They accuse the United States of 'cultural imperialism', of seeking to impose 'Western' values on Asian cultures (Stuart and Tow 1995: 12).

What has transpired is a strong support for Asia-Pacific regionalism in East Asia because of a high degree of shared economic and military interest between both sides of the Pacific. In terms of economic interest, the United States remains the largest export market for most of the region's economies. As regards security, most East Asian members trust the United States more than they trust their neighbours. The recent rise of China, and its involvement in territorial disputes with a number of Southeast Asian countries over several islands in the South China Sea, has rekindled and reinforced distrust of the region's historical power. Although there are disputes between the United States and several of its Asian allies over the distribution of costs of security provision, the overwhelming desire in East Asia is for the United States to be actively engaged in the region. This desire is further strengthened by the security uncertainties created by the two

Koreas and the two Chinas. In short, there is strong pragmatic and strategic support for APEC regionalism.

East Asian regionalism: from EAEC to 'ASEAN+3'

Like trans-Pacific regionalism, East Asian regionalism first reasserted itself after the Cold War, in response to the APEC initiative, to be more specific. As noted earlier, Malaysia responded to the APEC proposal by putting forward a rival plan based on an exclusive Asian membership. However, because of strong opposition from the United States, which was suspicious of Dr Mahathir's protectionist tendency, ambivalence from Japan, which was keen to engage the United States in Asian economy and security, and a cool reception from most other East Asian nations, Mahathir's plan was diluted. Instead of a separate EAEG, an East Asian Economic Caucus (EAEC) *within* APEC was set up, consisting of all the Asian members.

However, the 1997 financial crisis has been seen as a turning point in East Asian regionalism. Since then, a number of decisive steps have been taken, which are moving the region increasingly in the direction first mapped out by Dr Mahathir (Bergsten 2000). Most notably, an effective EAEG is beginning to take shape in the form of the so-called 'ASEAN+3', consisting of the ten ASEAN nations and the three Northeast Asian countries of China, Japan, and South Korea. The coordination of financial and trade policies is now on the regional agenda. According to Bergsten (ibid.), the 'ASEAN+3' 'has become the most active regional grouping outside Europe', boasting an institutional structure increasingly akin to G7 and already more sophisticated than NAFTA.

Driven by a desire to avoid a similar crisis to that experienced in 1997, regionalism is proceeding rapidly on financial cooperation. Initiatives adopted include a region-wide system of currency swaps to help members deal with future financial crises, a surveillance mechanism using early-warning indicators within ASEAN to try to anticipate and head off future crises, and mutual monitoring and sharing of information on short-term capital movements in the vicinity among Northeast Asian countries. There is also much talk of common currency baskets and joint intervention arrangements, to replace both the discredited dollar pegs of the past and the costly free floats imposed by the crisis.

These developments, suggests Dieter (2000), mark the beginning of 'monetary regionalism' in East Asia, an idea originating (again) with Malaysia, which, during the 1997–8 financial crisis, suggested the setting up of a Japan-led Asian Monetary Fund (AMF) to enable the region to tackle the then developing and future financial crisis. This was also envisaged as an important break away from the dominance of Western financial institutions such as the IMF. Precisely because of this, the United States mounted a

vigorous opposition to the proposal, which was eventually shelved largely
due to three factors: Japan's unwillingness to assert itself; the 'large dose
of "Asian way" hubris' accompanying it, and its ill-thought-out nature
(Higgott 2000b: 269). The revival of the plan barely 3 years later, this time
under a far more active Japanese leadership and with positive support from
China, argues Dieter (2000), demonstrates a determination on the part of
both Japan and the region as a whole to have an independent voice in the
global economy, a determination strengthened by the widespread perception
of the IMF's mismanagement of the 1997–8 financial crisis.

Since 1997, there has also been a flurry of activities on trade cooperation,
although this is not confined to East Asian nations. A growing number of
subregional agreements are being negotiated, both among East Asian
economies and along the Pacific rim, involving Japan, South Korea,
Singapore, Mexico, Canada, Australia and New Zealand (APEC 2000:
Chapter 2). However, what is notable is the incipient move signalling the
emergence of an East Asian Free Trade Area that covers the whole of Pacific
Asia, spanning Northeast and Southeast Asia. The basis of this speculation
is the fact that all three countries, namely China, Japan and South Korea,
are currently studying the plan for a North-East Asia Free Trade Area,
consisting of these countries, and its possible merger with AFTA.

It appears that since the 1997–8 crisis, the East Asian political leaders
have demonstrated more political willingness to engage in closer regional
cooperation, a willingness spurred partly by their dissatisfaction with the
slow global and regional movement towards the trade liberalisation on
which the region relies for its post-crisis economic recovery, and partly
by their resentment of what is perceived to be Western dominance of the
global economy. Consequently, regional integration in East Asia is now
characterised by three dimensions: an incipient move towards what Dieter
calls 'monetary regionalism', centred on a Japan-led AMF, a multiplication
of bilateral and plurilateral trade pacts both within the region and between
East Asian members and other regional members, and a closely integrated
regional production network centred on Japanese MNCs. But to what
extent, if at all, is this regional development being underpinned by a
Japanese-based Asian form of capitalism in contention with the West, as
claimed by some students of Pacific Asian affairs?

TOWARDS EAST ASIAN REGIONALISM: A CRITICAL ANALYSIS

The move towards East Asian regionalism has been moderate and remains at
an early stage. Its future development would depend as much on international
factors as on regional and national dynamics. As Bergsten (2000) points out,

any outbreak of US or European protectionism could serve as an extra push to East Asian regionalism. While it is difficult, if not impossible, to predict the future shape of East Asian regionalism, it is nevertheless instructive to highlight the major issues facing its development. For our purpose, I focus on the following two: the question of Japanese intellectual and political leadership, and the changing national political context in which the 'Asian way' is being defined and the Asian community imagined.

The question of Japanese leadership

Being the region's towering economic power, responsible for two-thirds of its output, Japan has long been expected to be the leading force behind East Asian regionalism. Indeed, it was mainly the Japanese model of capitalism, with its deep social embeddedness, that was hailed as the normative foundation for the emerging third, i.e. Asian, form of capitalism. East Asian regional integration is thus effectively seen as the regionalisation of the Japanese form of capitalism.

This perspective is accurate only in so far as regional production is concerned and in most other economic areas, Japan's leadership role is yet to come to the fore. This has less to do with Japan's weak military position resulting from its post-war 'peace constitution', which bars Japan from becoming a regional military power, than with its inability to shake off its inwardly looking mercantilist mentality and adapt to a changed world. Its long economic stagnation and political immobilism and deep involvement in the Asian financial crisis are but two of the most noteworthy indications of Japan's hitherto limited intellectual and political leadership in East Asian regional development.

As noted earlier, regional integration in East Asia has gone furthest in the form of production networks centred on Japanese MNCs. Inter-governmental cooperation, on the other hand, is prominent only by its absence. To note this, however, is different from saying that the Japanese government has played no role in East Asian regional integration. On the contrary, Pyle (1996: 132–3) has convincingly demonstrated how, in the late 1980s, the Japanese government engineered this *particular* form of regional integration by coordinating Japanese FDI, trade and official aid as 'three sides of one body' to ensure Japan's financial and industrial penetration of Pacific Asia. Therefore, what concerns us is not the lack of political leadership per se that characterises Japan's role in East Asian regionalisation but the nature and form that this leadership role has taken.

Like the US promotion of global liberalism and APEC regionalism, which is motivated partly by national interest, Japan's active promotion of Japanese FDI-led regionalisation in East Asia is motivated by similar considerations. The only difference is that Japan defines its national interest in *mercantilist* rather than liberal terms, an approach that became increasingly unsustainable after the end of the Cold War and its associated 'embedded liberalism' in the global economy. When the United States intensified its pressure on Japan to liberalise its economy so as to open its market to foreign trade and investment, the LDP found itself immobilised by the anti-liberal coalition, which it had long nurtured for its electoral survival. The bursting of its economic bubble in the early 1990s, which saddled many Japanese banks and *keiretsu* with bad loans, a situation similar to that in Thailand, Indonesia and South Korea which triggered the 1997–8 financial crisis, further reinforced the dilemma in which the Japanese government found itself. In an attempt to help Japan escape, delay or ease the pain of domestic reform, the Japanese government found in regional relocation of Japanese corporations an excellent solution to its domestic political immobilism. Hence its 'trinity' approach to East Asian regional integration based on the coordination of Japanese FDI, trade and aid in the region (ibid.).

A major consequence of Japan's mercantilist approach to East Asian regional integration is the generation of economic conflicts between Japan and its economic partners and the deepening mistrust between the two sides, a sentiment unconducive to inter-governmental collaboration. Japanese MNCs, for example, have been heavily criticised by their host governments for advancing Japanese interests at the expense of local economies. The issue often involves these companies' failure to 'localise' their management, as they tend to redeploy large numbers of excess Japanese employees to the Asian affiliates as a way of easing employment problems in Japan (Hatch 2000: 388–9). Another dispute involves trade between Japan and its East Asian partners, which have collectively replaced the United States as the largest export market for Japanese goods since 1991. This change in Japan's trade pattern has been accompanied by a repetition of similar trade disputes between Japan and the United States; since 1993, East Asia has replaced the United States as Japan's largest source of trade surplus while at the same time remaining overwhelmingly reliant on the US market for its manufactured goods (Friedland 1994: 40). In fact, the US market has been crucial to the region's post-1997 export-led recovery. All these have added new dimensions to the distrust between Japan and its Asian partners, preventing Japan from exercising a leadership role in East Asian regionalism.

The limit to Japan's mercantilist approach to East Asian regionalisation was exposed to the full both during and after the 1997–8 Asian financial crisis. As Higgott (2000a: 263–4) noted, Japan played a central role in the crisis by creating overcapacity in the region without fulfilling the role of a market of last resort to absorb it. Furthermore, when the financial crisis escalated into economic crisis, neither was Japan in a position to help its neighbours' economic recovery, as it was itself seeking to export out of its decade-long recession. This made East Asia's similar strategy of recovery much more difficult. It is therefore ironic that Japanese capitalism has been touted in some quarters of Pacific Asia and beyond as the normative basis of East Asian regionalism at a time when its fundamental weaknesses have been exposed to the full by the 1997–8 crisis.

The changing normative basis of the 'Asian way'

The limit to regionalising Japanese capitalism in East Asia is further reinforced by the increasingly divergent national development trajectories in the region. The much vaunted 'Asian way', which for a long time provided the region's political leaders with a cloak in which to dress up their authoritarian policies in the name of culture, has increasingly been subject to contested interpretations thanks to democratisation and the traumatic experience of the 1997–8 financial crisis. Consequently, both the Japanese model of political economy and the many aspects of the officially defined 'Asian way' have been called into question.

The divergent approaches to regional cooperation between the democratising countries and the rest were clearly identifiable during the 1997–8 crisis. In all the affected societies (and indeed in the West as well), there was widespread dissatisfaction with the way the IMF mishandled the crisis by demanding public expenditure cuts, whereas the cause of the crisis lay in private rather than public debt. However, few countries went as far as Malaysia by appealing to the 'Asian way' both to justify domestic cronyism and to promote East Asian regionalism. In fact, both South Korea and Thailand adopted opposite approaches in their efforts to tackle the crisis and to move towards regional cooperation. In South Korea, President Kim Dae Jung (1998), who took over office during the crisis, openly denounced the 'collusive links between companies and politicians' as the root cause of the crisis and unequivocally committed his country to 'democracy and a free market economy'.

Similarly, since 1997, Thailand, together with Singapore, has been instrumental within the ASEAN forum in moving the organisation away from its traditional 'ASEAN way' of regional cooperation to 'enhanced interaction' (Haacke 1999). The key feature of the 'ASEAN way' is its stress on the paramount importance of national sovereignty and non-interference in members' domestic affairs. Consequently, regional cooperation within ASEAN is characterised by a preference for dialogue and informal personal contact as against formal institutionalisation. In contrast, 'enhanced interaction' sees greater ASEAN transparency with regard to its members' economic and financial data as essential to strengthening the region's ability to deal with future economic problems. A concrete example of this is the endorsement by ASEAN finance ministers in October 1998 of a peer review and information exchange in areas such as interest and exchange rates as well as capital flows (Tassell, in Haacke 1999). As Haacke (1999: 605) explains, this in practice means that ASEAN finance ministers are now called upon to highlight economic risks in the economies of member states, to recommend policy responses, and to encourage early action in relation to these points. Therefore, 'enhanced interaction' almost certainly marks the beginning of a new vision of regional cooperation, one based on formal institutions rather than personal interactions.

What is emerging in East Asia today is thus more than one voice on the region's political and cultural identity, thanks to the spread of democracy and the need to establish new forms of state capacity in an age of globalisation and liberalisation. Gone are the days when the state monopolised both national and regional political decision making behind the mask of the 'Asian way'. Not only has the Japanese model of political economy lost its political and intellectual appeal as a normative basis for East Asian regionalism, the very notion of the 'Asian way' has come under increasing democratic contestation and been subject to new interpretations. Therefore, the question 'what sort of region in what sort of world?', to borrow from Buzan (1998), will be increasingly decided by the people of East Asia in partnership with their governments rather than by governments alone. An increasing number of political leaders in the region have now realised that the quest for regional equality in the international system is achievable only by according the same equality to their own people in national politics.

CONCLUSION

Regional development in East Asia has historically been subject to two conflicting influences: one based on the region's collective sense of humiliation suffered at the hands of the West and its resultant desire to be independent and equal to the West in the international community; the other based on trans-Pacific cooperation and shared liberal democratic values. During the Cold War, East Asia emerged as one of the tripartite regions that dominated the global economy against the background of US-sanctioned 'embedded liberalism'. However, increasing economic strength led to 'Asian way' hubris, which claimed the superiority of East Asian/Japanese capitalism over 'Western' capitalism. Despite the region's complex intertwining of national economic, security and geostrategic interests, which led to the parallel development of both strands of regionalism, 'Asian way' subscribers claimed the predominance of East Asian regionalism supposedly underpinned by Japanese mercantilism.

The end of the Cold War and the 1997–8 financial crisis have fundamentally transformed the international and national contexts of politics, the interplay of which shapes regional development. At the international level, despite the continuing dominance of the notion of national interest in the nation-state's pursuit of foreign policy, the increasing importance of liberal democratic values in international affairs has led to a demand for political as well as economic liberalisation. The notion of national sovereignty, which has long been the over-riding principle in international politics and thus jealously guarded by national governments, is being eroded, albeit slowly. The disputes on such issues as democracy and human rights, largely between the United States and some East Asian political leaders in Pacific Asia, testify to this changing reality.

However, it would be grossly wrong to deduce from the above that there is greater potential for East Asia to develop a regionalism based on illiberal values such as the so-called 'Asian way'. The end of the Cold War has not only reinstated the liberal democratic values at the level of international politics, but has also given ordinary people in Pacific Asia the opportunity to participate in national politics. Democratisation, a result partly of the changed international context of politics and partly of the changed domestic balance of power brought by decades of sustained economic development, has fundamentally transformed the national political context in which national interest is defined. The outbreak of the 1997–8 financial crisis in the region has further reinforced this development. Rather than sharing their national leaders' vision of a region governed by the illiberal values embodied in the 'Asian way', the people of Pacific Asia have increasingly realised that the best way to advance their national interest is to embrace liberal democracy at both national and regional levels. Nowhere is this better illustrated than in Japan, where long adherence to economic and political illiberalism has resulted in its loss of political leadership in Pacific Asia contrary to the much hyped anticipation. In short, the contested visions of regionalism in Pacific Asia have increasingly been fought in ideological rather than cultural terms. The difference between East Asian regionalism and Asia-Pacific regionalism is not about cultural difference between the East and West, nor about the geographical delineation of a region, but about its normative boundary between liberalism and illiberalism.

Conclusion

Since the end of World War II, which brought about worldwide decolonisation in the non-European parts of the world, Pacific Asia is the only region that has realised the dream of development thanks to decades of sustained economic growth. This remarkable achievement has not only lifted millions of the region's population out of poverty but has also sparked off an international debate on the lessons, both positive and negative, that can be drawn from the region's development experience.

This book is part of the ongoing debate on the nature and implications of post-war economic, social and political development in Pacific Asia. I began this study by noting the contested nature of the concept of development, suggesting that both the development process and the perception of it are inescapably influenced by political contestation and ideological differences. Based on this understanding, I focused my spotlight on the ideological nature of the cultural – New Orientalist – discourse, one of the influential perspectives on development in Pacific Asia. Throughout the study, I sought to demonstrate how, within Pacific Asia, New Orientalism was used by the political leadership as a powerful ideology to justify development policies necessitated by often very different national imperatives. The ascendance of New Orientalism in Pacific Asia, I suggested, was part of the global move towards economic liberalism and social conservatism, which was symptomatic of the backlash against the post-war liberal welfare state that was established in the West. It is from this perspective that I also sought to analyse the emerging discourse on East Asian regionalism, which claimed the latter's normative underpinning by Asian/Japanese capitalism. The 1997–8 Asian financial crisis, I argued, could be seen to have put paid to this apolitically conceived cultural wishful thinking as well as to the authoritarian developmental state, which had thrived in an age of Cold War-induced embedded liberalism.

The culturalist perspective is not the only perspective that has been subject to critical examination in this book. Our emphasis on the *politics* of development has also led to our questioning the other major perspective on development in Pacific Asia, which is equally deficient due to its apolitical conceptualisation of development. This is the neo-classical political economic perspective, which tends to see the construction of a market economy as a technical, as opposed to a political, process that requires little legitimation by the state. Economic development in Pacific Asia, which laid the basis for the region's social and political development, as we have seen, has demonstrated, by way of both the diversities and the similarities of the region's national experiences, the crucial role of the state in shaping national development. Although all the economies took off under the auspices of an authoritarian state, a situation abetted by the Cold War, the manner in which different states exercised control over their respective societies nevertheless differed a great deal, as reflected in their different institutional capacities to work *with* society. In many ways, these differences were themselves a legacy of the nation's unique history and social structure, which constrained the state's policy options. Hence the difference between the largely meritocratic states in the ethnically homogeneous East Asian NICs on the one hand, and the 'administocratic' states in the multi-ethnic Southeast Asian NECs on the other. The states *within* each group also differed for similar reasons, ranging from Malaysia's unashamedly 'ethnic state' to Indonesia's patrimonial state, which economically colluded with the Chinese and politically excluded them; from Taiwan's mainlander-dominated quasi-Leninist state, which kept the Taiwanese-dominated industries at arm's length, to South Korea's *chaebol* state, characterised by its strategic alliance with the *chaebols*; from Singapore's one-party Leninist state, which allied itself with foreign capital, to Thailand's bureaucratic state, which sought to assimilate the Chinese into Thai society and politics. As I have shown, these differences have had a profound impact on individual nation's political and social as well as economic development. In other words, the states in Pacific Asia, through their key – albeit different – roles in economic development, have been a major political force in shaping the region's national development.

The rise of Pacific Asia in the international community has undoubtedly raised many issues that will continue to be debated by historians, economists, sociologists and political scientists for many years to come. However, as the world has entered the twenty-first century, and as the intellectual and political search continues for solutions to the scourge of poverty, which still plagues the majority of the world's population, the second half of the twentieth century could well be seen as a period of history in which the people of Pacific Asia had to endure the burden of development under authoritarian governments, which nevertheless engineered the endeavour in a favourable international environment. It was also a time that witnessed the empowerment of the people by development; they then came to question not only their political leaders' version of their nations' cultural heritage and political future but also their monopoly on power. For those Western opinion leaders and policy makers, who worked in international agencies charged with assisting Third World development, the hardest lesson of Pacific Asian development must be the realisation that the market economy, which had hitherto proved the most effective system of wealth generation, needs a helping hand from the state both for its construction and successful functioning and for utilising its fruits for social and democratic development, without which economic growth can only bring about strife and instability rather than development.

Appendix 1: country timelines

JAPAN

1603–1868	Tokugawa shogunate
1868	Meiji Restoration
1889	Meiji Constitution
1890	Parliamentary government established
1894–5	Sino-Japanese War; annexation of Taiwan
1910	Annexation of Korea
1918	First party government formed; Taisho democracy begins
1925	Universal male suffrage
1931–45	Invasion and partial occupation of China
1941–5	Attacks on Pearl Harbor; occupation of Southeast Asia
1945	Atomic bombing of Hiroshima and Nagasaki; Allied Occupation begins
1947	New constitution and major political reforms
1948	'Reverse course' begins
1951	San Francisco Peace Treaty; US–Japan security pact signed
1952	Occupation ends
1954	Self-defence forces established
1955	JSP and LDP formed through merger, beginning of LDP supremacy
1960	Signing of new US–Japan security treaty amid mass protests; 'income-doubling' policy announced
1972	Diplomatic relations restored with China
1974	First oil shock; ambitious welfare policy abandoned
1976	Arrest of former Prime Minister Tanaka over Lockheed scandal
1980	Beginning of US–Japan trade disputes

1985	Plaza Accord to deflate the value of the US dollar against the yen
1988	Record trade surplus with the United States; US–Japan trade disputes intensified
1989	Death of Emperor Hirohito; Showa period ends and Heisei era begins; forced resignation of Prime Minister Takeshita over Recruit scandal; many leading politicians also implicated
1990–1	Tokyo stock market crashed; end of the bubble economy
1991	Gulf War raises issues about Japan's 'peace constitution'
1992	Economic slowdown begins; Japan New Party formed by an LDP breakaway faction led by Hosokawa; Sagawa Kyubin scandal breaks
1993	An LDP breakaway faction forms JRP; LDP loses power in 1993 general election; coalition formed under Hosokawa
1994	Electoral reforms implemented; coalition formed between LDP and the socialist party SDPJ, the leader of which, Murayama, takes over as prime minister
1995	Kobe earthquake; sarin gas attack by Aum Shinrikyo sect in Tokyo underground
1996	First general election held under the new electoral system; LDP leader Hashimoto becomes prime minister
1997	LDP regains majority position in the lower house of the Diet; continuing economic stagnation, falling consumer demand, rising public debt and unemployment; sharp increase in male suicide

INDONESIA

First to sixth century	Hindu and Buddhist cultural influences from India spread to Sumatra and Java
Seventh to twelfth century	Contact with Arabia, India, and China; Hinduism and Buddhism flourish on Java and Bali respectively
Fifteenth century	Rapid spread of Islam in Sumatra and Java
1619	Dutch build fort at Batavia (Jakarta)
Seventeenth century	Dutch East India Company monopolises spice trade, defeats native sultanates, and assumes sovereign powers

1799	The Netherlands assumes direct control of the East Indies
Nineteenth century	Commercial exploitation and plantation economy flourishes
1900–1930s	Development of Indonesian nationalism
1942–5	Japanese Occupation
1945–9	Nationalists proclaim Indonesian independence with Sukarno as first president; War of Independence fought with Dutch
1949	Dutch recognise Indonesian independence
1950–7	Ineffective parliamentary democracy under President Sukarno
1957–65	'Guided democracy'; Sukarno suspends Parliament and dissolves political parties; 'confrontation' policy against Malaysia
1965–7	General Suharto's 'incremental coups' lead to the massacre of alleged communists and Chinese; New Order proclaimed; end of confrontation with Malaysia
1968	Suharto 'elected' president (beginning of the seven successive 5-yearly terms)
1976	Indonesia invades East Timor
1980	Petition of the Fifty
1989	Student protests and social unrest
1991	Political campaigns banned on university campuses; freedom of speech restricted
1993	Suharto re-elected for a sixth term
1997	Asian financial crisis; IMF bail-out sought; ethnic violence and secessionist movements break out
1998	Suharto re-elected for the seventh term; mass protests and violence spread; Suharto forced to resign
1998–9	Vice-President Habibie takes over; ethnic violence and separatist movements continue in East Timor, Aceh, Irian Jaya and other parts of Indonesia
June 1999	First democratic election held for four decades; Over forty political parties contest the election
1999	Abdurrahman Wahid elected president; East Timor gains independence from Indonesia after a referendum
July 2001	Wahid dismissed by parliament based on charges of corruption and misrule; Megawati takes over as president

MALAYSIA

Eighth to thirteenth century	Sumatran Srivijayan Empire controls Malacca Strait
1403	Port of Malacca founded
Fifteenth century	Malacca centre of world spice trade; Islam becomes dominant
1511	Portuguese capture Malacca
1641	Dutch expel Portuguese and rule Malacca for 150 years
1786–1824	British and Dutch struggle for supremacy in the Malacca Strait
1819	British build fort at Singapore
1824	Anglo-Dutch treaty gives Penang, Malacca, and Singapore to Great Britain
1826	Straits Settlements administered from Singapore
1839–1942	'White Rajahs' (the Brooke family) rule Sarawak
1867	Straits Settlements placed under Colonial Office
1874–1925	British establish protectorate over inland and east coast sultanates on Malay peninsula
1881	British North Borneo Company controls Sabah
Late nineteenth century	Indians immigrate to work Malayan rubber plantations and Chinese immigrate to work Malayan tin mines
1942	Japan captures Malay peninsula and Singapore
1942–5	Japanese Occupation
1945–8	Malayan Union; growth of political movements
1947–60	Communist armed offensive; assassination of British high commissioner
1957	Independence for eleven states of Malay peninsula
1963	Federation of Malaysia established, consisting of Malaya, Singapore, Sarawak, and Sabah
1965	Singapore secedes from Malaysia
1966	Peace treaty with Indonesia
1969	Racial violence between Malays and Chinese; beginning of 'ethnic authoritarianism'
1971	New Economic Order introduced
1977	Violent political disturbances; state of emergency declared
1981	Mahathir elected prime minister

1987	106 people detained under Internal Security Act
1990	Mahathir re-elected prime minister
1993	Parliament curtails sultans' legal immunity
1995	Mahathir wins third term
1997	Asian financial crisis
2000	Mahathir wins fourth term

SINGAPORE

Eighth to thirteenth century	Sumatran Srivijayan Empire controls Malacca Strait
Thirteenth century	Unimportant settlement of Temasek renamed Singapura (Lion City), but it remains merely a fishing village
1786–1824	British and Dutch struggle for supremacy in the Malacca Strait
1819	British fort and trading post established by Sir Stamford Raffles
1824	Anglo-Dutch treaty gives Penang, Malacca, and Singapore to Great Britain
1826	Singapore incorporated into Straights Settlements along with Penang and Malacca; Singapore administered from British India
1832	Singapore becomes administrative centre of Straights settlements
1869	Opening of Suez Canal greatly increases importance of Singapore
1942–5	Japanese Occupation
1959	Singapore becomes an autonomous state within British Commonwealth; PAP comes to power; Lee Kuan Yew becomes prime minister
1963	Federation of Malaysia formed, with Singapore as a constituent state
1964	Communal riots
1965	Singapore expelled from Malaysia and forced to declare independence
1981	PAP loses its monopoly on parliament after the Workers' Party wins one seat through a by-election
1984	PAP electoral support drops to a historical low; launch

of political reforms and Confucianisation campaign to counter 'Western' influence of individualism

1990   Goh Chok Tong replaces Lee Kuan Yew as prime minister, but Lee remains powerful by virtue of being senior minister

1994   American citizen flogged with rattan cane as punishment for vandalism

1997   Prime Minister Goh hails PAP's increase share of the vote in the parliamentary election as a triumph of 'Asian democracy' over 'Western style liberalism'; Singapore escapes the worst of the Asian financial crisis

SOUTH KOREA

Seventh century   Unification of the Korean peninsula by the Kingdom of Silla

660–918   The Kingdom of Silla; widespread influence of Buddhism and Confucianism

918–1392   Koryo Dynasty

1392–1910   Choson (Yi) Dynasty; establishment of a Confucian state

1443   The Korean phonetic system, *Han'gul*, invented

Late sixteenth century to early seventeenth century   Repeated invasion by the Japanese and nomadic Manchu

Late seventeenth century to eighteenth century   Spread of Catholicism

Late nineteenth century to early twentieth century   Spread of Protestantism and *Tonghak* (Eastern Learning), social and political upheaval; great power rivalry over Korea between Japan, China and Russia

1905   Japan wins the Russo-Japanese War; Korea becomes a Japanese protectorate

1910   Korea annexed by Japan

1948   Republic of Korea established

1948–60   Ruled by Syngman Rhee; economic drift and political disturbances

1950–3   Korean War

1961–79	Ruled by General and later President Park Chung Hee; rapid economic development begins
1979	Park assassinated
May 1980	Kwangju Massacre
1980–7	Ruled by General Chun Doo Hwan
1985–7	Intensified opposition movements inside and outside parliament, calling for constitutional reform
June 1987	General Rho Tae Woo announces intention to hold direct presidential election and to initiate democratic reforms demanded by the public; beginning of Korea's democratisation
October 1987	New constitution approved by a referendum
December 1987	First direct presidential election held, Rho wins due to divided opposition
April 1988	President Rho's party fails to achieve an overall majority in parliament for the first time since the party's formation in 1980, setting the trend for US-style 'split government'
December 1992	Kim Young Sam is the first civilian to be elected president since 1961; economic and financial liberalisation pursued under Kim's presidency
1996	South Korea becomes a member of the OECD
1997–8	Financial crisis spreads to South Korea; IMF bail-out sought; Kim Dae Jung elected president

TAIWAN

1590	Portuguese arrive on Taiwan, calling it Ilha Formosa, 'Beautiful Island'
1646	Dutch seize control of the island from Spanish
Early seventeenth century	Large numbers of Chinese begin to settle on the island
1661	Dutch ousted by a large influx of Chinese Ming Dynasty refugees
1683	Manchu-established Ching Dynasty takes control of Taiwan
1858	Open to Europeans after nearly two centuries of seclusion
1894–5	China loses the Sino-Japanese War, Taiwan ceded to Japan

1895–1945	Japanese colony
1945	Taiwan returned to China, ruled by KMT government
1947	Taiwan Uprising; martial law introduced; beginning of Taiwan nationalism and democratic movement
1949	KMT flee to Taiwan after loss of the civil war to the communists on mainland China
1954	Taiwan–US mutual defence treaty signed
1960s–1980s	Rapid economic growth
1971	Taiwan loses its UN membership to the People's Republic of China, triggering mass mobilisation for democratisation
1979	Kaohsiung incident
Late 1970s to late 1980s	Steady Taiwanisation of the KMT and the state
1986	DPP formed despite martial law
1987	Martial law lifted; the democratic process begins
1988	Lee Tenghui becomes the first Taiwanese to hold both the KMT Chair and state presidency following the death of Chiang Chingkuo, his mainland predecessor
1989	Opposition parties legalised
1991–2	Direct legislative elections, ending the 'Long Parliament' first elected on mainland China in the late 1940s
1996	Lee Tenghui becomes the first directly elected president amid military threats from mainland China
1997	Taiwan survives the financial crisis largely unscathed
March 2001	Chen Shuibian, leader of the DPP, elected president

THAILAND

Eleventh century	Ethnic Tai begin migrating from Yunnan province of China
1238	Sukhothai Kingdom
1350	Ayutthayan Kingdom
1764	Burmese invade and destroy Ayutthayan but are expelled
1767–82	Thai makes a rapid recovery under military leader Taksin; Thai Kingdom united
1782	Chakri Dynasty begins
1851	Coronation of moderniser King Mongkut (Rama IV)
1855	King Mongkut signs treaty of friendship and commerce with Britain

1893	Fighting between French and Siamese forces; Laos becomes French protectorate
1896	Siam neutralised by both Britain and France
1909	Siam relinquishes northern Malay states to Britain
1912	Military revolt suppressed
1932	Bloodless coup leads to constitutional monarchy
1939	Name of country changed from Siam to Thailand
1941	Thailand sides with Japan; gains territory from all its neighbours
1946	Thailand returns territory to its neighbours
1947–73	Series of military coups and periodic elections; military-dominated bureaucratic authoritarianism
1957	Marshal Sarit Thanarat takes power and lays the foundation for Thailand's economic take-off during his 6-year rule
1973	Popular revolt; King Bhumipol Adulyadej (Rama IX) withdraws support from military regime; 3 years of civilian democratic rule follows
1974	New constitution legalises political parties
1975	Legislative elections
1976	Military seizes power; 1975 constitution annulled
1979–91	Legislative elections and semi-democracy; transition to liberal corporatism dominated by businesses
1991	Bloodless coup temporarily ends transition to democracy; provisional civilian prime minister
1992	General election won by a coalition of civilian parties following student-led uprisings against the military, which led to the tragedy of Black May; Chuan Leekpai becomes prime minister
1995	Constitutional reforms approved by parliament
1997	New constitution promulgated; the financial crisis breaks out; IMF bail-out sought
2000	First election to the Senate held under the new constitution
2001	Business tycoon Thaksin Shinawatra elected prime minister

Appendix 2: key historical and contemporary personalities in Pacific Asia

JAPAN

Post-war prime ministers

Prime minister	Date elected	Party
Prince Higashikuni	August 1945	–
Kijuro Shidehara	October 1945	–
Shigeru Yoshida	May 1946	JLP
Tetsu Katayama	May 1947	JSP
Hitoshi Ashida	March 1948	DP
Shigeru Yoshida	October 1948	DLP/LP
Ichiro Hatoyama	December 1954	JDP/LDP
Tanzan Ishibashi	December 1956	LDP
Nobusuke Kishi	February 1957	LDP
Hayato Ikeda	July 1960	LDP
Eisaku Sato	November 1964	LDP
Kakuei Tanaka	July 1972	LDP
Takeo Miki	December 1974	LDP
Masayoshi Ohira	December 1978	LDP
Zenko Suzuki	July 1980	LDP
Yasuhiro Nakasone	November 1982	LDP
Noboru Takeshita	November 1987	LDP
Sosuke Uno	June 1989	LDP
Toshiki Kaifu	August 1989	LDP
Kiichi Miyazawa	November 1991	LDP
Morihiro Hosokawa	August 1993	JNP
Tsutomu Hata	April 1994	JRP
Tomiichi Murayama	June 1994	SDPJ
Ryutaro Hashimoto	January 1996	LDP
Keizo Obuchi	July 1998	LDP
Yoshiro Mori	April 2000	LDP
Junichiro Koizumi	April 2001	LDP

DLP, Democratic Liberal Party; DP, Democratic Party; JDP, Japan Democratic Party; JLP, Japan Liberal Party; JSP, Japan Socialist Party; JNP, Japan New Party; JRP, Japan Renewal Party; LDP, Liberal Democratic Party; LP, Liberal Party; SDPJ, Social Democratic Party of Japan.

INDONESIA

Sukarno The founding father of the Indonesian nation and first president after Indonesia gained independence from the Netherlands in 1949. Ousted by General Suharto in the 1965–7 coups, Sukarno died in 1970, aged 69.

Suharto A military general, who seized power in 1967 through 2 years of 'incremental coups', in which hundreds of thousands of alleged communists and Chinese were killed. His highly personalised 'New Order' rule, which ended with his forced resignation in May 1998 amid widespread protests and violence, would go down in Indonesian history as both corrupt and an era of rapid economic growth.

Abdurrahman Wahid A moderate Muslim cleric educated in Indonesia, Egypt, Iraq and Canada, Wahid was elected president by the People's Consultative Committee (MPR) in October 1999 after his party, the National Awakening Party, had come fourth in the parliamentary elections held in June 1999, the first democratic elections since the late 1950s. However, his presidency ended in his dismissal by the MPR in July 2001, based on charges of corruption and misrule.

Megawati Sukarnoputri Daughter of Sukarno, Indonesia's first president, Megawati became Indonesia's Vice-President in October 1999, despite the fact that her party, the Indonesian Democratic Party of Struggle, won the largest proportion of popular vote. However, she replaced Wahid in July 2001 after his impeachment by the MPR.

MALAYSIA

Mahathir bin Mohamad Malaysia's prime minister since 1981 and best known on the world stage for his often acerbic attacks on the 'decadent' West and ardent championship of 'Asian values'.

SINGAPORE

Lee Kuan Yew Founder of the PAP, prime minister between 1959 and 1990 and now a senior minister. Educated in Britain, Lee was the architect of both Singapore's 'economic miracle' and the 'Asian values' discourse. Since his retirement from the prime ministership, Lee is regularly invited to other Pacific Asian countries to offer advice on the formula of development success.

Goh Chok Tung Singapore's prime minister since 1990.

SOUTH KOREA

Syngman Rhee First president of South Korea and first Korean to earn a PhD at a US university (Princeton). The Japanese annexation of Korea in 1910 forced him into exile in the United States, where he spoke for Korean independence. He returned to South Korea in 1948 and was elected president. He held that post until 1960, when opposition to his authoritarian rule forced his resignation. He died in exile in Hawaii.

Park Chung Hee A military general who ruled South Korea for the 1961–79 period, during which the Korean economy flourished. He was assassinated in 1979.

Chun Doo Hwan Shortly after Park's assassination, Chun Doo Hwan launched a military coup and took over the presidency. However, it was not until after he had brutally suppressed the civilian opposition in the Kwangju Massacre in May 1980 that he resigned from the military and became president. His 8-year rule (1980–8) was punctuated by economic scandals and political instabilities, although the economy continued to grow. In 1996, Chun was indicted for his role in the 1979 coup and the Kwangju Massacre, as well as for corruption during his rule and was sentenced to death. The sentence was later reduced to life imprisonment.

Rho Tae Woo Fellow military officer and political protégé of Chun Doo Hwan. Although guaranteed to win the 1987 presidential election as the official candidate, Rho put to an end the widespread popular democratic protests with the historic speech he made on 29 June that year promising wide-ranging democratic reforms. Rho won the ensuing direct election and became president in 1988. During his 5-year rule (1988–93), Rho oversaw the continuing democratisation of South Korea. In 1996, however, he was found guilty of crimes similar to those committed by his predecessor Chun Doo Hwan and was sentenced to life imprisonment.

Kim Young Sam The first civilian to be elected president after South Korea's democratisation in the late 1980s, Kim Young Sam ruled South Korea between 1993 and 1998. Kim's rule established firm civilian control over the military and implemented a wide range of reforms aimed at liberalising the economy and rooting out corruption in the Korean body politic.

Kim Dae Jung A veteran opposition leader, Kim Dae Jung became president in 1998. He first entered politics in 1954, opposing the policies of Syngman Rhee, but did not win a seat in government until 1961. After several arrests in the 1970s, Kim was sentenced to death on charges of sedition and conspiracy; that sentence was commuted to 20 years in prison. In 1985, after a brief exile in the United States, he resumed his role as one of the principal leaders of the political opposition. He was elected president in December 1997 in the height of the Asian financial crisis. He was awarded the Nobel Peace Prize in 2000 for his work for democracy and human rights in South Korea and in East Asia in general, and for peace and reconciliation with North Korea in particular.

TAIWAN

Sun Yat-sen Also known as Sun Zhongshan (1866–1925), he was the leader of the 1911 Chinese Republic revolution and the KMT. In both Taiwan and China he has been called the father of the Chinese nation. The doctrine of *sanminzhuyi*, three principles of the people, was first formulated by Sun and later became the KMT government's guiding principle on Taiwan.

Chiang Kaishek Head of the nationalist government in China (1928–49) and later in Taiwan (1949–75). After receiving military training in Tokyo, in 1918 he joined Sun Yat-sen, leader of the KMT, and later became Commander-in-Chief of the revolutionary army, which he sent to crush warlords active in the north of China. After his defeat by the communists in the civil war, he fled to Taiwan with about 2 million followers and ruled the island until his death in 1975. His rule, although dictatorial, oversaw Taiwan's rapid economic development with a remarkably high degree of equality. This can be largely attributed to his determination to avoid the same fate of government failure as happened on mainland China. The widely acclaimed land reform and the strict rules on clean government went a long way towards Taiwan's development success under his rule.

Chiang Chinkuo Son of Chiang Kaishek, and his successor as leader of Taiwan. He was formally elected by the National Assembly to a 6-year presidential term in 1978 and re-elected in 1984. He tried to maintain Taiwan's foreign-trade relationships and political independence as other countries began to break off diplomatic relations in order to establish ties with mainland China. The latter part of Chiang's rule was marked by his initiatives in guiding Taiwan towards democratisation. He died in 1988.

Lee Tenghui First Taiwan-born president (1988–2000) of Taiwan. He became president in 1988 after the death of Chiang Chingkuo. He was re-elected in 1990 and won a landslide victory in 1996 in the first direct presidential election. Although he favoured a policy of 'flexible diplomacy' in dealing with mainland China, Lee often attracted fierce attack from the latter for his perceived intention to create an independent Taiwan.

Chen Shuibian Leader of the DPP, Chen succeeded Lee Tenghui in May 2000 as Taiwan's first democratically elected president from an opposition party.

THAILAND

King Bhumibol Adulyadej Also known as Rama IX, Bhumibol was the ninth king of the Chakri Dynasty, which has ruled or reigned in Thailand since 1782. He succeeded his brother in 1946. Since the Thai revolution of 1932, when the absolute monarchy was abolished in Thailand, the king has been a figurehead, functioning as a living symbol of and a focus of unity for the Thai nation. However, since the 1960s, King Bhumibol has enjoyed enormous popularity with the Thai people by frequently intervening in public life to prevent excess political violence.

Sarit Thanarat A military marshal, who came to power through coups in 1957 and was credited for laying the foundation for Thailand's economic take-off during his 6-year rule, which came to an end in 1963.

Chuan Leekpai A charismatic politician, widely known and respected for his honesty and moderate approach to politics. After the tumultuous events that followed the 1991 military coup culminating in the 'Black May' of 1992 and subsequent elections, Chuan pulled together a multi-party coalition, which ruled Thailand until 1996. The outbreak of the Asian financial crisis in 1997 and the subsequent implementation of the stringent IMF austerity programmes by the Chavalit government triggered mass demonstrations against the government, which was seen to be corrupt and incompetent. As a result, the entire government resigned that year, replaced by one headed by Chuan Leekpai, who presided over Thailand's subsequent economic recovery. Chuan lost the 2001 general election to Thaksin Shinawatra, who became prime minister despite having to face corruption charges both before and after the election.

Thaksin Shinawatra Until he was elected prime minister in January 2001, Mr Thaksin was a highly successful businessman in Thailand and is believed to be the richest man in the country.

Bibliography

Adema, W., Tergeist, P. and Torres, R. (2000) 'Korea: better social policies for a stronger economy', *OECD Observer*, 9 November 2000, www.oecdobserver.org/news/fullstory.php/aid/372.

Ahmad, Z. H. (1993) 'Malaysia in an uncertain mode', in Morley, J. W. (ed.), *Driven by Growth: Political Change in the Asia Pacific Region*, New York: M. E. Sharpe.

Alam, M. (1989) *Governments and Markets in Economic Development Strategies: Lessons from Korea, Taiwan and Japan*, New York: Praeger.

Alatas, S. (1977) *The Myth of the Lazy Native*, London: Frank Cass.

Almond, G. and Powell, B. (1966) *Comparative Politics: A Developmental Approach*, Boston: Little, Brown.

Amin, S. (1976) *Unequal Development*, Hassocks: Harvester.

Amsden, A. H. (1985) 'The state and Taiwan's economic development', in Evans, P., Rueschemeyer, D. and Skocpol, T. (eds), *Bringing the State Back In*, Cambridge: Cambridge University Press.

—— (1989) *Asia's Next Giant: South Korea and Late Industrialisation*, New York: Oxford University Press.

Anek, L. (1992) *Business Associations and the New Political Economy of Thailand: From Bureaucratic Polity to Liberal Corporatism*, Singapore: Institute of Southeast Asian Studies.

APEC (2000) *APEC Economic Outlook 2000*, www.apecsec.org.sg.

Appelbaum, R. P. and Henderson, J. (eds) (1992) *States and Development in the Asian Pacific Rim*, London: Sage Publications.

Ariff, M. and Hill, H. (1985) *Export-Oriented Industrialisation: The ASEAN Experience*, London: Allen & Unwin.

Asian Development Bank (1998) *Asian Development Outlook 1998*, Oxford: Oxford University Press.

Aspinall, E. (1996) 'The broadening base of political opposition in Indonesia', in Rodan, G. (ed.), *Political Oppositions in Industrialising Asia*, London: Routledge.

Balassa, B. (1991) *Economic Policies in the Pacific Area Developing Countries*, New York: New York University Press.

Banfield, E. C. and Wilson, J. Q. (1963) *City Politics*, Cambridge, MA: Harvard University Press and the MIT Press.

BBC World Monitoring (2001) 'Indonesia press anger over Borneo', 27 February 2001, news.bbc.co.uk/hi/english/world/monitoring/media_reports/newsid_ 1192000/1192865.stm.

Beeson, M. and Jayasuriya, K. (1998) 'The political rationalities of regionalism: APEC and the EU in comparative perspective', *The Pacific Review* 11 (3): 311–36.

Beetham, D. (1992) 'Liberal democracy and the limits of democratisation', *Political Studies* 40 (special issue), *Prospects for Democracy*, 40–53.

Befu, H. (1993) 'Introduction', in Befu, H. (ed.), *Cultural Nationalism in East Asia: Representation and Identity*, Berkeley: University of California Press.

Bell, D. (1995) 'Democracy in Confucian societies: The challenge of justification', in Bell, D., Brown, D., Jayasuriya, K. and Jones, D. M. (eds), *Towards Illiberal Democracy in Pacific Asia*, London: Macmillan.

Bell, D., Brown, D., Jayasuriya, K. and Jones, D. M. (eds) (1995) *Towards Illiberal Democracy in Pacific Asia*, London: Macmillan.

Berger, M. T. (1997) 'Post-Cold War Indonesia and the revenge of history: The colonial legacy, nationalist vision and global capitalism', in Berger, M. T. and Borer, D. A. (eds), *The Rise of East Asia*, London: Routledge.

Berger, M. T. and Borer, D. A. (eds) (1997) *The Rise of East Asia*, London: Routledge.

Bergsten, F. (2000) 'Towards a tripartite world', *The Economist*, 15 July 2000.

Bernhard, M. (1993) 'Civil society and democratic transition in East Central Europe', *Political Science Quarterly* 108 (2): 307–26.

Bernstein, H. and Nicholas, H. (1983) 'Pessimism of the intellectual, pessimism of the will?: A response to Gunder Frank', *Development and Change* 14 (October): 609–24.

Bienefeld, M. and Godfrey, M. (eds) (1982) *The Struggle for Development: National Strategies in an International Context*, London: Wiley.

Booth, A. (1993) 'Counting the poor in Indonesia', *Bulletin of Indonesian Economic Studies* 29 (1): 53–83.

Borthwick, M. (1992) *Pacific Century: The Emergence of Modern Pacific Asia*, Boulder, CO: Westview Press.

Bouchlaka, R. (1999–2000) 'The genealogy of despotism', *Centre for the Study of Democracy Bulletin* 7 (1): 7–9.

Bowie, A. (1991) *Crossing the Industrial Divide: State, Society and the Politics of Economic Transformation in Malaysia*, New York: Columbia University Press.

Bresnan, J. (1993) *Managing Indonesia: The Modern Political Economy*, New York: Columbia University Press.

Bretherton, C. (1996) 'Introduction: Global politics in the 1990s', in Bretherton, C. and Poynter, G. (eds), *Global Politics*, Oxford: Blackwell.

Brook, C. (1998): 'Regionalism and globalism', in McGrew, A. and Brook, C. (eds), *Asia-Pacific in the New World Order*, London: Routledge.

Buckley, R. (1998) *Japan Today*, Cambridge: Cambridge University Press.

Bullard, N., Bello, W. and Mallhotra, K., (1998) 'Taming the tigers: The IMF and the Asian crisis', *Third World Quarterly* 19 (3): 505–55.

Burmeister, L. L. (1990) 'State, industrialization and agricultural policy in Korea', *Development and Change* 21 (2): 197–223.

Buzan, B. (1998) 'The Asia-Pacific: What sort of region in what sort of world?', in McGrew, A. and Brook, C. (eds), *Asia-Pacific in the New World Order*, London: Routledge.

Calder, K. E. (1993) *Strategic Capitalism*, Princeton, NJ: Princeton University Press.

Callahan, W. A. and McCargo, D. (1996) 'Vote-buying in Thailand's northeast: The July 1995 general election', *Asian Survey* 36 (4): 376–92.

Cardoso, F. H. (1973) 'Associated dependent development: Theoretical and practical implications', in Stepan, A. (ed.), *Authoritarian Brazil*, New Haven, CT: Yale University Press.

—— (1977) 'The consumption of dependency theory in the United States', *Latin American Research Review* 12 (3): 7–24.

Cardoso, F. H. and Faletto, E. (1979) *Dependency and Development in Latin America*, (trans. Urquidi, M. M.), Berkeley, CA: University of California Press.

Case, W. (1993) 'Semi-democracy in Malaysia: Withstanding the pressures for regime change', *Pacific Affairs* 66 (2): 183–205.

Castells, M. (1992) 'Four Asian tigers with a dragon head: A comparative analysis of the state, economy and society in the Asian Pacific rim', in Appelbaum, R. P. and Henderson, J. (eds), *States and Development in the Asian Pacific Rim*, London: Sage Publications.

Chai-Anan, S. (1989) 'Thailand: A Stable Semi-Democracy', in Diamond, L., Linz, J. J. and Lipset, S. M. (eds.), *Democracy in Developing Countries: Asia*, Boulder, CO: Lynne Rienner Publishers.

Chan, H. C. (1971) *Singapore: The Politics of Survival 1965–67*, Oxford: Oxford University Press.

—— (1993) 'Singapore: Coping with vulnerability', in Morley, J. W. (ed.), *Driven by Growth: Political Change in the Asia Pacific Region*, New York: M. E. Sharpe.

Chang, P. H. (1986) 'Taiwan in 1985: Quest for a brighter day', in Major, J. S. (ed.), *China Briefing 1985*, London: Westview Press.

Chen, F. (2000) *Working Women and State Policies in Taiwan*, Basingstoke: Palgrave.

Cheng, T. (1989) 'Democratising the quasi-Leninist regime in Taiwan', *World Politics* 41: 471–99.

Cheng, T. and Kim, E. M. (1994) 'Making democracy: Generalising the South Korean case', in Friedman, E. (ed.), *The Politics of Democratization: Generalizing East Asian Experiences*, Boulder, CO: Westview Press.

Choi, J. J. (1989) *Labour and the Authoritarian State: Labour Unions in South Korean Manufacturing Industries 1961–1980*, Seoul: Korea University Press.

—— (1993) 'Political cleavages in South Korea', in Koo, H. (ed.), *State and Society in Contemporary Korea*, Ithaca, NY: Cornell University Press.

Chu, J. J. (1993) 'Political liberalisation and the rise of Taiwanese labour radicalism', *Journal of Contemporary Asia* 23 (2): 173–88.

Chu, Y. (1989) 'State structure and economic adjustment of the East Asian newly industrialising countries', *International Organization* 43: 647–72.

—— (1994) 'Social protests and political democratization in Taiwan', in Rubenstein, M. A. (ed.), *The Other Taiwan*, Armonk, NY: M. E. Sharpe.

Chua, B.-H. (1995) *Communitarian Ideology and Democracy in Singapore*, London: Routledge.

Clark, R. (1979) *The Japanese Company*, New Haven, CT: York University Press.

Cohen, M. (1988) *Taiwan at the Crossroads: Human Rights, Political Development and Social Change on the Beautiful Island*, Washington, DC: Asia Resource Centre.

Corsetti, G., Pesenti, P., and Roubini, N. (1998) 'What caused the Asian currency and financial crisis, Part I: A macroeconomic overview', www.stern.nyu.edu/globalmacro/

Cotton, J. (1989) 'From authoritarianism to democracy in South Korea', *Political Studies* 37 (2): 244–59.

—— (2000) 'The Asian crisis and the perils of enterprise association: Explaining the different outcomes in Singapore, Taiwan and Korea', in Robison, R., Beeson, M., Jayasuriya, K. and Kim, H.-R. (eds), *Politics and Markets in the Wake of the Asian Crisis*, London: Routledge.

Crispin, S. W. and Tasker, R. (2001) 'Thailand Incorporated', *FEER*, 18 January 2001, www.feer.com/_0101_18/p016region.html.

Crouch, H. (1985) *Economic Change, Social Structure and the Political System in Southeast Asia*, Singapore: Institute of Southeast Asian Studies.

—— (1992) 'Authoritarian trends, the UMNO split and the limits of state power', in Kahn, J. S. and Loh, K. W. (eds), *Fragmented Vision: Culture and Politics in Contemporary Malaysia*, Sydney: Allen & Unwin.

—— (1993) 'Malaysia: Neither authoritarian nor democratic', in Hewison, K., Robison, R. and Rodan, G. (eds), *Southeast Asia in the 1990s: Authoritarianism, Democracy and Capitalism*, St Leonards, UK: Allen & Unwin.

—— (1996) 'Malaysia: Do elections make a difference?', in Taylor, R. H. (ed.), *The Politics of Elections in Southeast Asia*, Cambridge: Cambridge University Press.

Cumings, B. (1987) 'The origins and development of the Northeast Asian political economy: Industrial sectors, product cycles, and the political consequences', in Deyo, F. (ed.), *The Political Economy of the New Asian Industrialism*, Ithaca, NY: Cornell University Press.

—— (1998) 'The Korean crisis and the end of "late" development', *New Left Review* 231 (September–October): 43–72.

Curtis, G. L. (1988) *The Japanese Way of Politics*, New York: Columbia University Press.

—— (1997) 'Democracy in East Asia: The relevance of Japanese experience', in Yu, G. T. (ed.), *Asia's New World Order*, London: Macmillan.

Dahl, R. A. (1971) *Polyarchy: Participation and Opposition*, New Haven, CT: Yale University Press.

—— (1989) *Democracy and its Critics*, New Haven, CT: Yale University Press.

Dalton, B. and Cotton, J. (1996) 'New social movements and the changing nature of political opposition in South Korea', in Rodan, G. (ed.), *Political Oppositions in Industrialising Asia*, London: Routledge.

Department of Social Affairs, Ministry of the Interior (Taiwan), vol.moi.gov.tw/ sowf3w/eng/

Deyo, F. (ed.) (1987) *The Political Economy of the New Asian Industrialism*, Ithaca, NY: Cornell University Press.

—— (1992) 'The political economy of social policy formation: East Asia's newly industrialized countries', in Appelbaum, R. P. and Henderson, J. (eds), *States and Development in the Asian Pacific Rim*, London: Sage.

Dicken, P. (1998) *Global Shift*, London: Paul Chapman Publishing.

Dieter, H. (2000) 'The 5th column: Asia's monetary regionalism', *FEER* online, 6 July 2000 www.feer.com/_0007_06/p30.html.

Dixon, C. (1995) *Thailand – Economy, The Far East and Australasia*, London: Europa Publications.

—— (1999) 'The developmental implications of the Pacific Asian crises: the Thai experience', *Third World Quarterly* 20 (2): 439–52.

Doner, R. (1992) 'Limits of state strength: Toward an institutional view of economic development', *World Politics* 44 (3): 398–431.

Doner, R. and Unger, D. (1993) 'The politics of finance in Thai economic development', in Haggard, S. and Webb, S. B. (eds), *Democracy, Political Liberalization and Economic Adjustment*, Ithaca, NY: Cornell University Press.

Dong, W. (1993) 'The democratisation of South Korea: What role does the middle class play?', in Cotton, J. (ed.) *Korea under Rho Tae Woo*, London: Allen & Unwin.

Dore, R. (1987) *Taking Japan Seriously: A Confucian Perspective on Leading Economic Issues*, London: Athlone Press.

Eccleston, B. (1989) *State and Society in Post-War Japan*, Cambridge: Polity Press.

Economic Daily News, 23 May, 2000, www.taiwanheadlines.gov.tw/20000523/ 20000523o2.html.

Eisenstadt, S. N. (1966) *Modernization: Protest and Change*, Englewood Cliffs, NJ: Prentice Hall.

Esping-Andersen, G. (1990) *The Three Worlds of Welfare Capitalism*, Oxford: Polity.

—— (ed.) (1996) *Welfare States in Transition*, London: Sage.

Evans, P. (1979) *Dependent Development: The Alliance of Multinational, State and Local Capital*, Princeton, NJ: Princeton University Press.

—— (1992) 'The state as problem and solution: Embedded autonomy and structural change', in Haggard, S. and Kaufman, R. R. (eds), *The Politics of Economic Adjustment: International Constraints, Distributive Conflicts and the State*, Princeton, NJ: Princeton University Press.

—— (1995) *Embedded Autonomy: States and Industrial Transformation*, Princeton, NJ: Princeton University Press.

Ezrati, M. (1999) *Kawari*, Reading, MA: Perseus Books.

Fields, K. J. (1995) *Enterprise and the State in Korea and Taiwan*, Ithaca, NY: Cornell University Press.

Flanagan, S., Kohei, S., Miyake, I., Richardson, B. M. and Watanuki, J. (1991) *The Japanese Voter*, New Haven, CT: Yale University Press.

Fong, P. E., Tan, C. H. and Chen, S. M. (1989) 'The management of people', in Sandhu, K. S. and Wheatley, P (eds), *Management of Success: The Moulding of Modern Singapore*, Singapore: Institute of Southeast Asian Studies.

Francks, P. (1999) *Japanese Economic Development: Theory and Practice*, London: Routledge.

Frank, A. G. (1969) *Capitalism and Underdevelopment in Latin America*, New York: Monthly Review Press.

Friedland, J. (1994) 'The regional challenge', *FEER*, 9 June 1994.

Friedman, E. (1994) 'Introduction', in Friedman, E. (ed.), *The Politics of Democratization: Generalizing East Asian Experiences*, Boulder, CO: Westview Press.

—— (ed.) (1994) *The Politics of Democratization: Generalizing East Asian Experiences*, Boulder, CO: Westview Press.

Fukui, H. (1992) 'The Japanese state and economic development: A profile of a nationalist–paternalist capitalist state' in Appelbaum, R. P. and Henderson, J. (eds), *States and Development in the Asian Pacific Rim*, London: Sage.

Fukuyama, F. (1992) 'Asia's soft-authoritarian alternative', *New Perspectives Quarterly* 9 (2): 60–1.

—— (1995a) 'Democracy's future: The primacy of culture', *Journal of Democracy* 6 (1): 7–14.

—— (1995b) 'Confucianism and democracy' *Journal of Democracy* 6 (2): 20–33.

Garon, S. (1987) *The State and Labour in Modern Japan*, Berkeley: University of California Press.

Gayle, D. J. (1989) 'Singaporean market socialism: Some implications for development theory', *International Journal of Social Economics* 15 (7): 53–75.

Gerlach, M. L. (1992) *Alliance Capitalism: The Social Organization of Japanese Business*, Berkeley, CA: University of California Press.

Gerschenkron, A. (1962) *Economic Backwardness in Historical Perspective*, Cambridge, MA: Harvard University Press.

Gibney, F. (1992) *Korea's Quiet Revolution: From Garrison State to Democracy*, New York: Walker and Co.

—— (1998) 'Politics and governance in Japan', in R. Maidment, D. Goldblatt, and J. Mitchell (eds), *Governance in the Asia-Pacific*, London: Routledge.

Giddens, A. (1990) *The Consequences of Modernity*, Cambridge: Polity Press.

Girling, J. (1981) *Thailand: Society and Politics*, Ithaca, NY: Cornell University Press.

—— (1988) 'Development and democracy in Southeast Asia', *The Pacific Review* 1 (4): 332–40.

Gluck, C. (1985) *Japan's Modern Myth: Ideology in the Late Meiji Period*, Princeton, NJ: Princeton University Press.

Godement, F. (1999) *The Downsizing of Asia*, London: Routledge.

Golay, F., Anspach, R., Pfanner, M. R. and Ayal, E. B. (1969) *Underdevelopment and Economic Nationalism in Southeast Asia*, Ithaca, NY: Cornell University Press.

Gold, T. B. (1986) *State and Society in the Taiwan Miracle*, Armonk, NY: M. E. Sharpe.

—— (1990) 'The resurgence of civil society in China', *Journal of Democracy* 1 (1): 18–31.

Gomez, E. T. (1994) *Political Business: Corporate Involvement of Malaysian Political Parties*, Townsville, Queensland: Centre for Southeast Asian Studies, James Cook University.

Goodman, R. (ed.) (1996) *Welfare States in Transition*, London: Sage.

—— (1998) 'The "Japanese-style welfare state" and the delivery of personal social services', in Goodman, R., White, G. and Kwon, H. (eds), *The East Asian Welfare Model: Welfare Orientalism and the State*, London: Routledge.

Goodman, R. and Peng, I. (1996) 'The East Asian welfare state: Peripatetic learning, adaptive change, and nation-building', in Esping-Andersen, G. (ed.), *The Three Worlds of Welfare Capitalism*, Oxford: Polity.

Goodman, R. White, G. and Kwon, H. (eds) (1998) *The East Asian Welfare Model: Welfare Orientalism and the State*, London: Routledge.

Gould, A. (1993) *Capitalist Welfare Systems: A Comparison of Japan, Britain and Sweden*, London: Longman.

Goulet, D. (1992) 'Development: Creator and destroyer of values', *World Development*, 20 (3): 467–75.

Greenhalgh, S. (1988) 'Families and networks in Taiwan's economic development', in Winckler, E. A. and Greenhalgh, S. (eds), *Contending Approaches to the Political Economy of Taiwan*, Armonk, NY: M. E. Sharpe.

Haacke, J. (1999) 'The concept of flexible engagement and the practice of enhanced interaction: intramural challenges to the "ASEAN way"', *The Pacific Review* 12 (4): 581–611.

Haggard, S. (1989) 'Introduction', in Haggard, S and Moon, C (eds), *Pacific Dynamics: The International Politics of Industrial Change*, Boulder, CO: Westview Press.

—— (1990) *Pathways from the Periphery: The Politics of Growth in the Newly Industrializing Countries*, Ithaca, NY: Cornell University Press.

Haggard, S. and Kaufman, R. R. (1992) 'Introduction: Institutions and economic adjustment', in Haggard, S. and Kaufman, R. R. (eds), *The Politics of Economic Adjustment: International Constraints, Distributive Conflicts and the State*, Princeton, NJ: Princeton University Press.

—— (eds) (1992) *The Politics of Economic Adjustment: International Constraints, Distributive Conflicts and the State*, Princeton, NJ: Princeton University Press.

Hamilton, G. and Biggart, N. W. (1988) 'Market, culture and authority: A comparative analysis of management and organization in East Asia', *American Journal of Sociology* 94: 552–94.

Harrison, D. (1988) *The Sociology of Modernisation and Development*, London: Routledge.

Harvey, D. (1990) *The Condition of Postmodernity*, Oxford: Blackwell.

Hatch, W. (2000) 'Regionalization trumps globalization: Japanese production networks in Asia', in Stubbs, R. and Underhill, G. R. D. (eds), *Political Economy and the Changing Global Order*, Oxford: Oxford University Press.

Heidenheimer, A., Heclo, H. and Adams, C. T. (1990) *Comparative Public Policy*, New York: St. Martin's Press.

Heilbroner, R. L. (1985) *The Nature and Logic of Capitalism*, New York: W. W. Norton.

Held, D. (1995) *Democracy and the Global Order*, Cambridge: Polity Press.

Hewison, K. (1997) 'Thailand: Capitalist development and the state', in Rodan, G., Hewison, K. and Robison, R. (eds) *The Political Economy of South-East Asia: An Introduction*, Oxford: Oxford University Press.

—— (2000) 'Thailand's capitalism before and after the economic crisis', in Robison, R., Beeson, M., Jayasuriya, K. and Kim, H.-R. (eds), *Politics and Markets in the Wake of the Asian Crisis*, London: Routledge.

Higgott, R. (2000a) 'The international relations of the Asian economic crisis: A study in the politics of resentment', in Robison, R., Beeson, M., Jayasuriya, K. and Kim, H.-R. (eds), *Politics and Markets in the Wake of the Asian Crisis*, London: Routledge.

—— (2000b) 'Regionalism in the Asia-Pacific: Two steps forward, one step back?', in Stubbs, R. and Underhill, G. R. D. (eds), *Political Economy and the Changing Global Order*, Oxford: Oxford University Press.

Higgott, R. and Stubbs, R. (1995) 'Competing conceptions of East Asian regionalism: APEC versus the EAEC in the Asia-Pacific', *Review of International Political Economy* 2 (3): 516–35.

Hill, H. (1997) 'Myths about tigers: Indonesian development policy debates', *The Pacific Review* 10 (2): 256–73.

Hirst, P. (2000) 'The end of both roads?: The developmental state, economic liberalism and the Asian crisis', *The Journal of Interdisciplinary Economics* 11: 139–51.

Hiwatari, N. (1993) *Sustaining the Welfare State and International Competitiveness in Japan: The Welfare Reforms of the 1980s and the Political Economy*, discussion paper presented to the Institute of Social Science, Tokyo.

Hobsbawm, E. (1983a) 'Mass-producing traditions: Europe, 1870–1914', in Hobsbawm, E. and Rangers, T. (eds), *The Invention of Tradition*, Cambridge: Cambridge University Press.

—— (1983b) 'Introduction: Inventing traditions', in Hobsbawm, E. and Rangers, T. (eds), *The Invention of Tradition*, Cambridge: Cambridge University Press.

Hobsbawm, E. and Rangers, T. (1983) *The Invention of Tradition*, Cambridge: Cambridge University Press.

Holden, B. (1993) *Understanding Liberal Democracy*, London: Harvester Wheasheaf.

Hsiao, H. H. M. (1992) 'The labour movement in Taiwan: A retrospective and prospective look', in Simon, D. F. and Kau, M. Y. M. (eds), *Beyond the Economic Miracle*, Armonk, NY: M. E. Sharpe.

Huntington, S. P. (1968) *Political Order in Changing Societies*, New Haven, CT: Yale University Press.

—— (1984) 'Will more countries become democratic?', *Political Science Quarterly* 99 (2): 193–218.

—— (1987) 'The goals of development', in Weiner, M. and Huntington, S. P. (eds), *Understanding Political Development*, Boston: Little, Brown.

—— (1993a) 'The clash of civilizations?', *Foreign Affairs* 72 (3): 22–49.

—— (1993b) 'Democracy's third wave', in L. Diamond and M. F. Plattner (eds), *The Global Resurgence of Democracy*, Baltimore, MD: Johns Hopkins University.

Hveem, H. (2000) 'Explaining the regional phenomenon in an era of globalization', in Stubbs, R. and Underhill, G. R. D. (eds), *Political Economy and the Changing Global Order*, Oxford: Oxford University Press.

Inoguchi, K. (1987) 'Prosperity without the amenities', *Journal of Japanese Studies* 13 (1): 125–34.

Ishida, T. and Krauss, E. S. (1989) 'Democracy in Japan: Issues and questions', in Ishida, T. and Krauss, E. S. (eds), *Democracy in Japan*, Pittsburgh: University of Pittsburgh Press.

Ishida, T. and Krauss, E. S. (eds) (1989) *Democracy in Japan*, Pittsburgh, PA: University of Pittsburgh Press.

Islam, I. and Chowdhury, A. (1997) *Asia-Pacific Economies: A Survey*, London: Routledge.

Jansen, K. (1997) *External Finance in Thailand's Development*, Basingstoke: Macmillan.

Jesudason, J. (1989) *Ethnicity and the Economy: The State, Chinese Business, and Multinationals in Malaysia*, Oxford: Oxford University Press.

—— (1995) 'Statist democracy and the limits to civil society in Malaysia', *Journal of Commonwealth & Comparative Politics* 33 (3): 335–56.

—— (1996) 'The syncretic state and the structuring of oppositional politics in Malaysia', in Rodan, G. (ed.), *Political Oppositions in Industrialising Asia*, London: Routledge.

Johnson, C. (1982) *MITI and the Japanese Miracle: The Growth of Industrial Policy 1925–1975*, Stanford, CA: Stanford University Press.

—— (1987) 'Political institutions and economic performance: The government–business relationship in Japan, South Korea and Taiwan', in Deyo, F. (ed.), *The Political Economy of the New Asian Industrialism*, Ithaca, NY: Cornell University Press.

—— (1995a) 'Social values and the theory of late economic development in East Asia', in C. Johnson (ed.), *Japan: Who Governs?*, New York: W. W. Norton & Co.

—— (1995b) 'Comparative capitalism: The Japanese difference', in C. Johnson (ed.), *Japan: Who Governs?*, New York: W. W. Norton & Co.

Jomo, K. S. (1988) *A Question of Class: Capital, the State, and Uneven Development in Malaya*, New York: Monthly Review Press.

—— (2000) 'Comment: Crisis and the developmental state in East Asia', in Robison, R., Beeson, M., Jayasuriya, K. and Kim, H.-R. (eds), *Politics and Markets in the Wake of the Asian Crisis*, London: Routledge.

Jomo, K. S., Chung, C. Y., Folk, B. C., ul-Haque, I., Simatupang, P. P. B. and Tateishi, M. (1997) *Southeast Asia's Misunderstood Miracle*, Boulder, CO: Westview Press.

Jones, C. (1993) 'The Pacific challenge: Confucian welfare states' in Jones, C. (ed.), *New Perspectives on the Welfare State in Europe*, London: Routledge.

Jones, D. M. (1998) 'The politics of economic governance', in Maidment, R., Goldblatt, D. and Mitchell, J. (eds), *Governance in the Asia-Pacific*, London: Routledge.

Jones-Finer, C. (1999) 'Trends and developments in welfare states', in Clasen, J. (ed.) *Comparative Social Policy: Concepts, Theories and Methods*, Oxford: Blackwell.

Kabashima, I. (1993) 'Japan: There may be a choice', in Morley, J. W. (ed.), *Driven by Growth: Political Change in the Asia Pacific Region*, New York: M. E. Sharpe.

Kahn, J. S. (1996) 'Growth, economic transformation, culture and the middle classes in Malaysia', in Robison, R. and Goodman, D. S. G. (eds), *The New Rich in Asia: Mobile Phones, McDonald's and Middle-class Revolution*, London: Routledge.

Karl, T. L. (1991) 'Dilemmas of democratization in Latin America', in Rustow, D. A. and Erickson, K. P. (eds), *Comparative Political Dynamics*, New York: HarperCollins.

Keesing, R. M. (1991) 'Asian cultures?', *Asian Studies Review* 15 (2): 43–50.

Khong, C. O. (1995) 'Singapore: Political legitimacy through managing conformity', in Alagappa, M. (ed.), *Political Legitimacy in Southeast Asia: The Quest for Moral Authority*, Stanford, CA: Stanford University Press.

Khoo, B. T. (2000) 'Economic nationalism and its discontents: Malaysian political economy after July 1997', in Robison, R., Beeson, M., Jayasuriya, K. and Kim, H.-R. (eds), *Politics and Markets in the Wake of the Asian Crisis*, London: Routledge.

Kim, D. J. (1994) 'Is culture destiny? The myth of Asia's anti-democratic values: A response to Lee Kuan Yew, former Singapore prime minister', *Foreign Affairs* 73 (6): 2–7.

—— (1998) 'Economic reform in Korea: Establishment of a democratic market economy', *Korea and World Affairs* 22 (2): 279–83.

Kim, K. S. (1997) 'From neo-mercantilism to globalism: The changing role of the state and South Korea's economic prowess', in Berger, M. T. and Borer, D. A. (eds), *The Rise of East Asia*, London: Routledge.

Kim, K.-R. (1993) 'Divergent organizational paths of industrialization in East Asia', *Asian Perspective* 17: 105–35.

—— (1994) The state and economic organization in a comparative perspective: The organizing mode of the East Asian political economy', *Korean Social Science Journal* 20: 91–120.

—— (1998) 'Family capitalism and corporate structure in South Korea', *Korea Focus* 6: 55–67.

Kinzley, W. D. (1991) *Industrial Harmony in Modern Japan: The Invention of a Tradition*, London: Routledge.

Klintworth, G. (1995) *New Taiwan, New China*, Melbourne: Longman Cheshire.

Kolko, G. (1988) *Confronting the Third World: United States Foreign Policy, 1945–1980*, New York: Pantheon Books.

Koo, H. (1991) 'Middle classes, democratisation, and class formation: The case of South Korea', *Theory and Society* 20: 485–509.

—— (1993) 'The state, minjung and the working class in South Korea', in Koo, H. (ed.), *State and Society in Contemporary Korea*, Ithaca, NY: Cornell University Press.

—— (ed.) (1993) *State and Society in Contemporary Korea*, Ithaca, NY: Cornell University Press.

Korhonen, P. (1994) 'The theory of the flying geese pattern of development and its interpretations', *Journal of Peace Research* 31 (1): 93–108.

Krauss, E. S. (1989) 'Politics and the policy making process', in Ishida, T. and Krauss, E. S. (eds), *Democracy in Japan*, Pittsburgh, PA: University of Pittsburgh Press.

Krauss, E. S. and Muramatsu, M. (1988) 'The Japanese political economy today: The patterned pluralist model', in Okimoto, D. I. and Rohlen, T. P. (eds), *Inside the Japanese System*, Stanford, CA: Stanford University Press.

Krueger, A. O. (1992) *Economic Policy Reforms in Developing Countries*, Oxford: Blackwell.

—— (1999) 'Are preferential trading arrangements trade liberalizing or protectionist?' *Journal of Economic Perspectives* 13 (Fall): 105–24.

Kruger, D. (2001) 'If it's broken, fix it', *FEER*, 22 March 2001.

Krugman, P. (1994) 'The myth of Asia's miracle', *Foreign Affairs* 73 (6): 62–78.

Ku, Y. (1998) 'Can we afford it? The development of National Health Insurance in Taiwan', in Goodman, R. (ed.), *The East Asian Welfare Model: Welfare Orientalism and the State*, London: Routledge.

Kwon, H. (1998) 'Democracy and the politics of social welfare: A comparative analysis of welfare systems in East Asia', in Goodman, R. (ed.), *The East Asian Welfare Model: Welfare Orientalism and the State*, London: Routledge.

Lam, D. and Clark, C. (1998) 'The cultural roots of "Guerrilla capitalism" in Taiwan', in Chan, S., Clark, C. and Lam, D. (eds), *Beyond the Developmental State: East Asia's Political Economies Reconsidered*, London: Macmillan.

Lee, H. (1994) 'Uncertain promise: Democratic consolidation in South Korea', in Friedman, E. (ed.), *The Politics of Democratization: Generalizing East Asian Experiences,* Boulder, CO: Westview Press.

Lee, H. K. (1987) 'The Japanese welfare state in transition', in Friedmann R. (ed.), *Modern Welfare States*, Hemel Hempstead, UK: Wheatsheaf.

Lee, J.-W. and Rhee, C. (1998) 'Social impacts of the Asian crisis: Policy challenges and lessons', www.stern.nyu.edu/globalmacro/

Lee, Y.-H. and Kim, H.-R. (2000) 'The dilemma of market liberalization: The financial crisis and the transformation of capitalism', in Robison, R., Beeson, M., Jayasuriya, K. and Kim, H.-R. (eds), *Politics and Markets in the Wake of the Asian Crisis*, London: Routledge.

Leftwich, A. (1995) 'Bringing politics back in: Towards a model of the developmental state', *Journal of Development Studies* 31: 400–27.

—— (1996) 'Two cheers for democracy: Democracy and the developmental state', in Leftwich, A. (ed.), *Democracy and Development*, Cambridge: Polity Press.

Lerner, D. (1958) *The Passing of Traditional Society*, London: Macmillan.

Levi-Faur, D. (1997) 'Friedrich List and the political economy of nation-state, *Review of International Political Economy* 4 (1): 154–78.

Lie, J. (1991) 'Review: Rethinking the "Miracle" – economic growth and political struggles in South Korea', *Bulletin of Concerned Asian Scholars* 23 (4): 66–71.

Liddle, W. (1996) 'A useful fiction: Democratic legitimation in New Order Indonesia', in Taylor, R. H. (ed.), *The Politics of Elections in Southeast Asia*, Cambridge: Cambridge University Press.

Lin, W. and Yeh, H.-S. (1992) 'Social movements and social policy in Taiwan: The case of the disadvantaged groups movement', *Chinese Journal of Social Work* 2: 37–56 (in Chinese).

Linder, S. B. (1986) *The Pacific Century: Economic and Political Consequences of Asian-Pacific Dynamism*, Stanford, CA: Stanford University Press.

Lipset, S. M. (1959) 'Some social requisites of democracy: Economic development and political legitimacy', *American Political Science Review* 53: 69–105.

—— (1960) *Political Man*, London: Heinemann

Lubeck, P. M. (1992) 'Malaysian industrialization, ethnic divisions, and the NIC model: The limits to replication', in Appelbaum, R. P. and Henderson, J. (eds) *States and Development in the Asian Pacific Rim*, London: Sage.

—— (1998) 'Winners and losers in the Asia-Pacific', in Thompson, G. (ed.), *Economic Dynamism in the Asia-Pacific*, London: Routledge.

Mabbett, D. and Bolderson, H. (1999) 'Theories and methods in comparative social policy', in Clasen, J. (ed.), *Comparative Social Policy*, Oxford: Blackwell Publishers.

McCargo, D. (2000) *Contemporary Japan*, London: Macmillan.

McClelland, D. (1961) *The Achieving Society*, Princeton, NJ: Van Nostrand.

McGrew, A. and Brook, C. (eds) *Asia-Pacific in the New World Order*, London: Routledge.

McVey, R. (1992) 'The materialization of the Southeast Asian entrepreneur', in McVey, R. (ed.), *Southeast Asian Capitalists*, Ithaca, NY: Cornell University Press.

Macintyre, A. (1994) 'Power, prosperity and patrimonialism: Business and government in Indonesia', in Macintyre, A. (ed*.), Business and Government in Industrialising Asia*, St Leonards, UK: Allen & Unwin.

Mackerras, C. (ed.) (1992) *Eastern Asia: An Introductory History*, London: Longman.

Mahathir, M. and Ishihara, S. (1995) *The Voice of Asia: Two Leaders Discussing the Coming Century* (trans. Baldwin, F.), Tokyo: Kodansha International.

Majstorovic, S. (1997) 'The politics of ethnicity and post-Cold War Malaysia: The dynamics of an ethnic state', in Berger, M. T. and Borer, D. A. (eds), *The Rise of East Asia*, London: Routledge.

Marshall, T. H. (1963) 'Citizenship and social class', in Marshall, T. H. (ed.), *Sociology at the Cross Roads*, London: Heinemann.

Maruro, N. (1986) 'The development of the welfare mix in Japan', in Rose, R. and Shiratori, R. (eds), *Welfare State: East and West*, Oxford: Oxford University Press.

Mazower, M. (1998) *Dark Continent: Europe's Twentieth Century*, London: Penguin.

Means, G. P. (1991) *Malaysian Politics: The Second Generation*, Oxford: Oxford University Press.

Metzger, T. A and Myers, R. H. (1989) 'Understanding the Taiwan experience: An historical perspective', *The Pacific Review* 2 (4): 297–311.

Mikuriya, T. (1996) General election '96', *Japan Echo* 23 (4), www.japanecho.co.jp/docs/html/230404.html.

Ministry of Health, Labour and Welfare, Japan (2000) *Annual Reports on Health and Welfare1998–1999 Social Security and National Life*, www.mhlw.go.jp/english/wp/wp-hw/index.html.

Moody, P. R., Jr (1995) *Tradition and Modernisation in China and Japan*, Belmont, CA: Wadsworth Publishing.

Moon, C. I. and Rhyu, S. (2000) 'The state, structural rigidity and the end of Asian capitalism: A comparative study of Japan and South Korea', in Robison, R., Beeson, M., Jayasuriya, K. and Kim, H.-R. (eds), *Politics and Markets in the Wake of the Asian Crisis*, London: Routledge.

Moore, B. (1966) *Social Origins of Dictatorship and Democracy: Lord and Peasant in the Making of the Modern World*, Boston: Beacon Press.

Morishima, M. (1982): *Why Has Japan Succeeded?*, Cambridge: Cambridge University Press.

Morley, J. W. (ed.) (1993) *Driven by Growth: Political Change in the Asia Pacific Region*, New York: M. E. Sharpe.

Myrdal, G. (1968) *Asian Drama: An Inquiry into the Poverty of Nations*, New York: Pantheon.

Nakagawa, Y. (1979) 'Japan, the welfare super-power', *Journal of Japanese Studies* 5 (1): 5–51.

Nakano, M. (1997) *The Policy-making Process in Contemporary Japan*, Basingstoke: Macmillan.

Napier, C. 'Analysis: Indonesia's fragile archipelago', BBC Asia-Pacific, 13 September 2000, news.bbc.co.uk/hi/english/world/asia-pacific/newsid_270000/270462.stm.

Neher, C. D. (1999) *Southeast Asia in the New International Era*, Boulder, CO: Westview Press.

Neher, C. D. and Marlay, R. (1995) *Democracy and Development in Southeast Asia: The Winds of Change*, Boulder, CO: Westview Press

North, D. (1994) 'Economic performance through time', *American Economic Review* 84 (3): 359–68.

O'Donnell, G. and Schmitter, P. (1986) *Transitions from Authoritarian Rule: Tentative Conclusions about Uncertain Democracies*, Baltimore, MD: Johns Hopkins University Press.

OECD (2000) Social Expenditure Database: 1980/1997, Paris: OECD.

Ogle, G. (1990) *South Korea: Dissent Within the Economic Miracle*, London: Zed Books.

Ohmae, K. (1995) *The End of the Nation State: The Rise of Regional Economies*, New York: Free Press.

Onis, Z. (1991) 'The logic of the developmental state', *Comparative Politics* 24 (October): 109–26.

Palley, H. A. (1992) 'Social policy and the elderly in South Korea: Confucianism, modernization, and development', *Asian Survey* XXXII (9): 787–801.

Patrick, H. T. and Rosovsky, H. (1976) *Asia's New Giant*, Washington, DC: Brookings Institution.

Pempel, T. J. (1982) *Policy and Politics in Japan: Creative Conservatism*, Philadelphia, PA: Temple University Press.

—— (1992) 'Political parties and representation: The case of Japan', *PS: Political Science and Politics* 25 (March): 13–18.

Pempel, T. J. and Tsunekawa, K. (1979) 'Corporatism without labour?: The Japanese anomaly', in Lembruch, G. and Schmitter, P. (eds), *Trends Towards Corporatist Intermediation*, London: Sage.

Phongpaichit, P. and Piriyarangsan, S. (1994) *Corruption and Democracy in Thailand*, The Political Economy Centre, Chulalongkorn University, Bangkok.

Polanyi, K. (1944) *The Great Transformation: The Political and Economic Origins of Our Time*, New York: Rinehart.

Przeworski, A. (1988) 'Democracy as a contingent outcome of conflicts', in Elster, J. and Slagstad, R. (eds), *Constitutionalism and Democracy*, Cambridge: Cambridge University Press.

Purcell, R. P. (ed.) (1987) *The Newly Industrializing Countries in the World Economy*, Boulder, CO: Lynne Rienner.

Pye, L. W. (1985) *Asian Power and Politics: The Cultural Dimension of Authority*, Cambridge, MA: Harvard University Press.

—— (1988) 'The new Asian capitalism: A political portrait', in Berger, P. L. and Hsiao, H. M. (eds), *In Search of an East Asian Development Model*, New Brunswick, NJ: Transaction Publishers.

Pyle, K. B. (1996) *The Japanese Question: Power and Purpose in a New Era*, Washington DC: American Enterprise Institute for Public Policy Research.

Ramstetter, E. (1998) 'Measuring the size of foreign multinationals in the Asia-Pacific', in Thompson, G. (ed.), *Economic Dynamism in the Asia-Pacific*, London: Routledge.

Ramesh, M. (2000) *Welfare Capitalism in Southeast Asia*, London: Macmillan.

Randall, V. and Theobald, R. (1998) *Political Change and Underdevelopment: A Critical Introduction to Third World Politics*, Basingstoke: Macmillan.

Rao, M. G. (1995) *Public Expenditure Policies in High Performing Asian Economies*, Canberra: Australian South Asia Research Centre.

Rasiah, R. (1997) 'Class, ethnicity and economic development in Malaysia', in Rodan, G., Hewison, K. and Robison, R. (eds), *The Political Economy of South-East Asia: An Introduction*, Oxford: Oxford University Press.

Ravenhill, J. (1998) 'The growth of intergovernmental collaboration in the Asia-Pacific Region' in McGrew, A. and Brook, C. (eds), *Asia-Pacific in the New World Order*, London: Routledge.

Redding, S. G. (1990) *The Spirit of Chinese Capitalism*, Berlin: Walter de Gruyter.

Regnier, P. (1991) *Singapore: City-State in Southeast Asia* (trans. Hurst, C.), London: Hurst and Company.

Reid, A. (1988) *Southeast Asia in the Age of Commerce: 1450–1680*, Vol. 1, *The Lands below the Winds*, New Haven, CT: Yale University Press.

Rigg, J. (1997) *Southeast Asia: The Human Landscape of Modernization and Development*, London: Routledge.

Rigger, S. (1996) 'Mobilisational authoritarianism and political opposition in Taiwan', in Rodan, G. (ed.), *Political Oppositions in Industrialising Asia*, London: Routledge.

Riggs, F. W. (1966) *Thailand: The Modernization of a Bureaucratic Polity*, Honolulu: East–West Centre Press.

Robertson, R. (1992) *Globalization: Social Theory and Global Culture*, London: Sage.

Robison, R. (1986) *Indonesia: The Rise of Capital*, Sydney: Allen & Unwin.

—— (1997) 'Politics and markets in Indonesia's post-oil era', in Rodan, G., Hewison, K. and Robison, R. (eds), *The Political Economy of South-East Asia: An Introduction*, Oxford: Oxford University Press.

Robison, R., Beeson, M., Jayasuriya, K. and Kim, H.-R. (eds) (2000), *Politics and Markets in the Wake of the Asian Crisis*, London: Routledge.

Rodan, G. (1989) *The Political Economy of Singapore's Industrialization: National State and International Capital*, London: Macmillan.

—— (1992) 'Singapore's leadership transition: Erosion or refinement of authoritarian rule?', *Bulletin of Concerned Asian Scholars* 24 (1): 3–17.

—— (1996) 'Elections without representation: The Singapore experience under the PAP', in Taylor, R. H. (ed.), *The Politics of Elections in Southeast Asia*, Cambridge: Cambridge University Press.

—— (ed.) (1996) *Political Oppositions in Industrialising Asia*, London: Routledge.

—— (1997) 'Singapore: Economic diversification and social division', in Rodan, G., Hewison, K. and Robison, R. (eds) (1997) *The Political Economy of South-East Asia: An Introduction*, Oxford: Oxford University Press.

Rodan, G., Hewison, K. and Robison, R. (eds) (1997) *The Political Economy of South-East Asia: An Introduction*, Oxford: Oxford University Press.

Rostow, W. W. (1960) *The Stages of Economic Growth: A Non-Communist Manifesto*, Cambridge: Cambridge University Press.

Roy, D. (1994) 'Singapore, China and the "soft authoritarian" challenge', *Asian Survey* XXXIV (3): 231–42.

Rozman, G. (ed.) (1991) *The East Asian Region: Confucian Heritage and its Modern Adaptation*, Princeton, NJ: Princeton University Press.

—— (1992) 'The Confucian faces of capitalism', in Borthwick, M. (ed.), *Pacific Century: The Emergence of Modern Pacific Asia*, Boulder, CO: Westview Press.

Rudd, C. (1994) 'Japan's welfare mix', *Japan Foundation Newsletter* XXII (3): 14–17.

Rudolph, L. and Rudolph, S. (1967) *The Modernity of Tradition: Political Development in India*, Chicago: University of Chicago Press.

Rueschemeyer, D., Stephens, E. and Stephens, J. (1992) *Capitalist Development and Democracy*, Cambridge: Polity Press.

Ruggie, J. (1982) 'International regimes, transactions and change: Embedded liberalism in the postwar economic order', *International Organization* 36 (2): 379–415.

Ruigrok, W. and van Tulder, R. (1993) *The Logic of International Restructuring*, Routledge: London.

Rustow, D. A. (1970) 'Transitions to Democracy', *Comparative Politics* 2: 337–63

Sachs, J. 'IMF is a power unto itself', 11 December 1997, www.stern.nyu.edu/globalmacro/

Sakakibara, E. (1993) *Beyond Capitalism: The Japanese Model of Market Economics*, Lanham, MD: University Press.

Schlesinger, J. M. (1997) *Shadow Shoguns: The Rise and Fall of Japan's Postwar Political Machine*, New York: Simon & Schuster.

Schmitter, P. C. and Karl, T. L. (1991) 'What democracy is ... and is not', *Journal of Democracy* 2 (3): 75–88.

Schwarz, A. (1994) *A Nation in Waiting: Indonesia in the 1990s*, St Leonards, UK: Allen and Unwin.

Seow, F. (1994) *To Catch a Tartar: A Dissident in Lee Kuan Yew's Prison*, New Haven, CT: Yale University Press.

Shain, Y. and Linz, J. (eds) (1995) *Between States: Interim Governments and Democratic Transitions*, Cambridge: Cambridge University Press.

Simone, V. and Feraru, A. T. (1995) *The Asian Pacific: Political and Economic Development in a Global Context*, New York: Longman Publishers.

Soeda, Y. (1990) 'The development of the public assistance in Japan 1966–83', *Annals of the Institute of Social Science* 32: 31–65.

Song, B.-N. (1990) *The Rise of the Korean Economy*, Oxford: Oxford University Press.

Sorensen, G. (1998) *Democracy and Democratization*, Boulder, CO: Westview Press.

Stallings, B. (ed.) (1995) *Global Change, Regional Response: The New International Context of Development*, Cambridge: Cambridge University Press.

Stallings, B. and Streeck, W. (1995) 'Capitalism in conflict? The United States, Europe, and Japan in the post-Cold War world', in Stallings, B. (ed.), *Global Change, Regional Response: The New International Context of Development*, Cambridge: Cambridge University Press.

Stockwin, J. A. A. (1999) *Governing Japan*, Oxford: Blackwell Publishers.

Strange, S. (1996) *The Retreat of the State*, Cambridge: Cambridge University Press.

Stuart, D. T. and Tow, W. T. (1995) 'A US strategy for the Asia-Pacific', *Adelphi Paper No. 299*, International Institute for Strategic Studies, London.

Stubbs, R. (1995) 'Asia-Pacific regionalization and the global economy: A third form of capitalism?', *Asian Survey* XXXV (9): 785–87

Stubbs, R. (2000) 'Introduction: Regionalization and globalization', in Stubbs, R. and Underhill, G. R. D. (eds), *Political Economy and the Changing Global Order*, Oxford: Oxford University Press.

Sukatipan, S. (1995) 'Thailand: The evolution of legitimacy', in Alagappa, M. (ed.), *Political Legitimacy in Southeast Asia: The Quest for Moral Authority*, Stanford, CA: Stanford University Press.

Tabata, H. (1990) 'The Japanese welfare state: Its structure and transformation', *Annals of the Institute of Social Science* 32: 1–29.

Tai, H. (1989) 'The Oriental alternative: An hypothesis on culture and economy', in Tai, H. (ed.), *Confucianism and Economic Development: An Oriental Alternative?*, Washington, DC: The Washington Institute Press.

Tang, K. (2000) *Social Welfare Development in East Asia*, Basingstoke: Palgrave.

Taylor, R. H. (ed.) (1996) *The Politics of Elections in Southeast Asia*, Cambridge: Cambridge University Press.

Thurow, L. (1992) *Head to Head: The Coming Economic Battle Among Japan, Europe, and America*, New York: Morrow.

Tien, H. M. (1989) *The Great Transition: Political and Social Change in the Republic of China*, Stanford, CA: Hoover Institution Press.

Tremewan, C. (1994) *The Political Economy of Social Control in Singapore*, London: Macmillan.

—— (1998) 'Welfare and governance: Public housing under Singapore's party-state', in Goodman, R., White, G. and Kwon, H. (eds), *The East Asian Welfare Model: Welfare Orientalism and the State*, London: Routledge.

United Nations Development Programme (1995) *Report of The World Summit For Social Development*, www.un.org/documents/ga/conf166/aconf166-9.htm.

UNDP (2000) *Human Development Report*, Oxford: Oxford University Press.

UNDP (undated) *FAQs on the Human Development Indices*, www.undp.org/hdr2000/english/FAQs.html.

US Congress (1993) *APEC and US Policy Towards Asia*, Hearings, House Committee for Foreign Affairs, Washington DC: US Government Printing Office.

Vatikiotis, M. R. J. (1998) *Indonesian Politics Under Suharto*, London: Routledge.

Vennewald, W. (1994) *Technocrats in the State Enterprise System in Singapore*, Working Paper No. 32, Asia Research Centre, Murdoch University, Perth, WA.

Vogel, E. F. (1980) *Japan as Number One: Lessons for America*, Tokyo: Tuttle.

Vogel, S. K. (1996) *Freer Markets, More Rules: Regulatory Reform in Advanced Industrial Countries*, Ithaca, NY: Cornell University Press

Wade, R. (1990) *Governing the Market: Economic Theory and the Role of Government in East Asian Industrialisation*, Princeton, NJ: Princeton University Press

—— (1992) 'East Asian economic success: Conflicting perspectives, partial insight, shaky evidence', *World Politics* 44 (2): 270–320.

—— (1998) 'From 'miracle' to 'cronyism': explaining the Great Asian Slump', *Cambridge Journal of Economics* 2: 693–706

Wade, R. and Veneroso, F. (1998a) 'The gathering world slump and the battle over capital control', *New Left Review* 231 (September/October): 13–41.

—— (1998b) 'The Asian crisis: The high debt model versus the Wall Street–Treasury–IMF complex', *New Left Review* 228 (March/April): 3–23.

Wallerstein, I. (1979) 'The rise and future demise of the world capitalist system: Concepts for comparative analysis', in I. Wallerstein, *The Capitalist World Economy*, Cambridge: Cambridge University Press.

Watchman, A. (1994) *Taiwan: National Identity and Democratisation*, London: M. E. Sharpe.

Weber, M. (1957) [1922] *The Theory of Economic and Social Organization*, Berkeley: University of California Press.

Weiss, L. (1995) 'Governed interdependence: Rethinking the government–business relationship in East Asia', *The Pacific Review* 8 (4): 589–616.

Weiss, L. and Hobson, J. M. (1995) *States and Economic Development: A Comparative Historical Analysis*, Cambridge: Polity Press.

—— (2000) 'State power and economic strength revisited: What's so special about the Asian crisis?', in Robison, R., Beeson, M., Jayasuriya, K. and Kim, H.-R. (eds), *Politics and Markets in the Wake of the Asian Crisis*, London: Routledge.

Wells, K. M. (1995) *Korea's Minjung Movement*, Honolulu: University of Hawaii Press.

White, G. and Goodman, R. (1998) 'Welfare Orientalism and the search for an East Asian welfare model', in Goodman, R., White, G. and Kwon, H. (eds), *The East Asian Welfare Model: Welfare Orientalism and the State*, London: Routledge.

White, G. Goodman, R. and Kwon, H. (1998) 'The politics of welfare in East Asia' in Maidment, R., Goldblatt, D. and Mitchell, J. (eds), *Governance in the Asia-Pacific*, London: Routledge.

Williams, D. (1994) *Japan: Beyond the End of History*, London: Routledge.

Williamson, J. (1994) 'In search of a manual for technopols', in Williamson, J. (ed.), *The Political Economy of Policy Reform*, Washington, DC: Institute for International Economics.

Winters, J. A. (2000) 'The financial crisis in Southeast Asia', in Robison, R., Beeson, M., Jayasuriya, K. and Kim, H.-R. (eds), *Politics and Markets in the Wake of the Asian Crisis*, London: Routledge.

van Wolferen, K. (1989) *The Enigma of Japanese Power: People and Politics in a Stateless Nation*, London: Macmillan.

Woo-Cumings, M. (1993) 'East Asia's America problem', in Woo-Cumings, M. and Loriaux, M. (eds), *Past as Prelude: History in the Making of a New World Order*, Boulder, CO: Westview Press.

Wood, C. (1992) *The Bubble Economy: The Japanese Economic Collapse*, London: Sidgwick & Jackson.

Woodall, B. (1996) *Japan Under Construction: Corruption, Politics and Public Works*, Berkeley: University of California Press.

Woods, L. T. (1993) *Asia-Pacific Diplomacy: Nongovernmental Organizations and International Relations*, Vancouver: University of British Columbia.

World Bank (1991a) *World Development Report 1991: The Challenge of Development*, Oxford: Oxford University Press.

—— (1991b) *Managing Development: The Governance Dimension, A Discussion Paper*, Washington, DC: World Bank.

—— (1992) *Governance and Development*, Washington, DC: World Bank.

—— (1993) *The East Asian Miracle: Economic Growth and Public Policy*, Oxford: Oxford University Press.

—— (1997) *World Development Report 1997: The State in a Changing World*, Oxford: Oxford University Press.

—— (1998) *World Development Indicators 1998*, Washington, DC: World Bank (CD-ROM).

—— (2000) *East Asia: Recovery and Beyond*, Oxford: Oxford University Press.

Yoshihara, K. (1976) *Foreign Investment and Domestic Response*, Singapore: Eastern Universities Press.

—— (1988) *The Rise of Ersatz Capitalism in South-East Asia*, Oxford: Oxford University Press.

—— (1994) *Japanese Economic Development*, Oxford: Oxford University Press.

Index